Internet Made Easy™

A Guide to the Internet for CompuServe Members

Roelf Sluman

Internet Made Easy™

A Guide to the Internet for CompuServe Members

Roelf Sluman

INTERNATIONAL THOMSON COMPUTER PRESS
I Ⓣ P An International Thomson Publishing Company

London • Bonn • Boston • Johannesburg • Madrid • Melbourne • Mexico City • New York • Paris
Singapore • Tokyo • Toronto • Albany, NY • Belmont, CA • Cincinnati, OH • Detroit, MI

Internet Made Easy™
A Guide to the Internet for CompuServe Members

I(T)P A division of International Thomson Publishing Inc.
The ITP logo is a trademark under licence

British Library Cataloguing-in-Publication Data
A catalogue record for this book is available from the British Library

First printed 1995

Commissioning Editor: Liz Israel Oppedijk

Printed in the UK by Clays Ltd, St Ives plc

ISBN 1-85032-240-6

International Thomson Computer Press
Berkshire House
High Holborn
London WCIV 7AA
UK

International Thomson Computer Press
20 Park Plaza
14th Floor
Boston MA 02116
USA

Imprints of International Thomson Publishing

Contents

Chapter 1

The Internet: an introduction

- ❍ **What is the Internet?**
- ❍ **Internet Basics**
- ❍ **CompuServe and the Internet**

COMPUSERVE
Internet Services

What is the Internet?

One of the questions that almost every new Internet user asks is 'What exactly is the Internet?' Every now and then, you see forum messages from CompuServe members stating that they 'are happy to be on the Net', actually referring to CompuServe. So is CompuServe the same as the Internet? Well, not exactly. Like many computer networks, CompuServe is *part* of the Internet. And to make matters a little bit more complicated, CompuServe also functions as an **access provider**, giving you unlimited access to the complete Internet.

To discuss the differences between CompuServe and the Internet, we'll use a few keywords: **location**, **access** and **interface**.

The location

As a CompuServe member, you are probably aware of the fact that when you connect to CompuServe, you are actually accessing a number of computers based in Columbus, Ohio. In other words, you are accessing an information service that has a fixed location. That is not the case with the Internet, however. The Internet is a large collection of computer networks worldwide that are linked to each other. Basically, the Internet resembles a telephone network. Just like each telephone has its own telephone number, each computer on the Internet has its own **Internet address**. Once you know the Internet address of a particular computer, regardless of where that computer is physically located, you can connect to it.

There are two sorts of Internet addresses: **permanent** addresses (anyone who has the money and/or resources can connect his or her computer permanently to the Internet) and **temporary** addresses (you 'rent' these addresses, not unlike a surfboard on the beach, to get temporary access to the Internet).

Getting access

The large number of available CompuServe **dial-in nodes** makes it usually very easy to connect to CompuServe, from almost any place in the world. Just hook up your computer to a modem, install a version of CIM (the CompuServe Information Manager, available for several platforms such as Windows, Apple Macintosh, OS/2 and DOS), enter the phone number of the CompuServe dial-in node in or near the city where you are, and you are ready to connect.

The Internet is another story. To get access to the Internet, your computer has to become part of it, either permanently or temporarily. More and more companies provide their employees with permanent Internet access from their desktop computer: it is connected (via a **Local Area Network**, for instance) to a central computer, which in turn is connected to the Internet – not via a regular telephone line, but via a permanent data line. Permanent connections are by far the fastest way to retrieve information from the Internet: access speeds often exceed those of regular telephone connections by a factor of four or more.

The method described above can be used only if you are actually in the office, working on your desktop computer. But what if you are working at home, and you would like to collect your mail or access a few files located on the central office computer? In some cases, you might be able to **dial up** (via a regular telephone line, using a computer and modem) to the office. This way, you can even access your central office computer while you are on the road, logging in from your hotel (by far the quickest way to build up a huge phone bill, by the way).

But what if your company is not connected to the Internet? In that case, you need a **commercial access provider**. Using a computer and a modem, you call a phone number in your neighborhood, not unlike the way you connect to CompuServe. Once connected, you have full Internet access.

These days, more and more commercial access providers offer their services. But as a CompuServe member, you can save yourself the trouble of searching for a good and inexpensive access provider: you simply use your CompuServe account to 'dial up' to the Internet using a new CompuServe service called **Dial PPP**. We'll discuss Dial PPP in Chapter 3.

The interface

To access CompuServe, most members use the popular **WinCIM** software (**CompuServe Information Manager for Windows**), or a CIM version for another platform or operating system (Apple Macintosh computers, OS/2, DOS, or GEOS, for example). The structured menus and dialogs that are part of the CIM software make CompuServe very easy to use, without the need to type complicated commands. Actually, the CIM software often lets you forget that you are accessing information that resides on a computer other than your own!

Thanks to the **Internet made easy** program, CompuServe members can access the Internet using WinCIM's friendly pull-down menus and dialogs. But for people who are not CompuServe members, the Internet is another story. They need to run several programs for the activities they want to perform. Reading messages from USENET newsgroups calls for **news reader** software, whereas they need a **browser** to look at the World Wide Web.

Internet basics

Actually, you don't need to know much about the Internet's inner structure to be able to use it. But then, it doesn't hurt to take a closer look at what the Internet is really about. In this section, we'll give you some basic information about typical 'Net jargon', like routers, hosts and domains and TCP/IP.

The history of the Internet

In the early 1970s, the **ARPAnet** was developed. A product of the American Defense Department, the ARPAnet's purpose was to see if a secure way could be found to transfer vital military information from one computer to another during times of crisis. Special attention was given to the fact that, during such a crisis, any part of the connection between those two computers could collapse at any moment. It was therefore necessary to develop a 'routing' system, that would be able to re-route the information through other computers if necessary. To implement this system, the **Internet Protocol (IP)** was developed: more about that in the next section.

Soon, universities and parts of the American government discovered the possibilities of the Internet Protocol. The number of computers that were part of the 'Net' increased rapidly, making it possible to communicate with more and more networks.

A big step in the direction of the Internet in its current form was made by the **National Science Foundation**, an American government agency. They created **NSFNET**, a network that used the same technology as ARPAnet, but with faster computers and higher transfer speeds. One of their goals was to give every American college student access to the Internet. It is safe to say that they have succeeded; in the United States, every university is connected to the Internet.

More recently, the number of independent access providers (like CompuServe) has expanded rapidly, providing easy access to the Internet and resulting in more and more individuals getting access to the Net.

Hosts, IP addresses and domains

A computer that is connected to the Internet is called a **host**. Every host has its own **Internet Protocol Address** abbreviated to **IP address**. This address consists of four numbers (from 0 to 255), separated from each other by dots. An example of an IP address is 198.4.6.2. As you will understand, each host must have a unique address. To see to it that this is the case, a group called the **Internet Architecture Board** has been founded. This group provides rules that have to be followed by everyone who wants to assign an IP address to a computer.

Those series of four numbers are not too easy to remember. Therefore, there is another system available: a database of **host names**, called the **Domain Name System** or **DNS**. Those names correspond to the IP addresses discussed above; when you address a host by its host name, that name will be converted (by means of a series of queries to so-called DNS servers) into the four-number IP address.

A host name often consists of two parts: a 'name' (**system**) and 'address' (**domains**). The **system** part (which is not always present) tells you more about the name or purpose of that computer, whereas the **domains** part gives you information about the network to which it belongs, or its physical location. An example of a host name is *www.compuserve.com*: *www* is the system, and *compuserve.com* are the domains. As you see, the domains are separated by periods as well.

Looking at the host name, you can learn a lot about the computer that you are connecting to, as well as its location. For example, the host name *turing.cnrs.humboldt.edu* belongs to the computer named 'turing', which can be found in the College of Natural Resources and Sciences (*cnrs*), part of Humboldt State University. The last part, *edu*, tells you that this host belongs to a educational domain. Examples of domains are:

Domain	**Description**
com	Commercial
edu	Educational
gov	Governmental
mil	Military
net	Network
org	Other

These days, an extension of the original domain naming system is gaining more and more popularity. In that system, the last domain is a two-letter abbreviation, indicating the country where the computer is located. A few examples:

Last domain	**Location**
au	Australia
be	Belgium
br	Brazil
ca	Canada
ch	Switzerland
cn	China
de	Germany
dk	Denmark
fr	France
id	Indonesia
ie	Ireland
il	Israel
in	India
jp	Japan
nl	The Netherlands
ru	Russian Federation
tr	Turkey
uk	United Kingdom
us	United States

The basis of Internet communication: TCP/IP

Unlike a telephone call, communication between two computers on the Internet is not a 'one-on-one' dialog. You will understand that in order to regulate all the traffic that flows through the Net, the system behind it is pretty advanced. To get traffic (that is, data) to its destination (a computer) as soon as possible, **routers** are used. Every computer on the Internet is either a router, or in one way or another connected to one. As its name implies, a router decides what route the traffic should follow to arrive at its destination. The system used is very sophisticated: if a router goes down, other routers can take over to get information to its destination as quickly as possible.

To allow routers to do their work as quickly and efficiently as possible, two protocols have been developed: the **Internet Protocol**, almost always abbreviated to (IP), and the **Transmission Control Protocol** (TCP). As both protocols are often used together, the common abbreviation for both of them is **TCP/IP**.

Information sent over the Internet is often split up into several packets. Packets can be anywhere between 1 and 1,500 characters in length. Every packet contains a part of the data that needs to be transmitted, as well as the address information: the destination address (the four numbers, separated by dots), and the address of the sender. This is the Internet Protocol (IP), mentioned in the previous paragraph.

Because information is often sent as a series of packets, another protocol is needed to ensure that, once the packets arrive, the original information can be retrieved out of those packets. Keep in mind that the packets don't necessarily arrive in the correct order, and that data loss can occur occasionally.

And here is where TCP comes in. Not only does it split the data into packets, it also attaches a 'serial number' to each packet, as well as a checksum. That way, the receiving computer can check if the data is still intact (and request the sender to re-send the packet if that is not the case) and retrieve the original information by combining the packets in the right order.

The Internet for modem users: command line access, SLIP and PPP

As you know by now, every computer present on the Internet has its own IP address (the four numbers, separated by dots). These numbers are used by TCP/IP to ensure error-free connections between computers that are part of the Internet. But what if your computer is not a permanent part of the Internet, for instance because you dial up to an access provider? Because your computer doesn't have an IP address, it is not able to communicate with other Internet computers!

In that case, there are three options. Which of those options are available depends on a particular access provider:

- Command line access
- SLIP
- PPP

Command line access

Although SLIP and PPP (discussed in the following sections) are being used more and more frequently, command line access, often referred to as **shell account access**, is still a frequently used way of connecting to the Internet. After the connection with the access provider has been established, you can access the Net through the **host** of that access provider. Effectively, this means that the commands that you type on your keyboard will be sent to the host. Next, the Internet address of that host is used to communicate (via TCP/IP) with other computers. In turn, the information that the host receives will be echoed on your computer screen.

To the destination computer you are communicating with, things look pretty normal: it has a normal TCP/IP connection with another Internet computer. And because all retrieved data will be echoed on your screen, everything seems to work perfectly.

However, problems arise when you want to retrieve files. Whenever you request (actually, your access provider's host does it) a file to be sent to you from another computer, it will be stored **on the host computer**. You will therefore have to download that file from the host computer before you can access it. The reason is that your computer does not have its own TCP/IP address (see Figure 1.1).

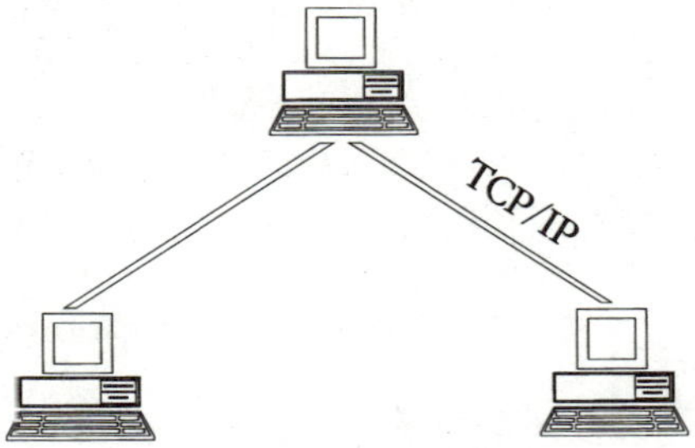

Figure 1.1 Command line access: you 'take over' your access provider's Internet host

There are other disadvantages. Firstly, new Internet services like the **World Wide Web**, which rely on transfers of large chunks of binary information, are not available to you when you use command line access. You will therefore need your own IP address to access those services. Fortunately, there is a way to do this without investing a lot of money in leased phone lines, expensive routers, etc.: choose an access provider that gives you a form of **IP access**. In that case, you use a special version of the Internet protocol (IP) to communicate with other Internet computers. Your computer actually gets its own IP address (only valid during the time you are actually connected), using one of two special TCP/IP versions: SLIP (**Serial Line Internet Protocol**), a slightly older version, or PPP (**Point-to-Point Protocol**), a more advanced version that gives your access provider better possibilities to get IP addresses for computers that dial up.

The following example might help to give you a clearer picture: a dial-in server maintains a bank of IP addresses (like a surfboard rental). When you log in, you rent an IP address for your surfing adventure. When you have finished, the IP address is returned for someone else's use.

Because your computer has its own IP address, it can communicate with other computers on the Internet - albeit it still through a so-called **dial-in server**, the computer you call which belongs to your access provider (see Figure 1.2).

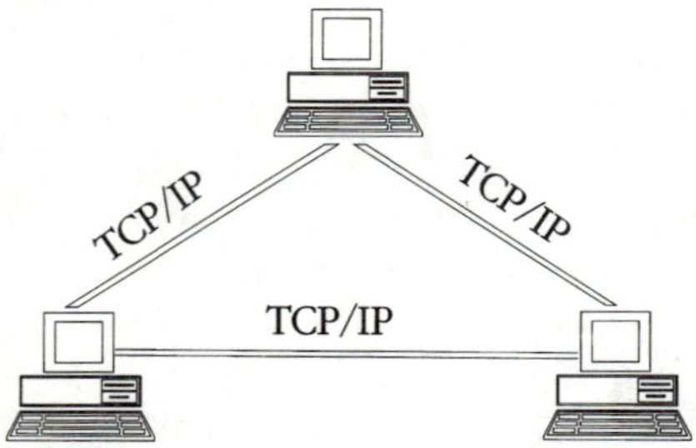

Figure 1.2 SLIP or PPP access: your computer has become part of the Internet

The power of TCP/IP: application programs

As we have seen, TCP/IP allows two computers to communicate, regardless of their physical location. Using TCP/IP, programmers have written software that allows you not only to connect to another computer, but to do useful things with it as well. A few examples of often-used Internet software applications are:

- **telnet**: Using telnet software, you can directly log in to other computers on the Internet. You will learn more about telnet in Chapter 8.

- **FTP (file transfer protocol)**: A variation on telnet, this program enables you to download files from another Internet site to your own computer or vice versa. More about FTP can be found in Chapter 7.

- **mail**: This software allows you to send mail through other Internet users, provided they have a **mail address** on another Internet computer. As a CompuServe member, you have your own mail address: it consists of your User ID (the comma replaced by a dot), followed by an @ sign and the text *compuserve.com*. My CompuServe User ID is 71333,1443; my Internet mail address is therefore:

  ```
  71333.1443@compuserve.com
  ```

Mail is covered in Chapter 5.

- **USENET News Reader**: This is the program used to read (most Internet applications are written in UNIX) USENET newsgroups: the Internet equivalent of CompuServe forums. You will find more information about USENET newsgroups in Chapter 6.

- **Archie**: If you are looking for a particular file, you can use the Archie system to see whether it exists and where it is located. After you have found the location, you use FTP, another Internet application, to retrieve it.
To use Archie, you **telnet** to an Archie server. If you want to know more about Archie, see page 186, under the heading 'Archie'.

- **Gopher**: Often referred to as the predecessor of the World Wide Web (WWW), Gopher is a program that lets you use menu structures to 'surf the Net'. It is much more limited than WWW in that it has limited hyperlink capacity. Another limitation is that you can't interact with Gopher as nicely as with WWW (you can't fill out forms, for instance). But there are still Gopher sites on the Internet, and the popular World Wide Web browsers provide you with easy access to them.

- **WWW**: According to many Internet users, the World Wide Web is the best thing that's happened to them in years. Resembling the structure and looks of a Windows help screen, the World Wide Web lets you view information about all kinds of topics by reading **pages** that reside on computers all around the world. One of the most powerful features is the **hyperlink**: when you click on a certain word or illustration, your **WWW browser software** will automatically show the WWW page connected to that word or illustration, regardless of where (on what computer) that page is stored. WWW is so famous that many people don't even know that the Internet has much more to offer!

The best way to connect to the World Wide Web through CompuServe is to use CompuServe's **NetLauncher**, a combination of dialer software (**Internet Dialer**), which establishes a temporary Internet connection, and browser software (**SPRY Mosaic**), which enables you to view World Wide Web pages. Both CompuServe NetLauncher and the World Wide Web are discussed extensively in Chapter 4.

CompuServe and the Internet

Until a few years ago, CompuServe was pretty much a 'closed network'. Access to the Internet was limited to electronic mail. To use popular Internet features like USENET newsgroups, FTP and the World Wide Web, you had to find a local access provider.

Happily, all that has changed. During the last two years, more and more Internet features have become available for CompuServe members. And today, CompuServe can be considered as the world's leading Internet access provider. Just take a look at the following summary:

- **Easy** access to the Internet through WinCIM's user-friendly menus and dialog windows.
- **Full** access to the Internet through the Internet dialer, allowing you to use all popular Internet software available.
- **Free** downloads of software that you need to browse the World Wide Web: SPRY Mosaic.
- **Low** rates: either three or twenty free Internet hours per month, and additional hourly rates that are currently amongst the lowest of all access providers.
- **Valuable** information online: a number of forums that are devoted to the Internet, as well as an extensive home page on the World Wide Web.

Although CompuServe offers its members a great way to access the Internet, there is more. If you are looking for great files (without viruses, of course), good advice and information that is hard to obtain otherwise, simply use the advanced, user-friendly CompuServe products! A few examples:

- **Forums**, the CompuServe equivalents of USENET newsgroups, are probably the most popular services. Almost every subject that you can think of is covered in one or more forums. There are forums with support for computer hardware and software, professional forums, entertainment forums and a growing number of 'local' forums, pertaining to a particular country (or even city). As a CompuServe member, you are welcome to visit all those forums! For a complete list, just `GO FORUMS`.

- **Databases**, filled with up-to-date information about a variety of subjects. Some databases (like the Hutchinson Encyclopedia (GO HUTCHINSON) are part of basic services and therefore free to members of the Standard Pricing Plan, whereas other databases are part of extended services, or, in some cases, surcharged. For a complete list of databases available on CompuServe, GO REFERENCE.

- **News** is available through a wealth of news services, covering information like the weather, daily news, stock quotes and the latest computer and software news. Some of them are free for members of the Standard Pricing Plan, others are part of extended services. There are also surcharged news services, amongst which one of the best news services available: the **Executive News Service** (GO ENS).

- **Entertainment** can be found on CompuServe as well. Just GO ENTERTAINMENT and read the latest editions of popular entertainment magazines, movie reviews, information about your favorite musicians and a large number of **syndicated columns** (GO COLUMNS, covering topics such as consumer and financial info, entertainment, family, politics and news events. All of those syndicated columns are part of basic services, by the way.

- **File Finders**, allowing you to search through the most popular forums for files containing one or more keywords, with a certain name or age, or upload by a particular person. File Finders can be a real time saver! GO FILEFINDER for more information, or refer to page 198, under the heading 'The CompuServe File Finders'.

Chapter 2

Finding Internet information on CompuServe

- ❍ **Useful places to GO**
- ❍ **Useful files**

Useful places to GO

Before you start your ventures on the Internet, you might want to spend some time on CompuServe itself, browsing through the vast amount of Internet information available. Just start WinCIM and `GO INTERNET`. The Internet menu, shown in Figure 2.1, contains entries for all Internet services that CompuServe provides for CIM users. There are also options to access the popular Internet Forums. Currently, there are three CompuServe Support forums for the Internet: the Internet New Users Forum (`GO INETFORUM`), the Internet Resources Forum (`GO INETRES`) and the Internet Publishing Forum (`GO INETPUB`). Besides this, Internet World magazine has its own forum on CompuServe (`GO IWORLD`).

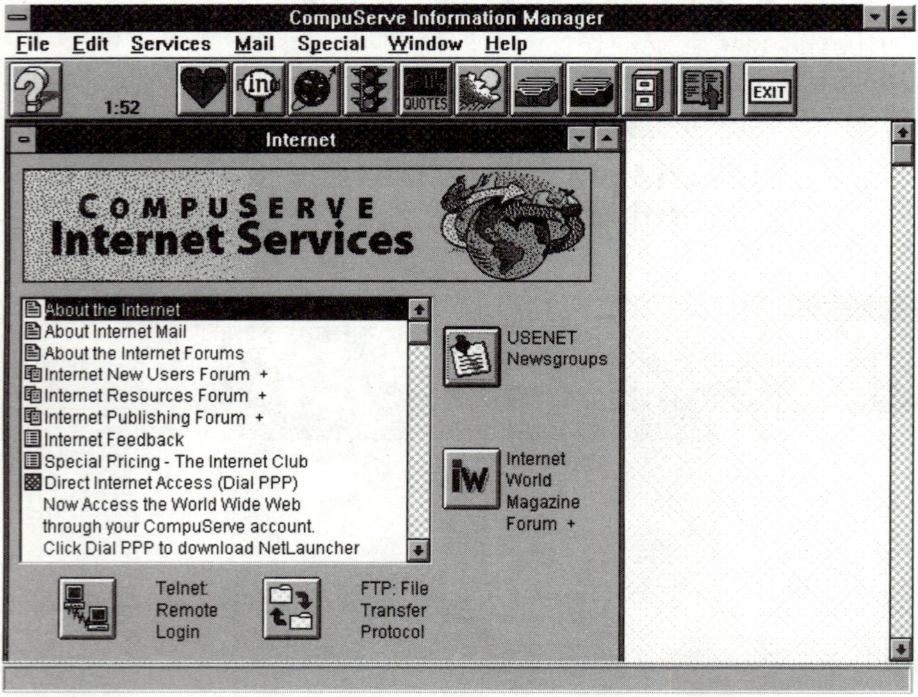

Figure 2.1 The CompuServe Internet menu

Watch the plus sign!

All forums mentioned in this chapter are part of CompuServe's extended services, unless indicated otherwise. Therefore, normal connect charges apply. For more information about costs, refer to page 67, under the heading 'Costs'.

The Internet New Users Forum

As its name implies, the Internet New Users Forum (see Figure 2.2) is aimed at CompuServe members who have little or no experience using the Internet. This very lively forum contains the following message sections and libraries:

```
 1 Chatter
 2 Internet Beginners
 3 Access: CompuServe
 4 Accessing the Net
 5 Using Email
 6 Using FTP & Archie
 7 Using USENET
 8 Using Mailing Lists
 9 Using WWW & Mosaic
10 Using Telnet
11 Using Gopher & WAIS
12 Finding People
13 Finding Resources
14 Business on the Net
15 Internet Society
```

Figure 2.2 The Internet New Users Forum (GO INETFORUM)

To go to the Internet New Users Forum directly, GO INETFORUM.

The Internet Resources Forum

If you are a skilled Internet user, or if you are looking for specific information and want to know where to find it on the Internet, GO INETRESOURCES to visit the Internet Resources Forum (see Figure 2.3).

The Internet Resources Forum contains the following message sections and libraries:

```
1 CIS Resources
2 Internet News
3 Books/Magazines
4 PC Internet S/W
5 Mac Internet S/W
6 Other Software
7 Where to find...
8 Mailing Lists
```

Figure 2.3 The Internet Resources Forum (GO INETRESOURCES)

```
 9 WWW/Hypertext Tools
10 Resources-Academic
11 Resources-Business
12 Resources-Community
13 Resources-Govt.
14 Resources-Technical
15 Resources-Personal
16 Resources-Other
17 Standards/RFC's
```

The Internet Publishing Forum

If you want to publish information on the Internet, or if you want to use the Internet as a marketing tool, visit the Internet Publishing forum (GO INETPUBLISH). This forum contains the following message sections and libraries:

```
 1 General Information
 2 Internet Marketing
 3 Internet PR
 4 Electronic Publish.
 5 Online News
 6 Online Commerce
 7 Design Resources
 8 HTML Language
 9 Server Tools
10 Server SW:PC/Win
11 Server SW:Mac
12 Graphics: Images
13 Graphic Tools:PC
14 Graphic Tools:Mac
15 HTML Editors:PC/Win
16 HTML Editors:Mac
17 Scripting: CGI
21 Payment Systems
22 Conferences
```

The Internet World Forum (GO IWORLD)

This is the support forum for the popular *Internet World* magazine. It contains the following message sections:

```
1 Hey, Editors!
2 Internet News
3 The Surfboard
4 Entry Level
5 IW's Feature Topic
6 Members' Picks
7 Subscription Info
8 Chatter Box
```

The libraries are named as follows:

```
1 Internet News
2 The Surfboard
3 Entry Level/Newbies
4 Editors' Toolbox
6 Members' Picks
```

Other useful forums on CompuServe

Apart from the three support forums mentioned in the previous sections, a number of other forums also have sections and libraries devoted to the Internet. You'll find a few examples in the following sections.

- The Aquaria/Fish Forum (`GO FISHNET`) has an *Internet Resources* library, containing information about interesting Internet sites and World Wide Web home pages.

- The Belgium Forum (`GO BELFORUM`), a forum aimed at CompuServe users in Belgium and Belgians all over the world, has a *CompuServe/Internet* message section and library. Although most files are in Dutch or French, there are some valuable English contributions, too. Amongst those files are my monthly newsletters (in the English language) about CompuServe and the Internet: just look for files named *NEWS01.TXT*, *NEWS02.TXT*, etc.

- Don't forget the free CompuServe Help Forum (`GO HELPFORUM`): it has a special *Internet Services* message section.

- The Court Reporters Forum (`GO CRFORUM`) has a special message and library section devoted to the Internet: *The Internet/VRC.* (VRC stands for Verbatim Resource Center, a World Wide Web site for the court reporting profession. If you want to take a look: their World Wide Web URL is *http://www.verbatim.com*).

- Is German your native language? Visit the Deutsches Computer Forum (`GO GERNET`) and take a look at the *Internet* message section and library. And while you're there, don't miss the *World Wide Web* section and library!

- The Education forum (GO EDFORUM) covers the Internet in the Internet message section, as well as in the Internet resources library. You'll find general Internet information, as well as information pertaining to educational matters.

- The Electronic Frontier Foundation, an organization that strives to assure freedom of expression in digital media, has its own forum on CompuServe: (GO EFFSIG). It contains numerous message sections and libraries pertaining to the Internet.

- If you use OS/2, you can't afford to miss the IBM OS/2 Users Forum (GO OS2USER). The Internet is covered in the *Internet access* message section, and scripts are available in the *Internet scripts* library.

- French CompuServe users can obtain information in their language in the Informatique France Forum (GO INFOFR). The special *Internet!* section and library contain informative files as well as interesting shareware.

- Are you from Japan, or are you interested in this country? Don't miss the *Networks-J/Internet* message section and library in the Japan Forum (GO JAPAN). If you can't speak Japanese, don't worry: the majority of forum messages and files are in English.

- Owners of Macintosh computers who are interested in the Internet have their own 'home' on CompuServe: the Macintosh Communications Forum (GO MACCOM). Look in the *Macs On*

Internet message section and library for informative files, popular software and useful tools.

- The NCSA (National Computer Security Association) has a couple of forums on CompuServe. Security matters pertaining to the Internet can be discussed in the *Unix/Internet* message section of the NCSA Info Security Forum (`GO NCSAFORUM`). Browse through the library of the same name for useful FAQs (files with frequently asked questions, hence the abbreviation) and informative files.

- The NL Computing Forum (`GO NLCOMP`), dedicated to Dutch computer users, has two message sections and libraries dedicated to the Internet: *Internet* and *World Wide Web*. This forum also publishes a monthly newsletter (in the English language) with up-to-date information about CompuServe and the Internet, written by me. You can download those newsletters from the *Internet* library of the NL Computing Forum: they are named *NEWS01.TXT*, *NEWS02.TXT*, etc.

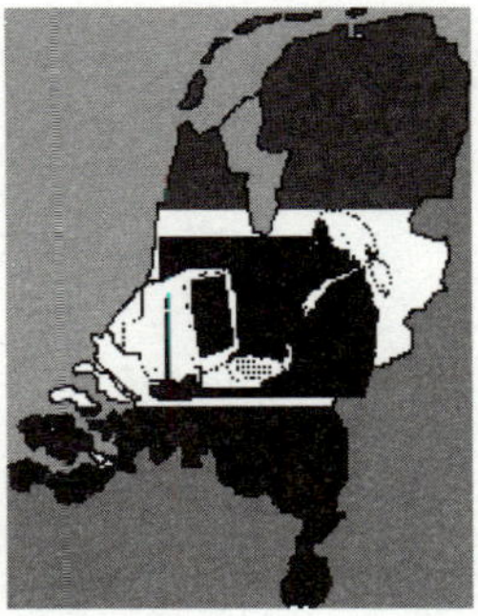

- The PR and Marketing Forum (`GO PRSIG`) also deals with the Internet, in its *Using Internet* message section and library.

- If you're from Spain, or if Spanish is your native language, GO SPFORUM to visit CompuServe's 'Foro Espadol': the Spanish Forum. Although the forum doesn't have a separate section and library dedicated to the Internet, the *Telecomunicationes* section and library offer plenty of information and useful files.

- The Telecommunications Forum (GO TELECOM) covers telecommunications services, products and related issues of interest. While you're there, don't forget to look in the *Internetworking* section and library.

- If you're in the United Kingdom, be sure to pay a visit to the UK Communications Forum (`GO UKCOMMS`). Besides the fact that this forum is the host for **WigWam**, a popular CompuServe navigation software package, it has an *Internet* message section and library.

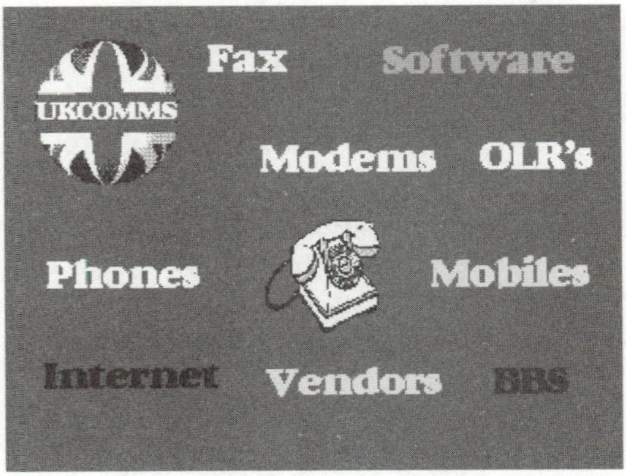

- UNIX, the 'Internet language by default', has its own forum on CompuServe. `GO UNIXFORUM` brings you there; if you like USENET newsgroups, be sure to take a look at the *USENET map entries*, descriptive files with information about USENET newsgroups and mailing lists, in the *Internet & Usenet* library.

- Windows users don't want to miss the Windows Connectivity Forum (`GO` WINCON) (nice logo, folks!) and check out the various Internet-related message sections and libraries. Very helpful sysops, good quality shareware: a great forum!

Finding more Internet resources
Select the Find option on WinCIM's Service menu and enter `internet` to find out about other CompuServe products that offer information about the Internet.

Useful files

If you want to know more about the latest Internet developments, or if you are looking for specific software to surf the Net, don't forget to look in the file libraries of the Internet Forums. The following sections contain an overview of some of the most popular files available.

The Internet New Users Forum (GO INETFORUM)

Protocols, technical information

- *[76703,407]   Lib:15*
  PCTCP.ZIP/Bin   Bytes: 54542

  Title   : IBM PC TCP/IP FAQs (Zipped)
  Keywords: IBM PC TCP TCPIP FAQ

  IBM PC TCP/IP FAQs (Zipped). Frequently asked questions and answers about TCP/IP networking on IBM PCs.

- *[75143,2171]   Lib: 2*
  HECKER.ZIP/Bin   Bytes: 36331

  Title   : Hecker: Personal Internet Access Using SLIP or PPP
  Keywords: HECKER SLIP PPP ACCESS

  September 26, 1994 update of Frank Hecker's "Personal Internet Access Using SLIP or PPP: How You Use It, How It Works". Plain English how-to for Mac and PC users. Very readable. Zipped file in Winword 6.0 format.

- *[74431,2303]   Lib: 2*
  SLIPFA.TXT/Text Bytes: 2815

  Title   : SLIP/PPP FAQ
  Keywords: SLIP

  A FAQ for getting started on SLIP or PPP.

- *[73710,1430]   Lib: 3*
  PPP.ZIP/Bin   Bytes: 26279

  Title   : Point-to-Point Protocol FAQ
  Keywords: PPP FAQ SERIAL IP CONFIGURATION SLIP

  Frequently Asked Questions about Point-to-Point Protocol, a serial-line protocol used for Internet transmission of data. A bibliography, list of software implementations, and configuration tips are included.

- *[76703,407]   Lib: 2*
  RF1208.TXT/Text Bytes: 41138

  Title   : RFC 1208 - Glossary of Networking Terms
  Keywords:

  This RFC is a glossary adapted from "The INTEROP Pocket Glossary of Networking Terms" distributed at Interop '90. This memo provides information for the Internet community. It does not specify an Internet standard. Distribution of this memo is unlimited.

- *[76703,407]   Lib:15*
  RF1600.TXT/Text Bytes: 82941

  Title   : RFC 1600 - Internet Official Protocol Standards
  Keywords: RFC 1600 PROTOCOL INTERNET STANDARDS

  This memo describes the state of standardization of protocols used in the Internet as determined by the Internet Architecture Board (IAB). This memo is an Internet Standard. Distribution of this memo is unlimited.

- *[74431,344]   Lib: 3*
  REGIST.TXT/Text Bytes: 16563

  Title   : How to get domain name & IP number; USA only!
  Keywords: REGISTER APPLY DOMAIN NAME IP NUMBER INTERNIC USA

  This file contains the text of two applications, one to get a domain name assigned, the other to get an IP address assigned.

  Note that both of these are ONLY valid for sites in the USA. Other countries have their own authorities and procedures!

User guides

- *[72401,233]   Lib: 2*
  NETDEM.ZIP/Bin Bytes: 61952

  Title   : NETDEMO - the Interactive Internet Guide
  Keywords: GUIDE INTERACTIVE DEMO BEGINNER INTERNET

  NETDEMO is an easy-to-use full-color interactive guide to the Internet. It includes guided interactive demos of mail, USENET news, Gopher, telnet, and FTP that look and act much like real Internet sessions. Also included is info on: getting access, resource listings, UNIX basics, Mosaic, World Wide Web, SLIP, and much more. DOS program. Shareware, $20.

- *[70404,3376]   Lib: 2*
  IPWIN.ZIP/Bin   Bytes: 475237

  Title   : InfoPop/Win Hypertext guide to Internet
  Keywords: INFOPOP GMUTANT HYPERTEXT WINHELP

  InfoPop/Win (1.24d) is a Windows 3.1 hypertext guide to the Internet, CompuServe, BBS systems and more. A WINHELP application, IPWIN offers basic Net info, screen snapshots of various tools (Gopher, Mosaic, etc.), address for hundreds of library catalogs; tutorial info; hundreds of interesting destinations; text of various RFCs; CIS access phone #'s & much more. Not a full encyclopedia (yet) but we're working on it. InfoPop is freeware from GMUtant Software.

- *[74431,2303]   Lib: 2*
  START.TXT/Text   Bytes: 6355

  Title   : "Where to Start" for Internet Beginners
  Keywords: WHERE START BEGINNER

  A document for the Internet "newbie".

- *[70322,2234]   Lib: 1*
  D_10IN.ZIP/Bin   Bytes:1204096

  Title   : The Desktop Internet Reference
  Keywords: INTERNET WINDOWS HELP HYPERTEXT

  The Desktop Internet Reference, a Windows hypertext reference to the Internet. Its 18,000 pages cover the following topics:

  1) What is the Internet? How does it work?
  2) How can I get connected to the Internet?
  3) What resources are available? How can I find things?
  4) How do I use these resources?
  5) Where can I find more about these topics?

- *[73564,347]   Lib: 1*
  BGI.ZIP/Bin   Bytes: 98040

  Title   : The Beginner's Guide to the Internet v 1.3a
  Keywords: TUTORIAL DOS INTERNET BEGINNER

  A full-color, computer-based Internet tutorial. Covers e-mail, telnet, FTP, newsgroups, mailing lists, Gopher, Veronica, WAIS, WWW, Archie, Internet Relay Chat, access methods, netiquette, freenets, and much more.

  The finest means for Internet newcomers to get acquainted with the Net. In plain English! Over 10,000 downloads to date. Shareware. $25, US Mastercard and Visa welcome.

- *[71750,3301]   Lib: 2*
  ZENART.ZIP/Bin Bytes: 74824

  Title   : Zen and the Art of the Internet (1st Ed. '92).
  Keywords: ZEN ART GUIDE HELP KEHOE

  Zen and the Art of the Internet. A Beginners's Guide to the Internet. 1st. Edition. Revised Feb. '92. By Brendan P. Kehoe. Uploaded by forum member.

- *[76703,407]   Lib: 2*
  NTGD23.ZIP/Bin Bytes: 136769

  Title   : EFF's Guide to the Internet, v. 2.3 (ZIP)
  Keywords: EFF GUIDE INTERNET

  EFF's Guide to the Internet, v. 2.3 (ZIP)

  Zipped version of the Electronic Frontier Foundation's Guide to the Internet. Excellent starting point to learn about the Internet.

  If you are not familiar with un-Zipping a file, there is a text version of this same document also available for downloading from this library as filename NTGD23.TXT.

Information about services

- *[72254,16] Lib: 1*
  ROADMA.ZIP/Bin Bytes: 101523

  Title : Official Roadmap to the Information Superhighway
  Keywords: ROADMAP GUIDE INTERNET WINDOWS HELP

  Windows Help File Format of the very popular Official Roadmap to the Information Superhighway, (TM) as found on the NETCENTER, the center of the Internet. Online Version actually links to hundreds of important and interesting places on the Internet, hundreds more added daily. This version allows you to get some of the same information offline. Get a feel for the Internet. Check here for updates. Windows required.

- *[72323,524] Lib: 1*
  MERITC.ZIP/Bin Bytes: 619025

  Title : Merit's Cruise through the Internet 2.0
  Keywords: INTERNET MERIT CRUISE ZIP 2.0

  A tour through the many facets of the Internet. Windows program featuring brief descriptions of various Internet features. Also includes 'Net addresses of many sites on the 'Net. Requires Windows 3.1. Free, public domain. Pkzipped.

- *[71573,2127] Lib: 2*
  GOPHER.ZIP/Bin Bytes: 83200

  Title : Navigating the Net: Let's Go Gopherin'
  Keywords: GOPHER

  Navigating the Net: Let's Go Gopherin' was a free Internet Workshop distributed weekly by mail to subscribers in late 1993. This zipped file archive contains 23 lessons on how to navigate around the Internet using the Net navigational tool called Gopher.

- *[71573,2127]   Lib: 9*
  GPHRMA.TXT/Text Bytes: 8280

  Title   : GopherMail Information
  Keywords: E-MAIL GOPHER

  A guide to accessing Gopher resources via mail. This is useful for people with no direct Internet access, but who have mail access.

- *[100020,2125]   Lib: 1*
  HUNT.ZIP/Bin   Bytes: 43263

  Title   : The Great Internet Hunt File
  Keywords: INTERNET HUNT QUIZ EXAMPLES HINTS TIPS FACTS FIGURES QUESTIONS

  Lots of files tell you what sources of information are available on the Internet, but I have seen very few which give examples of the sorts of questions that can be answered and how to go about this.

  This is a compilation of the Internet Hunt - a set of really hard posers and the answers and how they were found. I hope it proves useful in showing you just what you can find on the Internet and how to go about finding it.

  ZIP file, unzip with PKUNZIP

- *[74431,2303]   Lib: 2*
  BROWSE.NET/Text Bytes: 10016

  Title   : Browsing the Internet
  Keywords: BROWSE

  An informative file about using the Net to browse for information and how to browse the Net for your needs.

Book reviews, magazines, journals

- *[76703,407] Lib: 8*
  INTPRS.TXT/Text Bytes: 6199

  Title : The Internet Press - Electronic Journal Guide
  Keywords: INTERNET PRESS ELECTRONIC JOURNAL HIGGINS SAVETZ

  The Internet Press - A guide to electronic journals about the Internet. Version 1.0 - 1 September 1994 by Kevin M. Savetz - @savetznorthcoast.com and John M. Higgins - @higginsdorsai.dorsai.org. This document is copyright 1994 by Kevin M. Savetz and John M. Higgins. All rights reserved.

- *[74140,1247] Lib: 1*
  INBOOK.ZIP/Bin Bytes: 32212

  Title : The Internet Book List v0.8 - 8/23/94
  Keywords: BOOKS INTERNET SAVETZ LIST

  The Internet Book List by Kevin M. Savetz gives information on and short reviews of more than 100 books about the Internet.

  Use a PKZIP v.204g compatible unzip program to unpack the archive.

- *[76703,407] Lib: 1*
  UNIXBK.TXT/Text Bytes: 52588

  Title : Concise Guide to Unix Books
  Keywords: UNIX BOOKS

  Concise Guide to Unix Books. Looking to learn more about Unix? Here's a great list of Unix books for you to review before purchasing one.

- *[100020,2125]   Lib: 1*
  BKREV1.ZIP/Bin Bytes: 48190
  BKREV2.ZIP/Bin Bytes: 26605
  BKREV3.ZIP/Bin Bytes: 25796

  Title   : Internet Book Reviews Files 1 to 3
  Keywords: INTERNET BOOK BOOKS REVIEW REVIEWS NETTRAIN NETWORK TRAINERS

  With so many books being published about the Internet it is difficult to decide which to read and which to buy with your hard earned $$$. These files contain in depth book reviews by members of the NETTRAIN discussion list. These people teach others to use the Internet so they should know a good book when they see one! .ZIP files, use PKUNZIP v.2.0.4.G to unzip.

General information

- *[76703,407]   Lib: 1*
  CISFAQ.TXT/Text Bytes: 10866

  Title   : Frequently Asked Questions - CompuServe/Internet
  Keywords: FAQ FREQUENTLY ASKED QUESTIONS INTERNET COMPUSERVE

  Frequently Asked Questions and Answers about CompuServe's Internet Services. Version 1.5 - 9/17/94. Copyright (C) 1994, Glenbrook Systems, Inc. All Rights Reserved.

- *[74431,2003]   Lib:12*
  INET03.TXT/Text Bytes: 58658

  Title   : Software Distribution on the Internet - A Primer
  Keywords: SHAREWARE INTRODUCTION FTP BEGINNER

  A text file describing the Internet and how a shareware author can make software available on the Internet. Introductory material is included. Also described is the author's shareware file of more resources.

- *[76703,407] Lib: 1*
  TIMELN.TXT/Text Bytes: 10888

  Title : Internet Time Line 1.1 - History of the Internet
  Keywords: INTERNET TIME LINE HISTORY ARPANET

  Internet Time Line 1.1 - History of the Internet.

- *[70202,141] Lib: 3*
  ACCESS.TXT/Text Bytes: 2797

  Title : How to access CompuServe from the Internet.
  Keywords: ACCESS INTERNET TELNET

  You can now access CompuServe from the Internet. You will need an Internet connection with a telnet command. There is no additional charge for access from the Internet.

  ASCII text file; may be read online or downloaded. Please distribute freely.

Apple Macintosh

- *[76703,407] Lib: 2*
  TUTOR.SEA/Bin Bytes: 756480

  Title : Internet Tutorial HyperCard Stacks v1.3 (SEA)
  Keywords: INTERNET HYPERCARD TUTORIAL MACINTOSH

  Internet Tutorial HyperCard Stacks v1.3 (Macintosh Self-Extracting Archive)

  A general introduction to the Internet tools: FTP; telnet; and World Wide Web browsers. The Internet Tutorials stack provides a common starting point for all the stacks.

  The final stack, Internet Hunt, is a beginner's version of the Internet Hunt. It has questions that will stretch a beginner's ability to use the tools described in the other stacks.

  These stacks will run with Hypercard 2.1 or later.

- *[76703,407]   Lib:17*
  PERSNW.ZIP/Bin   Bytes: 34624

  Title   : Personal Networking w/SLIP or PPP (Zipped)
  Keywords: PERSONAL NETWORKING SLIP PPP

  Frank Hecker's excellent paper on Personal Networking w/SLIP or PPP in the Macintosh environment (zipped). See the file PERSNW.TXT or an ASCII text version of this file.

- *[76703,407]   Lib:17*
  MCIMCL.SIT/Bin   Bytes: 5632

  Title   : Internet CCL Script for use with MacCIM
  Keywords: MACCIM CCL SCRIPT INTERNET

  Internet CCL Script for use with MacCIM. Replacements for CONNECT.SCR and INTERNET.SCR in your CompuServe CCL folder. These versions enable MacCIM to access CompuServe over the Internet using a telnet tool.

- *[76703,407]   Lib:17*
  INSLIP.SEA/Bin   Bytes: 240896

  Title   : InterSLIP 1.0.1 from InterCon Systems
  Keywords: MACINTOSH SLIP INTERCON INTERSLIP

  InterSLIP 1.0.1 from InterCon Systems. Free SLIP software for the Macintosh. Requires a SLIP account with a local access provider and Apple's MacTCP to function.

The Internet Resources Forum (GO INETRES)

Protocols, technical information

- *[76703,407] Lib:14*
  INAFAQ.ZIP/Bin Bytes: 87889

  Title : Internet Access Provider FAQ (ZIP)
  Keywords: INTERNET ACCESS PROVIDER ISP FAQ

  Internet Access Provider FAQ (ZIP) Think you want to be an Internet access provider? This file (compressed in ZIP format) contains some basic information on what's involved.

- *[76703,407] Lib:17*
  RF1739.ZIP/Bin Bytes: 35759

  Title : RFC 1739 - A Primer on Internet and TCP/IP Tools
  Keywords: RFC 1739 PRIMER INTERNET TCP IP TOOLS

  A Primer On Internet and TCP/IP Tools (ZIP)

  This memo is an introductory guide to some of the TCP/IP and Internet tools and utilities that allow users to access the wide variety of information on the network, from determining if a particular host is up, to viewing a multimedia thesis on foreign policy. It also describes discussion lists accessible from the Internet, ways to obtain Internet documents, and resources that help users weave their way through the Internet.

- *[70303,2522] Lib:17*
  RFC103.ZIP/Text Bytes: 17390

  Title : Domain names - implementation and specification.
  Keywords: DOMAIN SYSTEM PROTOCOL

  This RFC describes the details of the domain system and protocol, and assumes that the reader is familiar with the concepts discussed in a companion RFC, 'Domain Names - Concepts and Facilities' [RFC-1034].

- *[70303,2522] Lib:17*
  RFC974.ZIP/Text Bytes: 3081

  Title : Mail routing and the domain system
  Keywords: MAIL MESSAGES DOMAIN

  This RFC presents a description of how mail systems on the Internet are expected to route messages based on information from the domain system described in RFCs 882, 883 and 973.

User guides

- *[74674,227] Lib: 4*
  ZEN10.HLP/Bin Bytes: 197804

  Title : Zen & the Art of the Internet
  Keywords: INTERNET HELP ZEN

  Zen and the Art of the Internet in Windows Help file format. Very cool!

Information about services

- *[72603,1671] Lib:12*
  NETGUI.TXT/Text Bytes: 109226

  Title : Library resources on the Internet
  Keywords: LIBRARIES RESOURCES STRATEGIES GUIDE

  Strategies for selection and use of library resources on the Internet. A 40+ page document includes how to get started, road maps, travel guides, search strategies and information about other library resources. (Downloaded from the Internet via anonymous FTP from dla.ucop.edu.)

General information

- ```
  [76703,407]      Lib:14
  INSEC.TXT/Text   Bytes:  46725

  Title    : Security on the Internet - NIST Testimony
  Keywords: SECURITY INTERNET NIST

  Security on the Internet - Statement of F. Lynn
  McNulty, Associate Director for Computer Security,
  National Institute of Standards and Technology, US
  Department of Commerce.
  ```

Access software

- ```
  [76703,407]      Lib: 4
  SLPKNT.ZIP/Bin   Bytes:1193552

  Title    : SlipKnot 1.0 WWW Browser by Peter Brooks (ZIP)
  Keywords: SLIPKNOT WWW BROWSER PETER BROOKS PC

  SlipKnot 1.0 by Peter Brooks (Zipped)

  SlipKnot is a graphical World Wide Web browser for PC
  users running Windows 3.1 or higher. It is designed for
  modem users with ordinary dial-up UNIX shell accounts.
  It does NOT require SLIP or PPP or TCP/IP services in
  any form (no TIA or remosock, etc. if you are familiar
  with these products).
  ```

The Internet Publishing Forum (GO INETPUB)

General information

- *[76703,407]   Lib: 4*
  HANDBOOK.PDF/Bin Bytes: 3102725

  Title   : Running a World Wide Web Service (PDF)
  Keywords: WWW WORLD WIDE WEB SERVICE SERVER PDF

  Running a World Wide Web Service (PDF)

  This handbook was written by Brian Kelly, Computing Service, University of Leeds. The handbook was funded by the Advisory Group On Computer Graphics (AGOCG) through the Support Initiative For Multimedia Applications (SIMA).

  This document is in Adobe Acrobat PDF format and requires Acrobat Reader to view.

HTML information

- *[76703,407]   Lib: 8*
  BEGGDE.TXT/Text   Bytes: 32015

  Title   : A Beginner's Guide to HTML (TXT)
  Keywords: HTML BEGINNERS GUIDE HYPERTEXT MARKUP LANGUAGE

  A Beginner's Guide to HTML

  This is a primer for producing documents in HTML, the markup language used by the World Wide Web.

- *[76703,407]   Lib: 8*
  GOODHT.HTM/Text   Bytes: 27289

  Title   : Composing Good HTML (HTM)
  Keywords: COMPOSING HTML HYPERTEXT MARKUP LANGUAGE

  Composing Good HTML (HTM)

  A guide to composing good HTML.

  This document is in HTML format (HTM) and requires a HTML Browser to read offline effectively.

- *[76703,407]   Lib: 8*
  HTMREF.TXT/Text   Bytes: 14182

  Title   : HTML Quick Reference (TXT)
  Keywords: HTML HYPERTEXT MARKUP LANGUAGE QUICK REFERENCE

  A quick reference to the HTML language.
  @LIBDES = [74011,233]   Lib: 3
  LCEMA.TXT/Text   Bytes: 7907

  Title   : Sending E-Mail Press Releases: A How to from
  Keywords: PRESS RELEASES E-MAIL PUBLIC RELATIONS MARKETING

  Kim LaSalle of LaSalle Communications did an informal survey with members of the Journet, SPJ and Online News LISTSERV discussion groups to find out the approach to sending e-mail press releases. Here are some responses from journalists in the field.

HTML Tools (Microsoft Windows)

- *[75141,1526]   Lib:15*
  HOTMET.ZIP/Bin   Bytes: 1358061

  Title   : HoTMetaL HTML editor
  Keywords: HTML WWW SGML

  This is the HoTMetaL software downloaded from ftp.ncsa.uiuc.edu.

  It is an SGML or HTML editor for Windows.

- *[76100,57]   Lib:15*
  WEBED1.ZIP/Bin   Bytes: 206104

  Title   : WebEdit 1.0a Windows HTML Editor
  Keywords: WEBEDIT WINDOWS WWW HTML HYPERTEXT MARKUP EDITOR

  WebEdit is a standalone Windows-based HTML editor designed for rapid creation and easy maintenance of Web documents. Includes support for every feature of HTML 1 and 2, plus most of HTML 3. Shareware. Uploaded by Author.

HTML Tools (Apple Macintosh)

- *[76703,407]   Lib:16*
  ARCHND.SEA/Bin   Bytes: 1449856

  Title   : Arachnid - Mac WYSIWYG HTML Editor (SEA)
  Keywords: ARACHNID HTML MACINTOSH EDITOR

  Arachnid is the first Macintosh application that offers a true graphical layout environment for building Internet Home Pages. Arachnid is being developed at the University of Iowa's WEEG Computing Center. This is the final beta version.

- *[76703,407]   Lib:16*
  BHE221.SIT/Bin   Bytes: 348544

  Title   : Bob's HTML Editor (for Macintosh) ver 2.2.1 (SIT
  Keywords: HTML EDITOR MACINTOSH HYPERTEXT MARKUP LANGUAGE

  Bob's HTML Editor (for Macintosh) ver 2.2.1 (SIT).

  Freeware HTML editor for Mac users.

- *[76703,407]   Lib:16*
  HTMLED.SIT/Bin   Bytes: 408490

  Title   : HTML Editor for the Macintosh - V1.0
  Keywords: HTML EDITOR MACINTOSH GILES

  HTML Editor for the Macintosh

  Copyright 1994, Rick Giles

  HTML Editor is a semi-WYSIWYG editor for an HTML document. HTML Editor requires:

  - a Macintosh SE/30, Mac II, or other Macintosh with a 68020-compatible CPU.
  - System 7 or higher.
  - at least 2 Megabytes RAM. A larger partition may be needed if you are running in greater than 16 bit color (millions of colors in the Monitors Control Panel).

- *[76703,407]   Lib:16*
  RFTHTM.SIT/Bin   Bytes: 189568

  Title   : RFT-to-HTML Converter (for Macintosh) (SIT)
  Keywords: RFT HTML WORD MACINTOSH

  RFT-to-HTML Converter (for Macintosh) (SIT)

  RTF is a document formatting language developed by Microsoft. There are many word processing packages (Microsoft Word, Word Perfect, Frame Maker...) that can read or write RTF format files. rtftohtml was designed to translate existing RTF documents into HTML - the format of the World Wide Web. It can also be used to author new documents specifically for the WWW.

  The latest version of rtftohtml is 2.7.5.

- *[76703,407] Lib:14*
  WEBMAP.SIT/Bin Bytes: 125056

  Title : WebMap 1.01 (Macintosh/SIT)
  Keywords: WEBMAP GIF PICT IMAGE EDITOR MACINTOSH

  WebMap reads GIF and PICT files, and allows you to draw out the various graphic primitives (rectangle, circle, and polygon) that represent the hot areas on an html image map. WebMap supports both the CERN and NCSA imagemap formats.

HTML extras

- *[76703,407] Lib:12*
  DOTS.ZIP/Bin Bytes: 28544

  Title : Dots/Cubes GIF Images for HTML Documents (ZIP)
  Keywords: DOTS CUBES GIF IMAGES HTML

  Dots/Cubes GIF Images for HTML Documents (ZIP)

- *[73232,3104] Lib:12*
  GIFS.ZIP/Bin Bytes: 412812

  Title : 300+ GIF Images and Icons from Stanford
  Keywords: GIFS BALLS DIAMONDS ICONS HTML DOCS

  This zip file of various GIFs for HTML publishing contains non-standard length file names. Unzip with the most recent version of WinZip (5.6) to convert in one easy step. Great collection of more than 300 GIFs.

- *[76703,407] Lib:12*
  STARS.ZIP/Bin Bytes: 5504

  Title : GIF images of stars, for use in HTML Documents
  Keywords: STARS IMAGES HTML

  GIF images of stars for use in HTML Documents (ZIP).

Chapter 3

How to access the Internet

- **WinCIM**
- **Dial PPP and the CompuServe NetLauncher**
- **Using other operating systems**
- **Costs**

COMPUSERVE Internet Services

CompuServe offers several ways to access the Internet. WinCIM users can benefit from its user-friendly menus and dialogs, while those who demand more freedom can use CompuServe's Dial PPP service. It is also possible to connect to the Internet using other operating systems such as OS/2 and Apple Macintosh.

WinCIM

Like most CompuServe members, you probably have some experience using the **CompuServe Information Manager** for Windows, or **WinCIM**, to access the service. Or, if your computer runs under another operating system (OS/2 or Macintosh, for instance), you probably have experience with the versions for those systems: CIM for OS/2 (OS2CIM) and CIM for the Macintosh (MacCIM), respectively.

Downloading the latest CIM version

If you use standard communications software to access CompuServe, you might consider downloading a version of CIM for your operating system. Downloading CompuServe Information Manager software is free, except for possible communication surcharges.

To download the latest version of WinCIM, `GO WINCIM`. Similarly, you can `GO OS2CIM` to download the latest version of the CompuServe Information Manager for OS/2, or `GO MACCIM` to download the Macintosh version.

Getting used to the CIM software

If you are a first-time CIM user, take some time to get acquainted with this software. You might want to visit a few forums (preferably the free forums, like the Practice Forum (`GO PRACTICE`) and the appropriate support forum for your version of CIM:

- `GO WCIMSUPPORT` if you use WinCIM
- `GO MCIMSUPPORT` if you use MacCIM

- GO OCIMSUPPORT if you work with CIM for OS/2.

Be sure to practice reading and posting forum messages, as well as downloading files. That way, you will be able to use CompuServe's forums as means of support when you experience problems while accessing the Internet.

Accessing the Internet with WinCIM

Do you use another CIM version?
The CompuServe Internet services are not limited to WinCIM. If you use the Macintosh or OS/2 version of the CompuServe Information Manager, you can access all services listed in the Internet menu.

To get access to the Internet with WinCIM, GO INTERNET. After a few seconds, the menu shown in Figure 3.1 is displayed. This menu contains the following options:

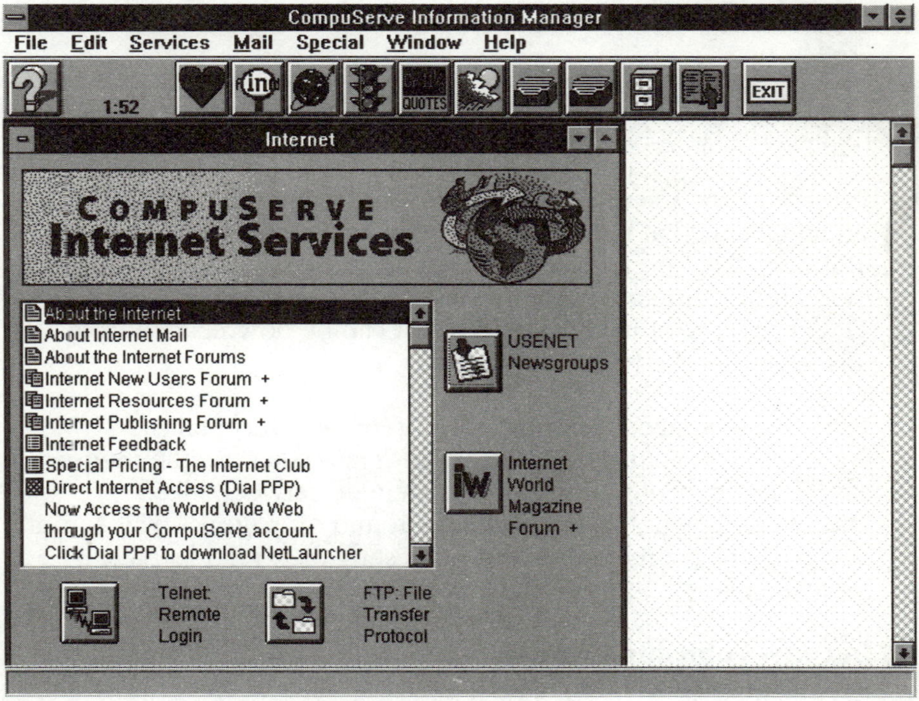

Figure 3.1 The CompuServe Internet menu

- **About the Internet**: This option provides a little background information about the Internet, as well as a summary of Internet services provided by CompuServe.

- **About Internet Mail**: Select this option to read more about the way CompuServe deals with Internet mail messages.

- **About the Internet Forums**: This option tells you more about the three regular Internet Forums available on CompuServe. See Chapter 2 for more information about those forums.

Save money!
Although CompuServe won't charge you for reading these articles, you might still save money (if you use an external network, or if you dial interlocally) by storing these articles into your WinCIM **Filing Cabinet**. Simply press the File It button. After you have disconnected from CompuServe, you can read the articles by selecting the Filing Cabinet option on the Mail menu, or by pressing the special Filing Cabinet button on the WinCIM Ribbon (see Figure 3.2).

Figure 3.2 The Filing Cabinet button

- **Internet New Users Forum**: Select this option to visit this forum, primarily aimed at new Internet Users. As the plus sign (+) indicates, this forum is part of CompuServe's extended services. For more information about the Internet New Users Forum, see page 17. A summary of interesting files that can be downloaded from this forum can be found on page 26

- **Internet Resources Forum**: This forum, which contains information about useful Internet sites, 'must-sees' on the Internet etc., is also part of CompuServe's extended services. More information about this forum can be found on page 18. This forum also contains a large number of interesting files; refer to page 37 for a summary.

- **Internet Publishing Forum**: If you plan to use the Internet as a marketing tool, or if you want to publish material on the Internet, pay this forum (also part of CompuServe's extended services) a visit. Don't forget to take a look in the forum libraries; you'll find a wealth of information about publishing on the Internet, useful tools etc. A few interesting files are listed from page 40 onwards.

- **Internet Feedback**: If you have comments about the way a particular Internet works, or if you have suggestions that might be useful to CompuServe, don't hesitate to select this option to let CompuServe know about them. Your input is very much appreciated!

- **Special Pricing: The Internet Club**: As a member of the Standard Pricing Plan, you get three free 'Internet hours' per month. That's right: except for possible communication surcharges and telephone costs, you don't pay anything during those three hours. This applies to all Internet services provided by CompuServe, except for the forums.

  If you find that you spend considerably more time on the Internet, select this option to sign-up for the **Internet Club**. You'll pay a higher monthly fee ($15 per month extra), but this gives you a total of 20 free hours on the Internet. Besides, the hourly rates that you pay when you use the Internet more often are lower, too. For more information about the costs, refer to page 67.

Standard Pricing Plan only!
If you are a member of CompuServe's Alternative Pricing Plan, you won't be able to sign-up to the Internet Club. To change your pricing plan, `GO CHOICES`.

- **Direct Internet Access (Dial PPP)**: CompuServe is striving to make all popular Internet products available for WinCIM users. But for members who want ultimate freedom in their choice of Internet applications, Dial PPP offers complete, unlimited access to the Internet. This means that you can surf the Web with your favorite Web browsers like SPRY Mosaic and Netscape CompuServe, and that you can use dedicated applications to FTP, telnet and read USENET newsgroup.

  By selecting this option, WinCIM users can download special, free software that makes PPP access very easy. This software package, **CompuServe NetLauncher**, contains the **Internet Dialer** (a program that uses your WinCIM settings to establish a temporary PPP account) and the CompuServe edition of **SPRY Mosaic**, a popular Web browser.

Don't worry if you haven't the vaguest idea what we're talking about... We'll explain Dial PPP and its possibilities from page 51 onwards. To get some background information about PPP, refer to Chapter 1.

- **USENET Newsgroups**: Press this button to get access to the numerous USENET newsgroups available. USENET newsgroups are a little bit like forums; they contain discussions about a range of topics, about all kinds of subjects (from scientific topics to, well, you probably don't want to know...). Chapter 6 discusses USENET newsgroups in detail.

- **Telnet: Remote Login**: This option gives you the possibility of communicating with thousands of computers all over the world that are connected to the Internet, without the need to call them directly. People use telnet to get access to their office computer, or to login to university libraries worldwide. You will learn more about telnet in Chapter 8.

- **FTP: File Transfer Protocol**: A seemingly endless number of files is available on the Internet, waiting for you to download. To transfer files from the Internet to your own computer, you select this option. More information about FTP can be found in Chapter 7.

Watch out for viruses!
Unlike files on CompuServe, Internet files are not by definition free from viruses! Therefore, you might want to use special software to check for potential viruses before you actually start using the files that you have downloaded through FTP.

- **WWW: World Wide Web**: When this book was written, the World Wide Web was not available as a service for WinCIM users. The only way to access the World Wide Web through CompuServe is to use **Dial PPP**. However, CompuServe has announced that it will provide World Wide Web access to WinCIM users as well. To see if this service is available yet, `GO WWW` or `GO INTERNET`. You might also want to check out the ***WebExtra*** for this book, on International Thomson Computer Press's site: *http://www.thomson.com.*

Dial PPP and the CompuServe NetLauncher

Although a number of Internet services have been available for quite some time, many CompuServe members indicated that they wanted more. Their wishes were granted: CompuServe now offers unlimited access to the Internet through their new **Dial PPP** service.

Undoubtedly, Dial PPP will have a big influence on the way that people look at Internet access providers. By launching Dial PPP, CompuServe has immediately become the world's largest Internet access provider. And the rates are, to say the least, very competitive. It will be very interesting to see how other providers react to this, but that's another story...

In short, Dial PPP allows you to establish a **temporary PPP connection**. As you have learned in Chapter 1, this means that, during this PPP connection, your computer is assigned an IP address so that it becomes visible to other computers on the Internet. (To use a metaphor, you 'rent a surfboard' to surf the Internet.) With this temporary IP address, you can use all available Internet applications (the World Wide Web, FTP, telnet, USENET newsgroups, IRC, Internet Phone etc.) without having to resort to WinCIM.

To use Dial PPP, you need two kinds of software:

- **Dialer software**, which connects your computer to CompuServe and establishes a PPP connection with the Internet.

- **Application software**, which you use to access specific features of the Internet, such as the World Wide Web.

You will learn more about the various application software packages in Chapters 4, 6, 7 and 8. The various types of dialer software are discussed in the next sections.

More about CompuServe NetLauncher

If you use a version of WinCIM, DOSCIM or CompuServe Navigator for Windows, you can download a free copy of CompuServe NetLauncher. (The reason you need one of the software packages mentioned above is that NetLauncher uses a file maintained by those packages to obtain information about your User ID, password, modem and CompuServe access number.) NetLauncher consists of two parts:

- The **Internet Dialer**, a Windows application that uses your WinCIM settings (User ID, password, modem configuration and CompuServe access number) to establish a PPP connection with CompuServe).
- **SPRY Mosaic**, an application that you can use to browse the World Wide Web.

Downloading NetLauncher

As mentioned before, you don't pay anything (except for telephone costs and eventual communication surcharges) to download CompuServe NetLauncher. GO NETLAUNCHER; after a few moments, CompuServe displays the CompuServe NetLauncher for Windows dialog, shown in Figure 3.3. This dialog contains a number of options. You might want to check the Hardware/Software Requirements option,

Figure 3.3 The CompuServe Netlauncher for Windows dialog

although NetLauncher works with every modern computer equipped with Microsoft Windows, version 3.1 or later.

Next, select the Download NetLauncher option to download the file *CNL.EXE* to your computer. CompuServe will ask for the directory to store this file. Typically, this will be *C:\CSERVE\DOWNLOAD*, but you can specify any directory you wish.

After you have successfully downloaded the file to your computer, disconnect from CompuServe. Next, exit WinCIM.

Installing NetLauncher

To install NetLauncher, select the Run option on the File menu in Windows Program Manager or File Manager and enter the name, including the complete path, of the NetLauncher file, for instance:

```
c:\cserve\download\cnl.exe
```

By default, NetLauncher will be installed in two separate directories on your hard disk:

- *C:\CSERVE\CID*: For the Internet Dialer;
- *C:\CSERVE\MOSAIC*: For SPRY Mosaic.

The installation software will do the following:

- It will copy the necessary files in the two directories mentioned above.
- It will create a CompuServe group in Program Manager, if such a group doesn't already exist. Four icons will be added to this group: SPRY Mosaic (for the Web browser application), CompuServe Internet Dialer (to establish a PPP connection with CompuServe), ImageView (this application can be used to view graphics and is invoked from SPRY Mosaic automatically) and a 'Read me' icon.

When the Installation procedure is completed, you can either copy the *CNL.EXE* file to a floppy disk or remove it altogether; you won't need it anymore. Provided all went well, you are now ready to 'surf the Net'!

Where to turn to for help

Although the installation of CompuServe NetLauncher is pretty easy, you might encounter a problem for which you have no immediate solution. In that case, use WinCIM to turn to the free NetLauncher Support Forum (`GO NLSUPPORT`) for help. Check out the library files for FAQs (files with **F**requently **A**sked **Q**uestions) about NetLauncher.

Testing NetLauncher

Naturally, you are eager to start exploring the World Wide Web. However, you might want to wait a few more moments and test your NetLauncher configuration. Here's what to do:

1 Double-click on the CompuServe Internet Dialer icon. After a few seconds, the screen shown in Figure 3.4 appears.

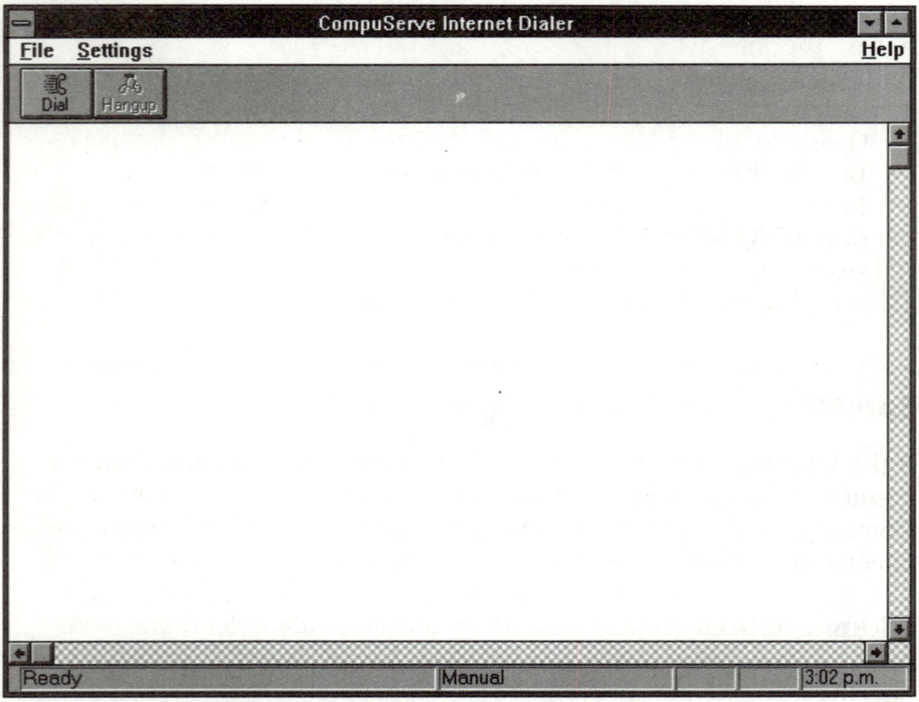

Figure 3.4 The CompuServe Internet Dialer

2 Select the Sessions option on the Settings Menu to display the Setup Session Settings window. WinCIM users might recognize this

window: it contains the same settings that you specified when you installed WinCIM. Check if all settings look alright (pay particular attention to the User ID, Network, Baud Rate and Access Phone fields) and press the OK button.

3 You are now ready to try your first PPP connection. Simply press the dial button. CompuServe will show the following messages:
- **Initializing modem**: The Internet Dialer checks if your modem is available and sends the initialization string.
- **Dialing ...**: The Internet Dialer chooses the telephone number that is specified in the Setup Session Settings dialog.
- **Connecting to CompuServe Network**: CompuServe has 'picked up the receiver'.
- **Logging onto CompuServe**: The Internet Dialer sends your User ID and password to CompuServe.
- **Negotiating**: CompuServe and the Internet Dialer try to establish a PPP connection.
- **Connected!**: The PPP connection has been established. Your computer now has a temporary IP address, and can communicate with all other computers that are connected to the Internet.

4 Did you make it all the way through the latest message? Congratulations! You are ready to start your Internet explorations. But for now, press the Hangup button (on the Internet Dialer Ribbon), or select the Hangup option on the File menu. This will disconnect you from CompuServe. We'll start our first real Internet session in a few moments.

Something went wrong: now what?

If the Internet Dialer gave up, the first important question is 'Can you connect with WinCIM?' If you can, there might be a problem on CompuServe's part – simply try again a little later (an hour or so), or check the NetLauncher Support Forum (`GO NLSUPPORT`).

If logging in with WinCIM doesn't give you any problems, you will have to do some troubleshooting. Take a look at the following checklist:

- **Problems during or before 'Initializing modem'**: Is your modem connected and switched on? You might also want to check the Setup Session Settings window (select the Sessions option on the Settings menu). Look at the Connector field; is the right COM port selected? Is the setting in the Baud Rate field correct? It should be either 9600, 14400 or 19200. Your modem does support connect speeds from 9600 bps onwards, doesn't it? 9600 bps is the minimum speed to establish a Dial PPP connection. If you still don't succeed, press the Modem button in the Setup Session Settings window.

- **Problems during or before 'Dialing ...'**: Is the access phone number correct? Select the Sessions option on the Settings menu and check the Access Phone field.

- **Problems during or before 'Connecting to CompuServe Network'**: Is the baud rate correct? If you entered 19200 in the Baud Rate field (in the Setup Session Settings window), you might want to try changing that to 14400 or 9600.

- **Problems during or before 'Logging onto CompuServe'**: There might be a problem with your User ID and password. When in doubt, just re-enter them in the Setup Session Settings window.

- **Problems during or before 'Negotiating'**: There might be a problem on the CompuServe network. However, check the Baud Rate field first and try entering another value (choose from 9600, 14400 and 19200). If you still can't get through, try again later. If your problems persist, post a message on the free NetLauncher Support Forum (`GO NLSUPPORT`).

Let's browse!

Once you have downloaded, installed and tested CompuServe NetLauncher, nothing can stop you from starting your travels on the World Wide Web. There's plenty to see there and you are in for a thrilling experience! And since the first three hours on the Internet are free for members of the Standard Pricing Plan, you have plenty of time to look around.

Watch out for communication surcharges!
If you use an external network to access CompuServe, the chances are that you have to pay a special fee, the so-called **communication surcharges**. When in doubt, `GO PHONES` for more information. If those surcharges apply to you, note that you

will still have to pay them, even during your free hours on the Internet.

To browse the World Wide Web, you'll initially use SPRY Mosaic. In Windows Program Manager, you'll find the icon in your CompuServe window. Double-click on it. No need to worry about the Internet Dialer; it will be launched automatically.

After a few moments, the SPRY Mosaic application window is displayed (see Figure 3.5). Look at the minimized Internet Dialer at the bottom of the screen; in the background, the connection with CompuServe is being established. You can follow the progress on your screen.

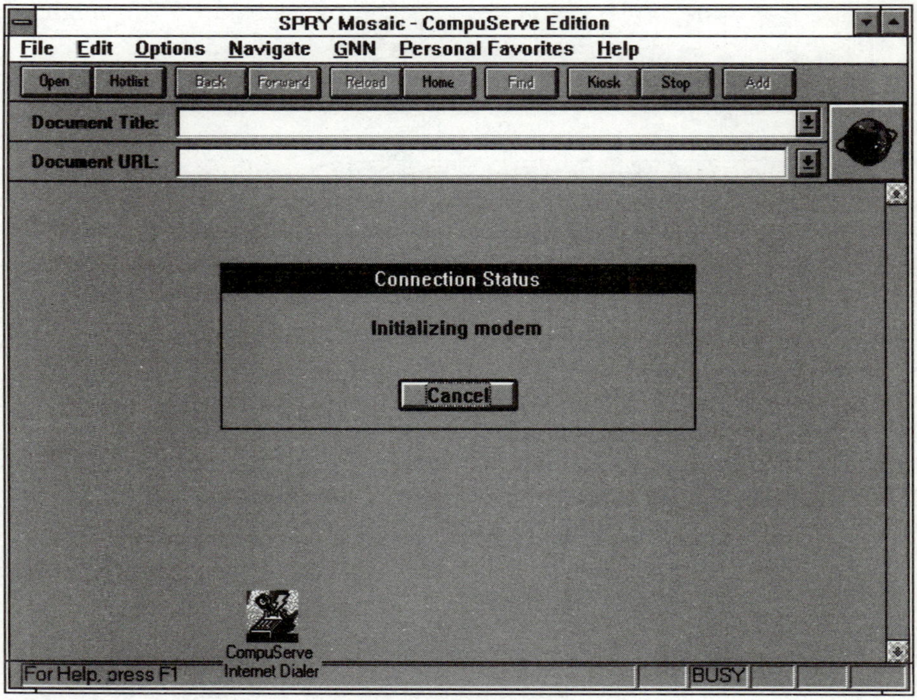

Figure 3.5 The Spry Mosaic application window

When the 'Connected!' message appears, just wait a few more moments. SPRY Mosaic will now try to access CompuServe's home page on the World Wide Web. The results are shown in Figure 3.6: Welcome to CompuServe's Web Home Page!

Do you see the blue, underlined text on your screen? Those are **hyperlinks**. They point to another place on the World Wide Web:

Figure 3.6 CompuServe's home page on the World Wide Web

another place on the current page, another place on CompuServe's computers, or a place on a computer that is located in another country, or even on another continent! Just click on one of those hyperlinks. SPRY Mosaic will clear the screen and **look up** the accompanying page. Would you like to go back to where you came from? Simply press the Back button (on the SPRY Mosaic toolbar), or select the Back option on the Navigate menu). You will soon see that SPRY Mosaic 'traces' your steps: you can 'rewind' and 'fast forward' through your entire World Wide Web session.

Try and experiment a little with the hyperlinks (try clicking on a graphic, too!) and the Back and Forward buttons. If a page doesn't show up, simply try another one.

I don't see the CompuServe home page: what now?
It could take some time before the CompuServe Home Page is displayed on your screen. If nothing seems to be happening, simply select another home page. You can either select a home page on the GNN menu, or you can type one in yourself, in the Document URL: field. A nice home page that you should visit as soon as possible:

`http://www.thomson.com/intlitcp.html`

This is the home page of International Thomson Computer Press, the publisher of the book you are currently reading. It will lead you to a ***WebExtra***: a special home page that contains valuable information for the readers of this book. Look it up and read all about the latest developments on CompuServe and the Internet!

Well, it's time to put this book aside for a few moments. Simply browse the Web and enjoy! After that, look up the following chapter for additional information about SPRY Mosaic, other browser programs, nice World Wide Web features and lots of other interesting stuff. Have fun!

Using other operating systems

You can also use Dial PPP to connect to the Internet if you don't use Dial PPP. The following section contains information for users of:

- Microsoft Windows, who don't want to use the CompuServe NetLauncher;
- OS/2;
- Apple Macintosh

Connecting with Microsoft Windows

You can use Trumpet Winsock, a very popular shareware program written by Peter Tattam, to establish a PPP connection with CompuServe. To download the latest version of Trumpet Winsock from the Internet Resources Forum, `GO INETRES` and look for the following file:

- ```
  [111111,156]        Lib: 4
  WINSOC.EXE/Bin      Bytes:    195921

  Title    : Trumpet Winsock self extracting archive
  preset f
  Keywords: TRUMPET WINSOCK TCPMAN PPP SLIP

  This is a self extracting archive of Trumpet 2.0b with
  the login.cmd where all you have to do is make the
  icon, enter your init string, local access number, user
  id, and password. Enclosed is a file called SETUP.WRI
  which will give you specific instructions on how to
  edit the login.cmd file and the trumpwsk.ini to work
  with your specific system.
  ```

As the description indicates, it is really very easy to install. After you have downloaded the file, execute it in a separate directory. Finally, edit the *LOGIN.CMD* script and the *TRUMPWSK.INI* file. That's all there's to it!

If a copy of Trumpet Winsock is already installed on your system, for instance because you have access to the Internet through another provider, the best thing to do is to make a complete copy of all the files in the Winsock directory to another directory, for instance *\CSERVE\WINSOCK*. That way, you can keep using both access providers without having to make changes in the following files all the time:

- *TRUMPWSK.INI*: This file contains settings that Trumpet Winsock needs to connect to your access provider, such as the Name Server address, the temporary connection protocol (SLIP or PPP), etc.

- *LOGIN.CMD*: This file contains a script with commands that will log you on to CompuServe and establish a PPP connection.

Modifying TRUMPWSK.INI

The best way to change the contents of *TRUMPWSK.INI* is through the Setup option on the File menu.

In the Name Server field, enter one of the following strings:

- 149.174.64.42

- 149.174.64.41
  ```

Finally, check the Internal PPP box. If the Internal SLIP box is checked, uncheck it.

Manual logins

With these changed settings, you are already able to establish a manual Dial PPP connection. Proceed as follows:

1 Restart Trumpet Winsock, to activate the new settings.

2 Select the Manual login option on the Dialler menu. The text 'PPP disabled' should now appear on your screen.

3 Type the following command to let your modem dial the CompuServe access number:

```
atdt123-4567
```

Replace *123-4567* by the phone number that you use to access CompuServe.

4 Your modem should now dial the CompuServe access number. After the CONNECTED message appears on your screen, press the Enter button. You should now see the following prompt:

```
Host Name:
```

5 Type `cis` and press the Enter button. CompuServe will now ask for your User ID:

```
User ID:
```

Enter your user ID, followed by a slash and the text `GO:PPPCONNECT` in capitals, like this:

```
100123,456/GO:PPPCONNECT
```

6 Press the Enter key. CompuServe will now ask for your password. After you have typed it in and pressed the Enter key, some garbage should appear on your screen (this can take a few seconds).

7 The garbage is actually part of the PPP code: you have established a PPP connection. Simply press the Esc key to indicate that you are done. You are now ready to launch SPRY Mosaic, Netscape and other Internet applications.

Modifying LOGIN.CMD

You can also write a script to connect to CompuServe. Or better, you can modify the contents of the *LOGIN.CMD* script. Replace it with the following information:

```
# initialize modem, try settings from CIM if having problems
# This string is for a US Robotics Sportster 14.4.
# Some generics strings to try:
# AT&F
# AT&F&Q0&K4
# AT&F%C0\N0
# AT&F2
# AT&F1
#
output AT&FS0=0 Q0 V1 &C1&D2B0&B1&M0&H2&I2\13
input 10 OK\n
#
# send phone number, change this to your local access number
#
output atdt555-1212\13
#
# now we are connected.
input 30 CONNECT
#
#  wait till it's safe to send, because some modems hang up
#  if you transmit during the connection phase. Try
#  removing the # before sleep 10 if you do not see a
#  Host Name: prompt
#
# sleep 10
#
# now send to wake up the terminal server
output \13
#  wait for the Host Name: prompt
#
sleep 5
output +\13
#
input 30 Name:
output CIS\13
#
# and wait for the ID: prompt
input 30 ID:
#
```

```
# Replace 70006,100 with your CompuServe ID number
output 70006,100/GO:PPPCONNECT\13
input 30 Password:
#
# replace pass-word with your password
output pass-word\13
#
# wait for the address string
#
# input 30 Your IP ADDRESS is
#
# parse address
#
# address 30
# input 30 \n
# we are now connected, logged in and in PPP mode.
# display \n
# display Connected.  Your IP address is \i.\n
```

Check the NetLauncher Support Forum!
For the latest scripts, GO NLSUPPORT to visit the free NetLauncher Support Forum.

Disconnecting

The fastest way to disconnect is by hanging up. CompuServe's Internet routes will detect your disconnection within a few seconds. One way to hang up is by executing the BYE.CMD script; select the Bye option on Trumpet Winsock's Dialler menu.

Disconnecting from CompuServe
If you want to disconnect from CompuServe when you use other products (like forums or databases), resist the temptation to disconnect by simply switching off your modem. Instead, select the Disconnect option (when you use WinCIM) or type `off` and press the Enter key (if you are online in ASCII mode).

Connecting with OS/2

To establish a PPP connection with CompuServe, you will need a copy of the Warp Internet Access Kit. Also, you must install the PPP Update. This file can be downloaded from the OS/2 Users Forum (GO OS2USER):

- ```
  [76011,3435]      Lib:20
  $PP.ZIP/Bin       Bytes:   462115

  Title   : PPP Protocol for Internet Warp Connection
  94/12/13
  Keywords: PPP WARP OS 2 INTERNET SLIP

  This file was downloaded from IBM's Watson Research
  Center.
  ```

After you have installed the PPP update, open the Other Internet Providers object in the Internet Utilities folder. Select the Add Entry option on the Configure menu and enter a name and description. Next, edit the following settings:

- **Login ID**: Type your User ID.
- **Password**: Type your password.
- **Phone Number**: Type the CompuServe access phone number.
- **Connection Type**: Select the PPP option.

In the Login Sequence field, enter the following script:

```
\r
ame:
CIS
ID:
[LOGINID]/GO:PPPCONNECT
ord:
[PASSWORD]
PPP
```

Note that this script applies to official CompuServe access numbers only. If you login through an external network, you'll probably have to modify this script. When in doubt, leave a message in the NetLauncher Support Forum (GO `NLSUPPORT`).

Now, go to the Connect Info page of the Settings notebook and edit the following fields:

- **MRU**: 1500.
- **VJ Compression**: Turn this option on.
```

- **Domain Nameserver**: 149.174.64.42
- **Your Domain Name**: compuserve.com

On the Modem Info page of the Settings notebook, enter or change the following values:

- **Data Bits**: 8
- **Parity**: None

After you have saved these settings, try to establish a PPP connection: select the name that you have given to these session settings and select the Dial option. Once your computer has established a PPP connection with CompuServe, you can switch to an Internet application.

Connecting with the Apple Macintosh

You will find the necessary software on the Internet Resources Forum (`GO INETRES`). Download the following file:

- ```
  [73766,267]     Lib: 5
  MACPPP.SIT/Bin  Bytes:  53760

  Title    : MacPPP 2.0.1
  Keywords: MACPPP PPP SLIP TCP IP

  Here is a copy of the Freeware MacPPP which inplements
  PPP for Internet use. PPP is a TCP/IP Protocol similar
  to SLIP.
  ```

After you have installed the file (since it is stored in compressed format, you need to 'unstuff' it first), proceed as follows:

1. Open the disk or folder where the PPP files are located.
2. Drag the PPP icon to the Extension folder, which is part of the System folder.
3. Drag the ConfigPPP Icon to your Control Panel folder.
4. Restart your computer.
  ```

5 Open the MacTCP Control Panel (you will find it in the Control Panel folder; select the Control Panel option on the Apple menu to open it).

6 Click on the More... button. Next, edit the following settings:
- **Obtain Address**: select the Server option.
- **IP Address**: set the Class option to C.
- **Domain Name Server Information**: set **Domain** to compuserve.com; set **IP Address** to 149.174.64.42 and select CompuServe as the default entry.

7 Open the ConfigPPP Control Panel. On the **Idle Timeout** menu, select None. On the **Echo Interval** menu, select OFF.

8 Click on the New... button and type in a name that you want to use for this configuration. Press OK and click on the Config... button. Enter the correct baud rate (9600, 14400 or 19200) and the CompuServe access phone number.

9 Finally, click on Connect Script... and specify the following script, provided you login through an official CompuServe access number:

```
OUT                                          <CR>
   WAIT   Host Name:
OUT       CIS

   WAIT   User ID:
OUT       your ppn/GO:PPPCONNECT   <CR>
   WAIT   Password:
OUT       your password            <CR>
OUT
```

Note that this script applies to official CompuServe access numbers only. If you login through an external network, you'll probably have to modify this script. When in doubt, leave a message in the NetLauncher Support Forum (GO NLSUPPORT).

You are now ready to establish a PPP connection with CompuServe. Select Config PPP and click on the Open button. To indicate that the PPP connection between your computer and CompuServe has been established, the status window displays 'Network'. You can now switch to an Internet application.

Costs

Although the pricing systems for CompuServe's Internet services look a little bit complicated at first, things aren't as bad as they seem. Here's all the information you need:

- Members of the Standard Pricing Plan (the default pricing plan for new CompuServe members – you pay $9.95 per month) get three hours of Internet usage per month for free. Every additional hour will be charged at $2.50. The new billing month starts on the last Sunday of the current month.

- If you spend more than nine hours per month on the Internet, you might consider joining the 'Internet Club'. You will be charged $15 per month extra, but you get 17 additional free hours of Internet usage in return. That gives you a total of 20 free hours per month; every additional hour costs you only $1.95. A terrific bargain! To become a member of the Internet Club, or to cancel your Internet Club membership, `GO INTERNET`.

- The rates for sending mail messages to the Internet are identical to those for CompuServe Mail messages: $0.10 for the first 7,500 characters, and $0.02 for each additional 2,500 characters. Unlike regular CompuServe Mail, retrieving mail from the Internet costs money, too: $0.10 for the first 7,500 characters, and $0.02 for each additional 2,500 characters. Note that as a member of the Standard Pricing Plan, you receive a monthly mail allowance of $9.

- Watch out: the special Internet rates don't apply to the Internet Forums that are part of extended services. When you visit those forums, you pay the normal rates for extended services, currently $4.80 per hour.

- If you access CompuServe through an external network, note that you might have to pay special communication surcharges in addition to the regular Internet fees. When in doubt, `GO PHONES`.

- To get the latest information about CompuServe rates, `GO RATES`. To get the latest information about the charges you have incurred, `GO BILLING`.

Chapter 4

The World Wide Web

- World Wide Web backgrounder
- World Wide Web terminology
- Ways to surf the Net: WWW browsers
- Browsing the Web with SPRY Mosaic
- Another way to browse the Web: Netscape
- Finding your way around the World Wide Web

CompuServe Internet Services

World Wide Web backgrounder

For a growing number of people, the World Wide Web is their first Internet experience. Happily, CompuServe members can 'surf the Web' as well, by using popular **browsers** like SPRY Mosaic and Netscape. A browser is a piece of software that allows you to see the contents of the World Wide Web on your computer.

The World Wide Web, often abbreviated to **WWW** or **W3**, consists of many, many thousands of **documents** or **pages**, stored on numerous computers all over the Internet. A World Wide Web document looks a lot like a Windows Help screen or an Apple Macintosh HyperCard, in that it can contain text, graphics, sound and sometimes even video clips. But that's not all: the most powerful features of a World Wide Web document are **hyperlinks**. A hyperlink is a pointer to another document on the World Wide Web. When you click on a hyperlink, the accompanying document will be retrieved and displayed on your computer screen. Again, this resembles the way that Windows Help files or Apple Macintosh HyperCard stacks work, yet with a big difference: one moment, you might be viewing a document stored in San Francisco, whereas two seconds later you could be looking at a document that resides on a computer in Amsterdam... A truly amazing aspect!

World Wide Web terminology

As soon as you start browsing the World Wide Web, you will be confronted with some new keywords and terms. Although you don't need to know the precise meaning of them to be able to use the World Wide Web, it helps to have at least a basic understanding.

- **Document**: This is the commonly used term for a document stored on the World Wide Web. (You will also see the word **page** used instead.) As stated earlier, documents can contain text, graphics, sounds as well as **hyperlinks** to other documents on the World Wide Web.

- **Home page**: This is either the entry page on a specific World Wide Web site, or the index page of a particular information provider.

- **Browser**: This is a piece of software that you use to look at World Wide Web documents. Two of the most popular browsers are

SPRY Mosaic and **Netscape**. We'll discuss browsers in the next section.

- **Hyperlink**: Often displayed as underlined text, a hyperlink 'points' to another World Wide Web document. This document can reside on the same computer as the current document, or on another computer elsewhere on the Internet. When you click on a hyperlink, your browser will retrieve the accompanying document and display it on your computer screen. So how does the browser know where those documents are located? It uses the **URL** information that is attached to each and every hyperlink.
  Often, hyperlinks are also 'hidden' behind graphics. You can easily check if a graphic contains a hyperlink: just move the mouse pointer over the graphic. If its appearance changes, you have located a hyperlink. The latest hyperlink fashion is the so-called **clickable map**: a graphic that contains not one, but several hyperlinks.

- **URL**: This is the abbreviation for **Uniform Resource Locator**, actually an Internet address for a certain file, newsgroup or site. When you know the URL of an Internet product, you know everything you need to reach it. For example, the Macintosh version of Netscape has the following URL:

  ```
  ftp://ftp.mcom.com/netscape/mac/netscape.sea.hqx
  ```

  The URL of the CompuServe home page on the World Wide Web is:

  ```
  http://www.compuserve.com/
  ```

  Since every World Wide Web document is actually a file stored somewhere on the Internet, every document has its own URL as well. By using these URLs, your browser can retrieve documents and display them on your computer screen.

- **HTML**: This is the abbreviation for **HyperText Markup Language**, a coding standard used to format documents that are placed on the World Wide Web. Using HTML, features like graphics, sounds and video clips can be added to a document, as can the most important feature: the hyperlink!

  Writing an HTML document is not as difficult as it may seem. More and more software companies are developing HTML converters that work together with popular word processor packages like

Microsoft Word and WordPerfect. You might like to check the Internet New Users Forum (GO INETFORUM) for details.

- **HTTP**: This is the abbreviation for **HyperText Transfer Protocol**. This protocol is used to transfer **documents** that have been prepared using HTML.

Ways to surf the Net: WWW browsers

Unlike Internet features such as USENET newsgroups, telnet and FTP, which can be accessed using either WinCIM or Dial PPP, the World Wide Web can currently only be accessed through Dial PPP. Will the World Wide Web eventually become available for WinCIM users, too? Probably. When WinCIM 1.4 was published, users already got a chance to GO ESM and view the new hypertext pages that CompuServe provides. The step from these pages to complete World Wide Web access with WinCIM looks like a small one, so let's wait and see what CompuServe has in store. For now, CompuServe members can surf the World Wide Web through Dial PPP, using the browser software that they prefer. A next to perfect facility!

The first step: your PPP connection

To access the World Wide Web, you need a PPP connection that allows your computer to communicate with all other computers on the Internet. As a CompuServe member, you can establish a temporary PPP connection. If you don't know how to do this, refer to page 51 (if you use WinCIM or CompuServe Navigator for Windows), or to page 59, under the heading 'Using other operating systems'.

If you have downloaded and installed CompuServe NetLauncher (GO NETLAUNCHER; the download is free!), you have automatically obtained a copy of SPRY Mosaic, CompuServe's official browser software for the World Wide Web. Since most CompuServe members will use SPRY Mosaic as their very first WWW browser, we'll spend a couple of pages discussing this software. Once you have gained some experience on the World Wide Web, you will want to take a look at what some people call the very best browser software available: Netscape. Not too strange, if you realize that Netscape has been developed by the original programmers of SPRY Mosaic, who decided to start a company on their own...

But we're moving too quickly. In the next section, we'll explore the World Wide Web using SPRY Mosaic.

Browsing the Web with SPRY Mosaic

Some experience required!
By now, we assume that you are able to establish a (temporary) PPP connection without any problems. If you need additional information, refer to Chapter 2.

SPRY Mosaic's basic features

Although the version of SPRY Mosaic that CompuServe provides is slightly outdated (the current version had been available for a year when CompuServe 'adopted' it), it does contain most of the features that you will find useful when you access the World Wide Web. The most important of these features are:

- **Primary navigational tools**: previous document, history list, 'home' page (initial document), etc.

- **Secondary navigational tools**: the possibility to create hotlists, in which you can store your favorite **links** to World Wide Web documents.

- **Support for graphics and audio**: using an external viewer program called **ImageViewer**, you can view graphic information in GIF and JPG format. Also, SPRY Mosaic can play audio files in .AU and .AIFF format, and it will redirect .WAV files (recorded sounds) and .MID files (musical information in MIDI format) to the Windows Media Player. You can also install your own tools to view other retrieved information, like video files.

- **Information storage**: When you see a document you like, you can save it to your hard disk. Also, you can use drag & drop to transfer a document to other software that supports drag & drop.

- **Development support**: Because SPRY Mosaic allows you to review an HTML document that is stored on your own computer, you can use it to write your own HTML files. Also, you can look at the source code (in HTML format) of every document that SPRY Mosaic has retrieved. This allows you to learn some 'tricks of the trade'. If you are going to develop your own World Wide Web documents, you will soon learn to appreciate this feature!

Obtaining new versions of Mosaic

Naturally, the best way to get informed about new updates to the CompuServe version of SPRY Mosaic is to `GO INTERNET`. But there are other versions of Mosaic available, too. You might therefore want to take a look at the following files, all located in the Internet Resources Forum (`GO INETRES`):

- ```
  [76703,407]        Lib: 4
  MOS20B4.EXE/Bin    Bytes:  1160079

  Title   : NCSA Mosaic for Windows 2.0b4 (EXE)
  Keywords: NCSA MOSAIC WINDOWS WWW WORLD WIDE WEB

  NCSA Mosaic for Windows 2.0b4 (EXE)

  Requires a TCP/IP stack and a direct connection to the
  Internet for online operation with the World Wide Web.
  ```

- ```
  [76703,407]        Lib: 5
  NCSAMO.68K/Bin     Bytes:   880896

  Title   : NCSA Mosaic for Macintosh (68000) (SIT)
  Keywords: NCSA MOSAIC MACINTOSH WWW WORLD WIDE WEB

  NCSA Mosaic for Macintosh (68000) (SIT)

  Latest version of NCSA's Mosaic for Macintosh.
  ```

- ```
  [76703,407]         Lib: 5
  NCSAMO.PPC/Bin      Bytes:  1103744

  Title    : NCSA Mosaic for Macintosh (PowerPC) (SIT)
  Keywords: NCSA MOSAIC MACINTOSH POWERPC WWW WEB

  NCSA Mosaic for Macintosh (PowerPC) (SIT)

  Latest version of NCSA's Mosaic for Macintosh.  This
  version supports PowerPC-based Macs.  See the file
  NCSAMO.68K for a version supporting 68000-based Macs.
  ```

The screen elements of SPRY Mosaic

Figure 4.1 shows the SPRY Mosaic application window. Besides the common objects (title bar, menu bar etc.), this window contains a number of special features, which will be discussed in the next sections.

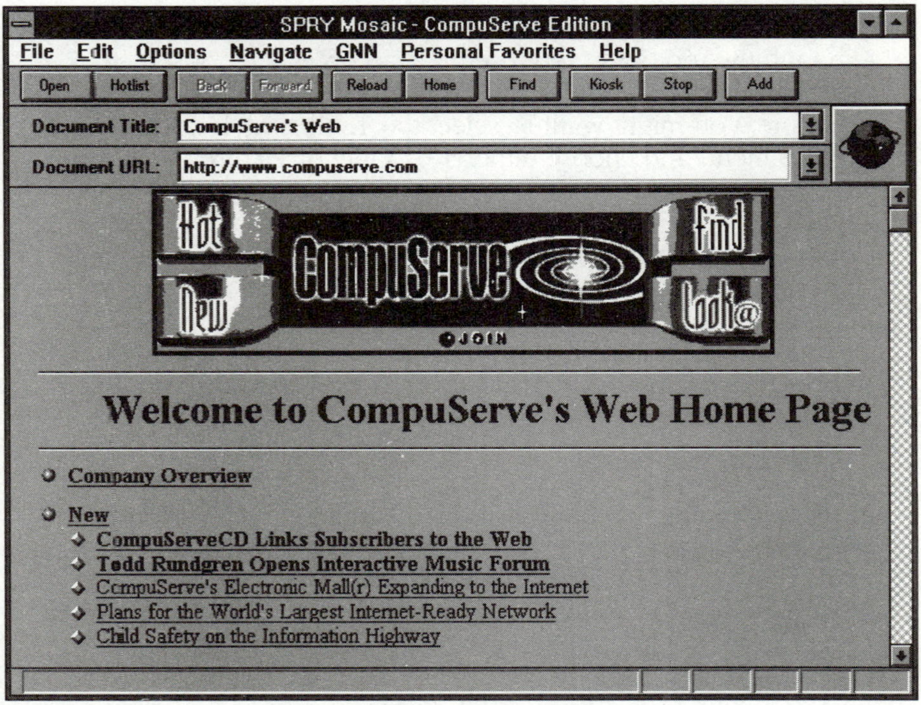

Figure 4.1 The Spry Mosaic application window – the CompuServe home page on the World Wide Web is being displayed
  ```

The Document Title field

This field shows the title of the current document. If you choose to add this document to one of the **hotlists** (lists with links to your favorite places on the World Wide Web), SPRY Mosaic will show this title in that particular hotlist.

The Document URL field

Every document on the World Wide Web has its own **Uniform Resource Locator** (URL): a 'filename' that provides information about its location on the Internet. If you want to see a particular World Wide Web document, you can enter its URL in this field. Don't forget to press the Stop button first, to indicate that SPRY Mosaic should stop loading the current document.

The SPRY Mosaic toolbar

The toolbar contains buttons for a number of actions that you'll perform frequently.

Reducing the size of the toolbar
Although the toolbar is very useful, it occupies a lot of screen space, especially if you use one of the lower screen resolutions. Therefore, you might want to select the Toolbar Style option on the Options menu and choose either Text Only or Picture Only.

- **Open**: Allows you to open a **local file**, an HTML file stored on your hard disk. You can save any HTML document to your hard disk. One way to do this is to hold down the Shift key while you click on a hyperlink. Another way is by selecting the Load to Disk option on the Options menu (this option is actually a toggle; from now on, all documents will be saved to your hard disk until you select the Load to Disk option again) and pressing the Reload button.

- **Hotlist**: Pressing this button shows a summary with **hotlists**: lists with links to your favorite places on the World Wide Web. As you can see in Figure 4.2, several hotlists are already available, like *Personal Favorites, Baby Boomers, Business* etc. You can also add one or more hotlists to Mosaic's menu bar, which allows you to access the hotlist through one mouse click. More information about hotlists can be found on page 82, under the heading 'Hotlists'.

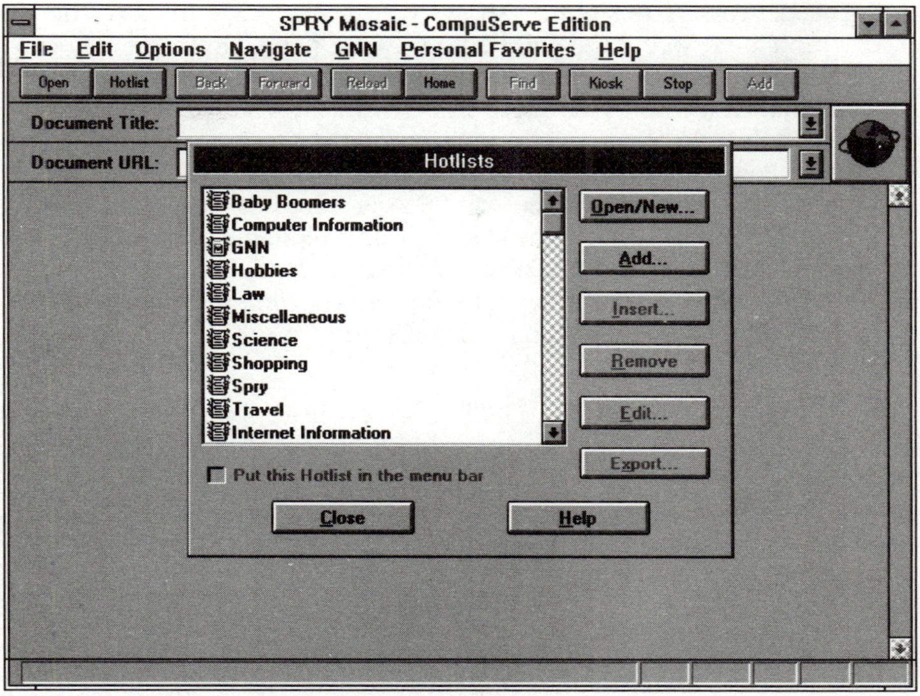

Figure 4.2 Readily available hotlists in Spry Mosaic

- **Back**: Press this button to go back to the last document you reviewed during the current session.

  Tip: You can also select the History option on the Navigate menu, for a summary of documents that were retrieved during the current session. To view a particular document again, just select it from the History dialog.

- **Forward**: If you used the Back button or the History option to look again at a previously loaded document, you can press this button to 'replay' the other documents, up to the last one that you retrieved.

- **Reload**: Press this button to reload the current document. This button can be handy to redisplay a document of which the contents change. A nice, albeit not too practical example of a document where the Reload button can come in handy is the **Trojan Room Coffee Machine** (*http://www.cl.cam.ac.uk/coffee/coffee.html*), a World Wide Web document that shows a continuously updated picture of the coffee pot at the University of Cambridge Computer Laboratory.

- **Home**: Pressing this button shows your home page. Initially, the CompuServe Web page will be your home page. However, you can change this to any document on the World Wide Web – or even to one that resides on your hard disk! To specify your personal home page, select the Configuration option on the Options menu. In the Home Page box, enter the complete URL of your home page. If you want to specify a home page that is stored on your hard disk, enter *file://*, followed by the directory and filename. Instead of backslashes, uses slashes to specify a path name. For example, to indicate that you want to use the file *mypage.htm* residing in the directory *\www* as your home page, enter:

  ```
  file:///www/mypage.htm
  ```

  You can also add a drive specification. However, note that the drive letter should be preceded by an extra slash, and that the colon must be replaced by a pipe symbol (|). For example:

  ```
  file:///c|/www/mypage.htm
  ```

  For more information about specifying the addresses of local files, see page 88, under the heading 'Browsers and local files'

  Tip: Since SPRY Mosaic allows you to save a hotlist in HTML format, you can use a hotlist as your personal offline home page. That way, your favorite links will appear on your screen every time you start SPRY Mosaic. For more information about this option, see page 82, under the heading 'Hotlists'.

- **Find**: If you want to search through the text displayed on the current document, press this button.

- **Kiosk**: Pressing this button switches SPRY Mosaic into 'Kiosk mode': all screen elements will be removed to leave as much room as possible for the actual document. To leave Kiosk mode, press the Escape key.

- **Stop**: If you find that a particular document doesn't load quickly enough, or if you want to cancel the transfer in progress, press this button. You need to press the Stop button before you can enter or select another document.

- **Add**: Press this button to add the document displayed on your screen to your current hotlist. To see what your 'current hotlist' is press the Hotlist button. More information about hotlists can be found on page 82, under the heading 'Hotlists'.

Putting SPRY Mosaic to work

As you have seen in Chapter 3, working with SPRY Mosaic is really very easy. Browsing the World Wide Web is merely a matter of selecting the appropriate home pages and clicking on hyperlinks. But still, those numerous menus and options aren't there without a purpose. In fact, they can help you to spend your time on the Web as economically as possible. In this section, you will learn some basic skills that are not hard to master, but that give you a head-on advantage over other Mosaic users.

Navigating through the World Wide Web

Basically, there are three ways to go from document to document:

- **Hyperlinks**: Virtually every World Wide Web document contains one or more hyperlinks (blue, underlined text) to another document. In many cases, graphics can be hyperlinks as well. To see if a document element is actually a hyperlink, simply place the mouse pointer on it. If the arrow changes into a hand with a pointing finger, you have found a hyperlink. By pressing the left mouse button, you're on your way to the accompanying document. **Tip**: If you click on a hyperlink accidentally, press the Stop button to stop the transfer of the new document, followed by the Back button to bring you back to the last document that was retrieved.

- **Document URLs**: If you know the 'address' of a World Wide Web document, you can enter it in the Document URL field, or you can select the Open URL option on the File menu. As soon as you press the Enter button, SPRY Mosaic will try to locate the document and retrieve it to your computer. Note that it might be necessary to press the Stop button first, to cancel a transfer in progress.

- **Hotlists**: When you start to build up your collection of favorite documents on the Web, you will want to put links to them in one or more hotlists. That way, you can access them easily in the future by selecting them from a dialog or menu. You'll read more about hotlists on page 82, under the heading 'Hotlists'.

Saving a document to disk

In many cases, a document will contain information that you want to save, for instance because you want to read it offline. The quickest way to do this is to select the Load to Disk Mode option on the Options menu. This option acts like a switch: you'll have to turn it off when you have saved all the documents that you need. Next, click on the appropriate hyperlink (if you want to save a document that is not currently shown on your screen) or press the Reload button (to save the current document to your hard disk).

Opening a document from disk

You can use SPRY Mosaic to read documents you have saved to disk, with one exception: since graphics are not saved to disk automatically, they will be replaced by a **placeholder** (the 'Mosaic' globe). Simply press the Open button, or select the Open Local File option on the File menu.

Selecting another default home page

By default, SPRY Mosaic will try to retrieve CompuServe's Home Page on the World Wide Web whenever you start the application. However, you can specify another home page easily: select the Configuration option on the Options menu to display the Configuration window. In this window, specify the address of the new home page in the URL field:

- If the home page resides on your hard disk: type `file:///`, followed by the address of the home page. For instance, `file:///c|/pages/mypage.htm`.
  For more information about specifying the addresses of local files, see page 88, under the heading 'Browsers and local files'.

- If SPRY Mosaic should retrieve the home page from the World Wide Web: type `http://`, followed by the address of the home page.

Disabling the auto-dial feature

When you start SPRY Mosaic, the application will try to load your default home page. If your default home page resides on the World Wide Web (its address starts with *http* as opposed to *file*), SPRY Mosaic will check if a PPP connection has already been established and try to retrieve it. If you're not connected yet, SPRY Mosaic will launch Internet Dialer automatically.

If you don't want SPRY Mosaic to connect to CompuServe every time you start the application, select the Configuration option on the Option menu and uncheck the Load automatically at startup box, or specify (in the Home Page field) a home page that resides on your hard disk.

Disconnecting from CompuServe

PPP allows you to access more Internet facilities simultaneously. For instance, you can access CompuServe with WinCIM through PPP while browsing the World Wide Web with SPRY Mosaic. However, since both applications will send and receive their information through the same channel, the data transfer speed for both applications will be reduced by at least 50 percent. And should you decide to launch another Internet application (telnet, for instance), the average data transfer speed per application will be even lower: less than 33.3 percent.

Because of the way PPP works, SPRY Mosaic doesn't have a Disconnect button. The reason is that SPRY Mosaic simply can't know what other applications on your PC currently use the PPP connection. Simply 'hanging up on them' by breaking the PPP connection wouldn't be a very nice thing to do and could lead to problems, like incomplete downloads, unsent mail messages etc.

The only way to cancel your temporary PPP connection is to switch to the Internet Dialer (press the Alt-Tab key combination one or more times, or press Ctrl-Esc to activate the Windows Task Manager) and press the Hang Up button. However, check if all other Internet applications (if any) have finished their work before you do this.

WinCIM's Disconnect button

If you use WinCIM to connect to CompuServe through a PPP connection, pressing its Disconnect button will not end the PPP connection; it will merely end the communication between WinCIM and CompuServe. To learn more about accessing CompuServe with WinCIM through a PPP connection, refer to page 221, under the heading 'Connecting to CompuServe through telnet'.

Hotlists

SPRY Mosaic contains a powerful means to store the links to your favorite World Wide Web documents. Just like WinCIM has its Favorite Places feature, SPRY Mosaic has its **hotlists** that allow you to collect links to your favorite World Wide Web documents. That way, you don't have to keep typing in URLs; whenever you want to review a particular document, you simply select it from the appropriate hotlist.

The following summary proves that hotlists are very powerful tools indeed:

- You can make as many hotlists as you like, with each hotlist pertaining to a particular topic. Every hotlist is saved as a separate file (with the extension *.HOT*). By adding hotlists to the Hotlists dialog and removing the hotlists that you don't need, you can configure this dialog to your own needs.

- Each hotlist can contain one or more **folders**, which help you to categorize your documents even better. For instance, the Computer hotlist that comes with SPRY Mosaic contains four folders: Services, Hardware, Software and Internet.

- Hotlists can be added to the menu bar, making them very easy to access.

- Hotlists can be exported to an HTML file. This is a great way to make your own default home page, even if you don't know how to write text in HTML, the 'Language of the World Wide Web'. You'll learn how to do this in this section.

Hotlists: indexes only!
Note that hotlists don't contain the documents themselves. They simply contain address information about the document, just like WinCIM's Favorite Places.

To open the Hotlist dialog, shown in Figure 4.3, press the Hotlist button or select the Hotlists option on the File menu. Figure 4.4 shows the symbols that are used to indicate hotlists, folders and documents.

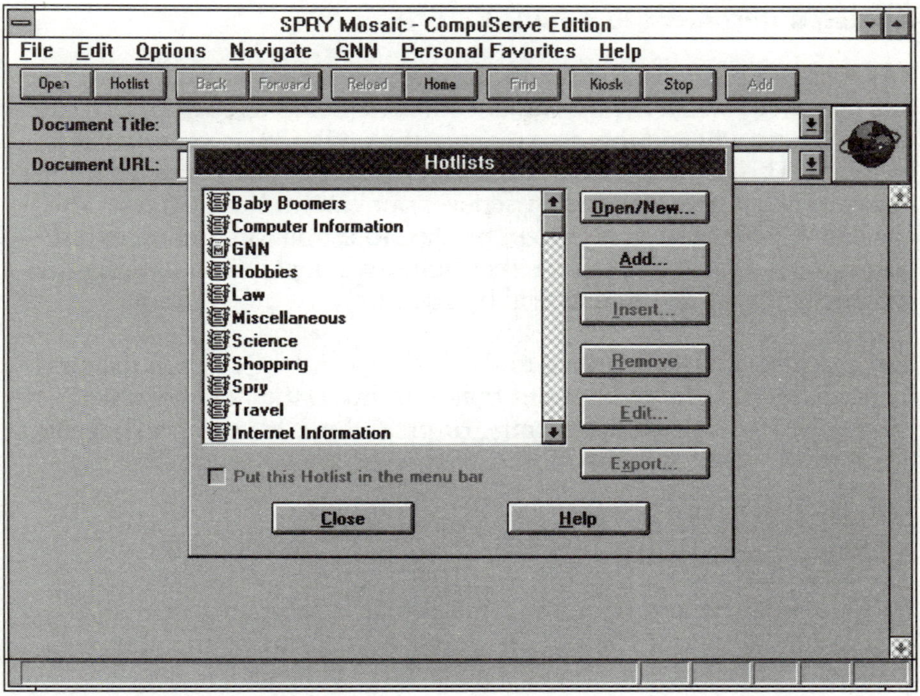

Figure 4.3 The Hotlists dialog

Hotlist, also available as a menu on the menu bar
Hotlist
Folder (heading), closed
Folder (heading), open
Item, contains link to a World Wide Web document

Figure 4.4 Common symbols in Spry Mosaic's Hotlist dialog

Browsing through a hotlist

To review the contents of a hotlist, press the Hotlist button to review the Hotlists dialog. If the hotlist is added to the menu bar, you can also open its menu. By default, both the Personal Favorites hotlist and the GNN hotlist are added to the menu bar.

In the Hotlists dialog, double-click on the hotlist entry, or select it and press the Enter key. If the entry is a folder, it will be opened and all documents in that folder will be displayed. If the entry is a document, SPRY Mosaic will retrieve it and show it on your screen.

Adding a document to a hotlist

To add a document to the hotlist, simply press the Add button (on the SPRY Mosaic toolbar) while the document is being displayed. SPRY Mosaic will add the document at the end of your *current* hotlist or folder. This sometimes confuses users, because it is not really apparent what hotlist is being used as your current hotlist. To review or change your current hotlist, press the Hotlist button and see what hotlist is selected. Selecting another hotlist will make it the current one, to which all new documents will be added.

You can also add a document to the hotlist while the Hotlists dialog is being displayed. Press the Insert button to insert the new document before the currently selected entry, or press the Add button to add it to the current folder or hotlist.

Editing a hotlist entry

To edit a hotlist entry, open the Hotlists dialog, select the item and press the Edit button. The options you have depend on the entry: if it is a hotlist or folder, you can change its title, whereas if it is a document, you can change its title as well as its address.

Removing an item from the hotlist dialog

To remove an item, open the Hotlists dialog, select the item and press the Remove button. Note that you can also remove folders and even complete hotlists.

Adding a hotlist to the dialog

There are two ways to add a hotlist to the Hotlists dialog:

- If there is already a file for the hotlist (all hotlist files have the extension *.hot*) on your hard disk: press the Open/New button and select the file.

- If you want to make an entirely new hotlist: press the Open/New button and type a filename in the Open Hotlist/Create New Hotlist dialog. You don't need to type the *.hot* extension. After you have typed the name, SPRY Mosaic will ask for the **title** that will be used in the Hotlists dialog. The new hotlist will be added at the end of the current entries.

Adding a hotlist to SPRY Mosaic's menu bar

To get even quicker access to your most frequently used hotlists, you can put them onto the menu bar. Similarly, you can remove one or more hotlists from the menu bar. Press the Hotlist button to display the Hotlists dialog: check or uncheck the Put this Hotlist in the menu bar option for each appropriate hotlist.

Converting a hotlist into a World Wide Web document

If you are like me, you will want easy access to your favorite World Wide Web pages. A perfect way to do this is to make your own 'offline home page', a World Wide Web document that resides on your hard disk and loaded automatically whenever you launch SPRY Mosaic, and add your favorite links to it.

The following procedure describes how to make your own default offline home page, loaded automatically every time you start SPRY Mosaic.

1 Press the Hotlist button. In this example, we'll use the Computer Information hotlist, but you can take another hotlist as well.

2 Select the Computer Information hotlist and press the Export button. As a result, the Export Hotlist to HTML File dialog is shown.

3 Type a filename, for instance `mypage.htm`, and press the OK button. You may now close the Hotlists dialog.

4 You have now created a World Wide Web document! To view it on your screen, press the Open button on SPRY Mosaic's toolbar, or select the Open Local File option on the File menu. The entry for *mypage.htm* should be listed in the Open Local File dialog. Select it and press the OK button. If all went well, your screen now looks like the one shown in Figure 4.5. There it is: your personal home page!

5 You can now setup this document page as your default home page. With the mouse, click in the Document URL field to select the text that is listed there. On the screen in Figure 4.5, this text is: *file:///c |/cserve/mosaic/mypage.htm*. After you have selected the text, press Ctrl-C to copy it to the Windows Clipboard.

6 Now select the Configuration option on the Options menu. Go to the Home Page box and delete the text in the URL field.

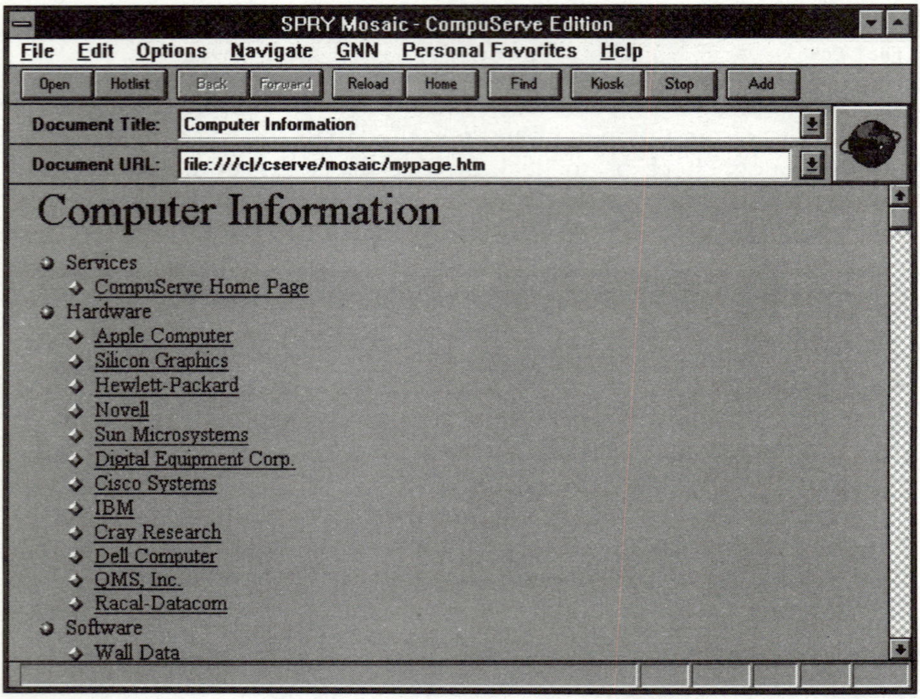

Figure 4.5 Your own home page, with a collection of hyperlinks

7 With the cursor still in the (now empty) URL field, press Ctrl-V to paste the contents of the Windows Clipboard into this field. The URL field should now look like the one in Figure 4.6, although the filename might be different.

8 Make sure that the Load automatically at startup box is checked and press OK to close the Configuration dialog.

9 That's all! To check if it worked, press the Home button on the SPRY Mosaic toolbar. If all went well, the Computer Information document should now be redisplayed. As a final test, exit the SPRY Mosaic application and launch it again. And there it is: your first offline home page (see Figure 4.7).

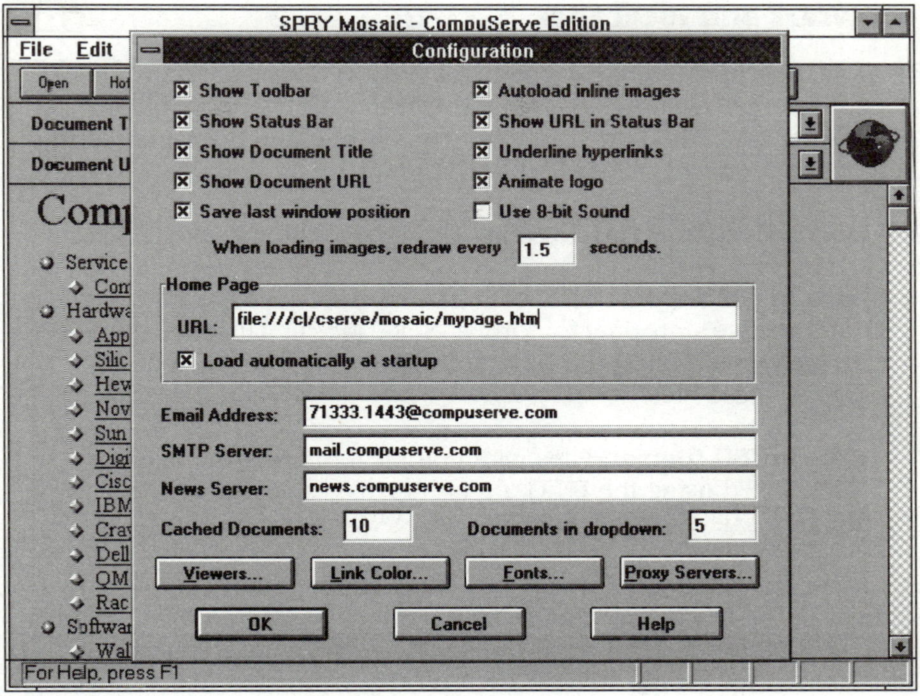

Figure 4.6 Specifying a new default home page

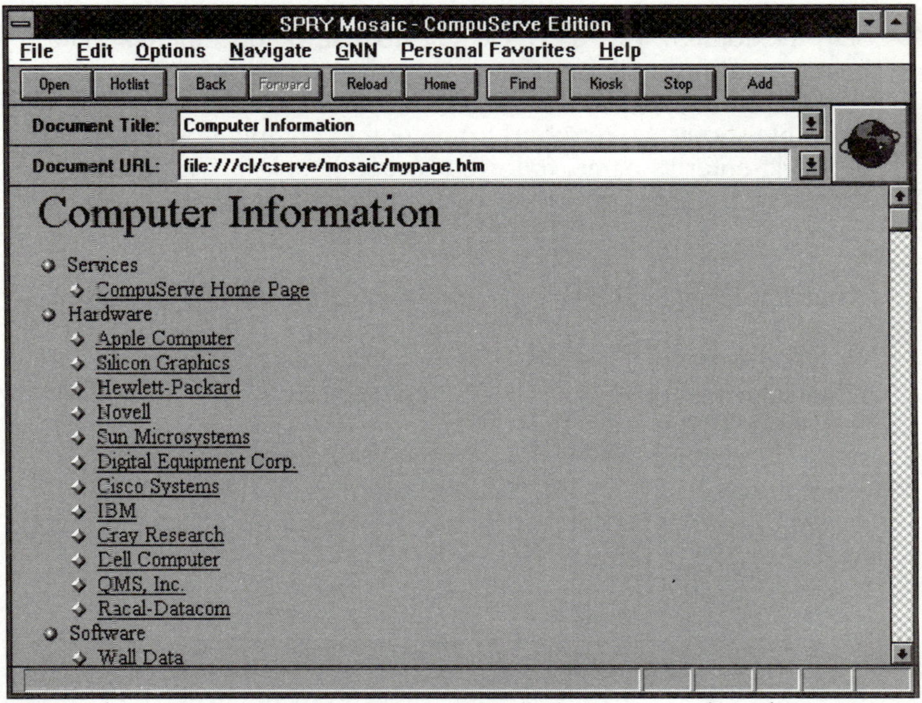

Figure 4.7 Your own home page, displayed whenever you launch Mosaic

Browsers and local files

By now, you have seen that you can use SPRY Mosaic to view documents that are published on the World Wide Web as well as documents that reside on your own hard disk. Using the Open Local File option, you can open the following files:

- **Documents in HTML format**: These have the extension *.htm.*
- **Files in GIF format**: Files with graphical information, in CompuServe's proprietary format. SPRY Mosaic launches the **SPRY ImageView** application, part of CompuServe NetLauncher, to display these files.
- **Files in JPG format**: Files with graphical information that are compressed using the JPEG algorithm. To display these files, SPRY Mosaic also uses the SPRY ImageView application.

After you have opened a local HTML document, you'll see its local address in the Document URL field. By entering other addresses in that field, you can open other local files. You can also specify those addresses as hyperlinks in your own HTML documents. When entering data into the Document URL field, the following rules apply:

- Start the address with *file://*, to indicate that the document should be retrieved from a local disk.
- If the file should be retrieved from another computer within your network, enter its name, followed by another slash (/). If the file should be retrieved from your own computer, simply add an extra slash (/).
- When specifying a drive name, type a pipe symbol (|) instead of a colon (:).
- When specifying a directory path, type slashes (/) instead of backslashes (\).

For example, to display the file *mypage.htm* that resides in the *\homepage* directory on your own hard disk, enter the following information in the Document URL field:

```
file:///homepage/mypage.htm
```

If you want to include a drive name, don't forget to use the pipe symbol instead of the colon. For example, to display the file *mypage.htm* in the directory *\homepage* on your *C:* hard disk, type the following information in the Document URL field:

```
file:///c|/homepage/mypage.htm
```

Another way to browse the Web: Netscape

Although Mosaic is undoubtedly a good, rugged piece of software, there are also other browsers available. One of the most popular programs is **Netscape**. A great program, which has been created by the Mosaic developers, by the way...

To download the latest version of Netscape, you FTP (see Chapter 7) to a mirror site close to the location of your PPP access provider. Since you use CompuServe to access the Internet, your 'location' is Ohio, in the United States. Therefore, pick one of the following FTP sites:

```
ftp://ftp.netscape.com/netscape1.1/
ftp://ftp2.netscape.com/netscape1.1/
download1.netscape.com/

ftp://wuarchive.wustl.edu/packages/www/Netscape/netscape1.1/
ftp://ftp.cps.cmich.edu/pub/netscape/
ftp://ftp.utdallas.edu/pub/netscape/netscape1.1/
ftp://ftp.micro.caltech.edu/pub/netscape/
ftp://unicron.unomaha.edu/pub/netscape/netscape1.1/
ftp://server.berkeley.edu/pub/netscape/
ftp://SunSITE.unc.edu/pub/packages/infosystems/WWW/clients/Nets
cape/
ftp://ftp.orst.edu/pub/packages/netscape/
ftp://magic.umeche.maine.edu/pub/Mirrors/nscape
```

This list was taken from a Netscape World Wide Web document; its URL is *http://home.netscape.com/comprod/mirror/index.html.*

Using SPRY Mosaic to download Netscape

If you have installed SPRY Mosaic (the World Wide Web browser that comes with CompuServe NetLauncher), you can download the latest copy of Netscape without the need to start an FTP session.

From the Netscape Home Page, simply follow the hyperlinks to one of the appropriate FTP sites.

After you have installed your copy of Netscape, simply connect to CompuServe's Dial PPP service using either the Internet Dialer or your socket program (`GO PPP` for more details) and start Netscape. As you can see from Netscape's initial screen, the program tries to connect to Netscape's home page on the World Wide Web, *http://home.netscape.com* (see Figure 4.8). The infamous 'N' will be animated, showing dropping meteors while the data transfer is in progress.

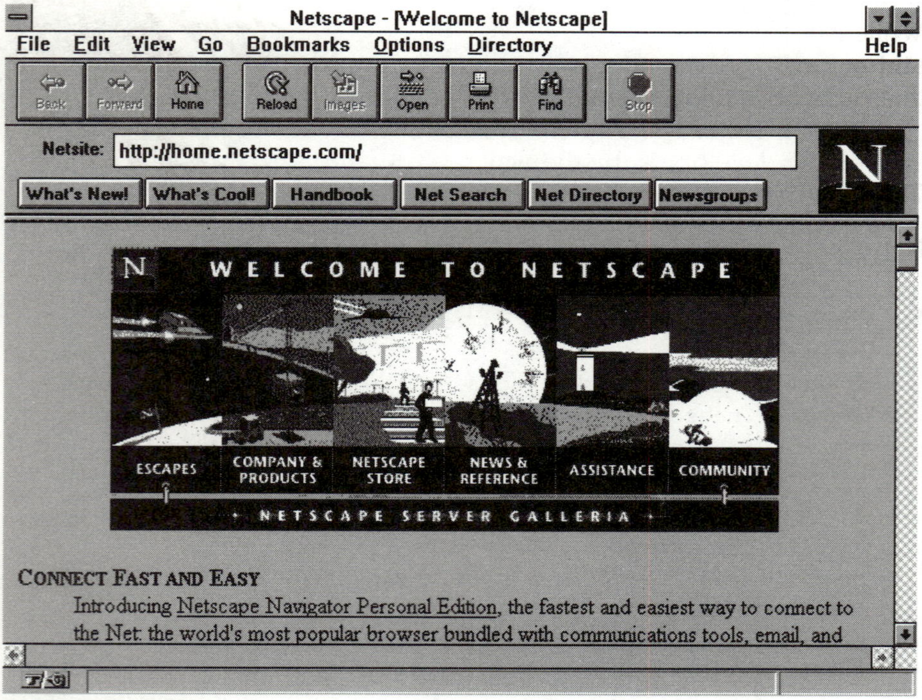

Figure 4.8 Netscape's home page on the World Wide Web

A quick way to the Netscape Home Page: the logo!
Most Netscape users will eventually change the default home page to one of their own favorites. However, you can return to Netscape's Home Page at any moment by pressing the 'N' logo.

Netscape's basic features

The following section lists the most important elements that can be found in the Netscape application window.

The status bar

Netscape's status bar contains some interesting information. First, the key symbol on the left side shows whether or not you are using a **secure connection**. As long as the key is broken, don't send any sensitive information (like credit card numbers).

While Netscape retrieves documents from the World Wide Web, the **status indicator** (on the right-hand side) shows the amount of data that has been downloaded. A real nice feature!

The Toolbar

Netscape's Toolbar contains the following buttons:

- **Back**: Pressing this button displays the document that you viewed before the current one. It takes you one document back in the so-called **history list**. You will also see a number of previously viewed documents on the Go menu.

  If you look at Figure 4.8, you will see that the Back button is greyed out. The reason is that there isn't a 'history' yet: Netscape has displayed only one document. Now look at Figure 4.9. This document was displayed because we have clicked on the **Netscape store** hyperlink. Do you notice that the Back button is now available? Clicking on it would result in the first document (Figure 4.8) being displayed again.

- **Forward button**: This button is only available when you are viewing documents that are part of the history list. (That is, if you went 'back'.) Press it to view the next document in the history list.

- **Home button**: Press this button to display your **home page**: the basic document that you want to be displayed whenever you start Netscape. By default, this will be the 'Welcome to Netscape' document, shown in Figure 4.8. However, you can assign any document you wish to be your personal home page: on Netscape's Options menu, select Preferences. From the combo box displayed in the Preferences window, select the first option, Styles. In the

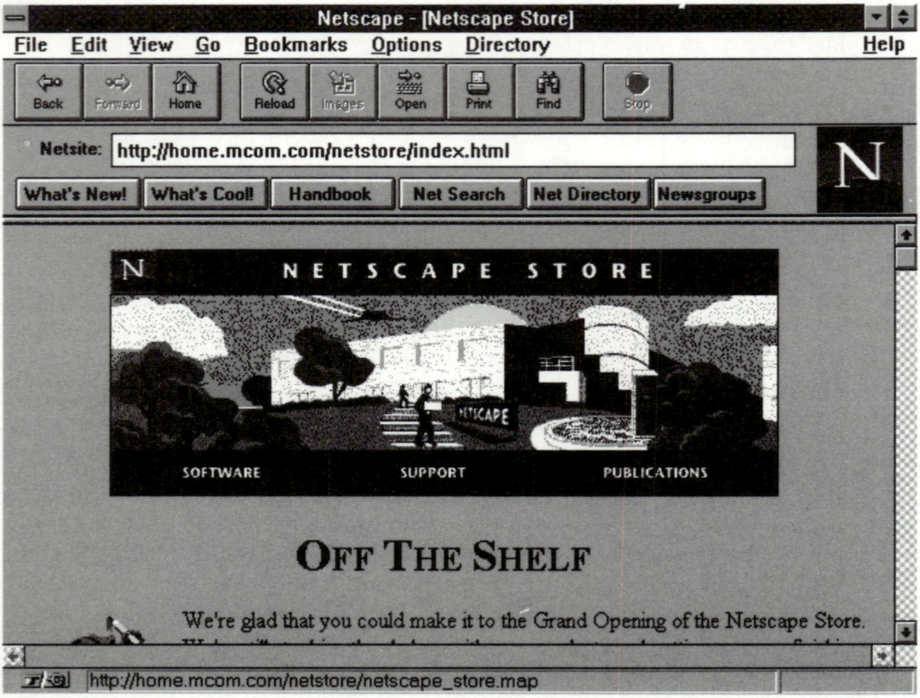

Figure 4.9 After following displaying more than one page, Netscape's Back button becomes available

resulting window, you can enter your home page location: the complete URL of the document you would like to be retrieved by default.

As a CompuServe member, you might initially want to select the CompuServe Home Page for this purpose (see Figure 4.10). Its URL is:

```
http://www.compuserve.com/
```

The CompuServe Home Page contains useful information about CompuServe and is updated frequently. Documents are being added regularly. Of course, you can always go back to the default Netscape URL:

```
http://home.netscape.com/welcome.html
```

- **Reload button**: Press this button to reload the current document, for instance if the transmission was interrupted, or when you have reason to believe that the original document has changed since the last time you retrieved it.

- **Open button**: If you press this button, you can enter the URL of a specific document (or even a USENET newsgroup, FTP site or Gopher page – Netscape can be used to view those Internet features as well!). You can also click directly in the Location text box and either edit the current URL or enter a new one.

- **Find button**: Don't be fooled by this one! Pressing this button allows you to search for text **in the current document only**. Therefore, this button can't be compared with WinCIM's famous Find button that actually scans CompuServe for products you are interested in.

  If you are looking for specific information on the World Wide Web, you might consider using one of the special URLs available. Refer to page 109, under the heading 'Finding your way around the World Wide Web', for more information.

Figure 4.10 CompuServe's home page on the World Wide Web

The Netsite field

The Netsite field contains the URL of the current page. You can edit the Netsite field directly, or you can use one of the following techniques to retrieve another document:

- Click on a hyperlink.
- Press one of the Directory buttons, or select an option on the Directory menu.
- Select the Open Location or Open File option on the File Menu.
- Select an option on the Go menu, or press one of the corresponding Toolbar buttons.
- Select an option on the Bookmarks menu. Just like the Hotlists in SPRY Mosaic, the Netscape Bookmarks menu helps you to organize your links to World Wide Web documents. More information about the Bookmarks menu can be found on page 97.

The Directory buttons

The Directory buttons correspond are actually shortcuts to options on the Directory menu. They all point to documents on the Netscape site, like information about the latest additions to the World Wide Web ('What's New'), a list of 'real cool' World Wide Web documents ('What's Cool') and the Netscape documentation ('Handbook').

The Newsgroups button
A special Directory button, Newgroups, provides access to the USENET newsgroups. To be able to access USENET newsgroups with Netscape, you'll have to specify a **news server**. As a CompuServe member, you can specify **news.compuserve.com**: select the Preferences option on the Options menu and select Mail and News from the Set Preferences On combo box. Next, enter `news.compuserve.com` in the News (NTTP) Server field.

Putting Netscape to work

Press the right mouse button!
In many cases, pressing the right mouse button will show a pop-up menu with context-specific options. To save time, use the right mouse button as often as you can.

Navigating through the World Wide Web

Basically, there are three ways to go from document to document:

- **Hyperlinks**: Virtually every World Wide Web document contains one or more hyperlinks (blue, underlined text) to another document. Netscape also uses purple-colored hyperlinks to indicate that you have retrieved that page earlier.

In many cases, graphics can be hyperlinks as well. To see if a document element is actually a hyperlink, simply place the mouse pointer on it. If the arrow changes into a hand with a pointing finger, you have found a hyperlink. By pressing the left mouse button, you're on your way to the accompanying document.

Tip: If you click on a hyperlink accidentally, press the Stop button to stop the transfer of the new document, followed by the Back button to bring you back to the last document that was retrieved.

- **Document URLs**: If you know the 'address' of a World Wide Web document, you can enter it in the Location field (the word 'Location' will change to 'Go to'), or you can select the Open Location option on the File menu. As soon as you press the Enter button, Netscape Mosaic will try to locate the document and retrieve it to your computer. Any previous transfer will be cancelled.

- **Bookmarks**: Once you start collecting your favorite Web documents, you will want to save links to those documents for future reference. All you have to do is place those links in Netscape's Bookmarks menu. The next time you want to look at the document, simply select on the Bookmarks menu. Bookmarks are discussed on page 97, under the heading 'Bookmarks'.

Opening another document window

One of the nice features of Netscape is the ability to have multiple document windows open at the same time. If you find yourself 'standing in line' before a document is transferred to your computer, select the New Window option on the File menu. While the transfer of the original document is still in progress, you can browse through other World Wide Web documents. (Naturally, it takes twice as long to transfer each individual document. But in many cases, it beats looking at the Netscape logo for minutes at a time, doesn't it?

Initially, you can have four windows open at once. If you need more windows, select the Preferences option on the Options menu, and select the Cache and Network option from the Set Preferences On combo box. The last option in the dialog, Connections, allows you to specify the maximum number of document windows.

The right mouse button
If you select the New Window option on the File menu, the new window will initially show the current page. However, you can also specify that the new window should show the document pointed to by the current hyperlink. Put the mouse pointer on the hyperlink and press the right mouse button. When a pop-up menu appears, select the New Window with this Link option. Netscape will now open a new window and retrieve the appropriate document.

Saving a document to disk

To save the current document to disk, select the Save As option on the File menu.

Saving an HTML page in text format
A real time-saver: if you want to save the document text without the HTML codes, select the Save As option and, in the Save file as combo box, choose Plain Text. Netscape will strip all HTML codes and leave you with a clean ANSI document.

Opening a document from disk

To view documents you have saved to disk, select the Open File option on the File menu. If you know the filename of the document, you can also press the Open key. Start the filename specification with *file://* and use slashes instead of backslashes in directory paths. Also, use a pipe symbol (|) instead of the colon when you specify a drive name, and precede the drive name by an extra slash.

An example: to open the file *c:\homepage\index.htm*, press the Open button and type the following:

`file:///c|/homepage/index.htm.`

When you open an HTML document from disk, it will be displayed just like a regular World Wide Web document, with one exception: if you retrieved the document from the World Wide Web, its graphics will be replaced by a **placeholder** (the folder with the question mark).

Saving illustrations
If you want to save an illustration that is part of a World Wide Web document, place the mouse pointer onto the illustration and press the *right mouse button*. A pop-up menu appears: select the Save this Image as option.

Selecting another default home page

By default, Netscape will try to load the Netscape Home Page (*http://home.netscape.com*) when you start the application. However, you can specify another home page easily: select the Preferences option on the Options menu, and select Styles from the Set Preferences On combo box. Next, select the Home Page Location option button and type the address of the new home page in the accompanying text box:

- If the home page resides on your hard disk: type `file://`, followed by the address of the home page. For instance, `file:///c|/pages/mypage.htm`.
  For more information about specifying the addresses of local files, see page 88, under the heading 'Browsers and local files'.

- If SPRY Mosaic should retrieve the home page from the World Wide Web: type `http://`, followed by the address of the home page.

Bookmarks

Just as SPRY Mosaic has its hotlists, Netscape has **bookmarks** that allow you to keep track of your favorite World Wide Web documents. All bookmarks are visible as items in the Bookmarks menu; to retrieve a World Wide Web document, simple select the respective item from the Bookmarks menu. It's as simple as that!

You will soon see that it's not difficult at all to add a link to the Bookmarks menu. However, there are some other activities pertaining to bookmarks that can take a little bit longer to master. In this section, we'll discuss the most important things you need to know to get the most out of this versatile Netscape feature.

Converting SPRY Mosaic hotlists into bookmarks
If you have used SPRY Mosaic before, and if you want to take your hotlists with you, you can convert them into bookmarks. First, use SPRY Mosaic to convert your hotlists into an HTML document (see page 85, under the heading 'Converting a hotlist into a World Wide Web document', for more information). Next, switch to Netscape. Press Ctrl-B or select the View Bookmarks option on the Bookmarks menu. Press the Edit button to expand the Bookmark List dialog and press the Import button to import the HTML document into your list with bookmarks.

Adding a bookmark

There are a few ways to add a link to the Bookmarks menu. The new link will become the last item.

- To add the document you are currently looking at: Press Ctrl-A, or select the Add Bookmark option on the Bookmarks menu.
- To add the document pointed to by a hyperlink: place the mouse pointer on the link and press the right mouse button. Next, select the Add Bookmark for this Link option on the pop-up menu.

Once you have added an item to the Bookmarks menu, simply select it to retrieve the accompanying document.

Deleting a bookmark

Press Ctrl-B, or select the View Bookmarks option on the Bookmarks menu. After a few moments, the Bookmark List dialog is shown (see Figure 4.11).

Press the Edit button to expand the dialog (see Figure 4.12). Next, select the item you want to delete and press the Remove Item button. Finally, press the Close button to remove the dialog from your screen.

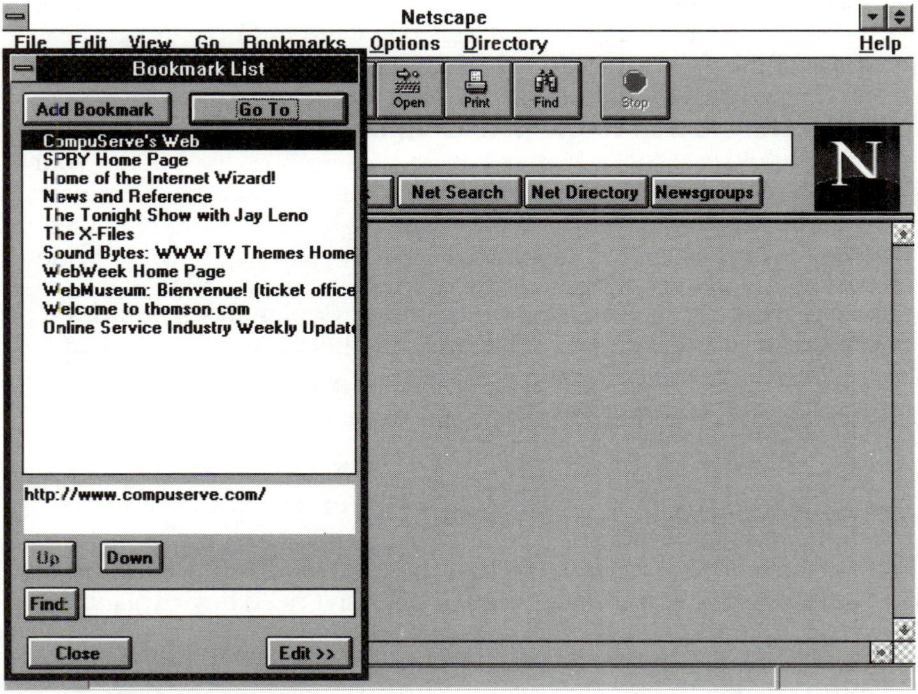

Figure 4.11 The Bookmark List dialog

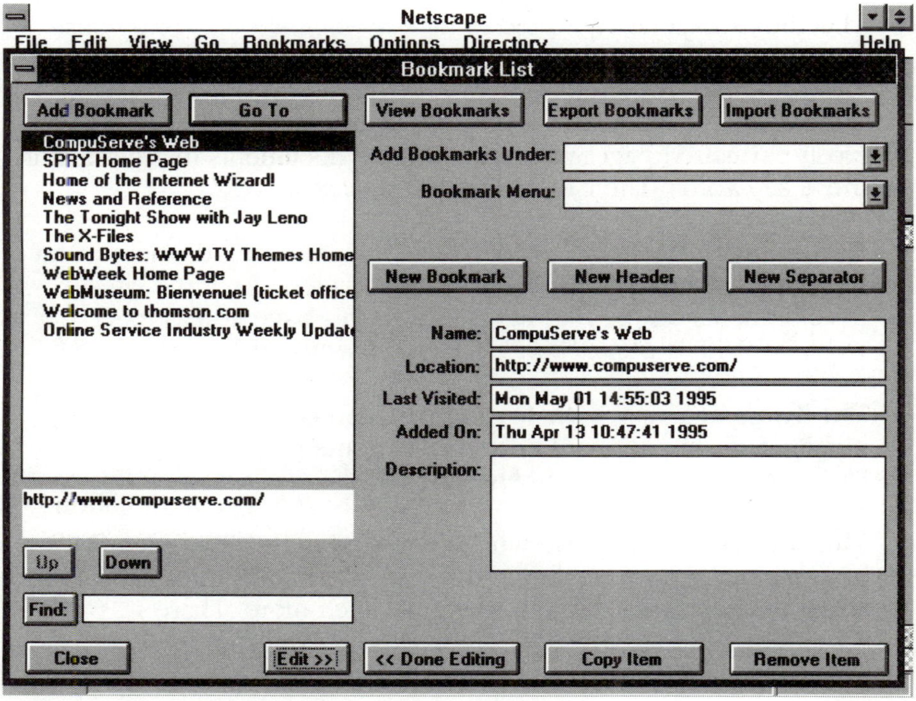

Figure 4.12 The expanded Bookmark List dialog

Changing a bookmark title

Press Ctrl-B, or select the View Bookmarks option on the Bookmarks menu. Next, press the Edit button to expand the Bookmark Lists dialog. Select the item you want to change and type the new title in the Name field.

Putting things in order: submenus

Most Netscape users soon discover that their Bookmarks menu has become almost useless due to the large number of items they've added to it. Time to do some housekeeping! A nice way to do this is to group related items in **submenus**. This is not really difficult to do, once you get the hang of it.

In the following example, we'll use a subset of my own Bookmarks menu. It contains 11 items:

- **CompuServe's Web Page**: this one doesn't need any explanation, does it? Its URL is *http://www.compuserve.com/*.
- **SPRY Home Page**: this home page contains information about SPRY, as well as links to a good search engine and some nice sites. The URL is *http://www.spry.com/*
- **Home of the Internet Wizard**: A nice (and fast!) search engine. After you have entered one or more keywords, it will return a nicely formatted page with hyperlinks to documents that pertain to those keywords. The URL is *http://wizard.spry.com/*.
- **News and reference**: One of the many interesting documents on Netscape's site, this page provides information about the latest developments on the Internet. I turn to this page at least once per week. Its URL is *http://home.netscape.com/newsref/*
- **The Tonight Show with Jay Leno**: Video clips, peeks backstage, highlights from Jay's conferences: this home page has it all. The URL is *http://www.nbctonightshow.com/*.
- **The X-Files**: for everyone who is addicted to this TV series (I became totally hooked during the second season), information about new episodes, biographies and much more. There's something out there on *http://www.rutgers.edu/xfiles.html*.

- **Sound Bytes: The WWW TV Themes Home Page**: Patrick Kenny did a terrific job compiling themes from hundreds and hundreds of famous TV series. You'll find them all on this page. Its URL is *http://ai.eecs.umich.edu/people/kennyp/sounds.html.*

- **WebWeek Home Page**: WebWeek is a newspaper for people who develop World Wide Web pages. Although it is primarily a paper-based publication, this home page contains highlights, as well as articles that are published on the Web only. The URL is *http://www.mecklerweb.com/mags/ww/wwhome.htm.*

- **Bienvenue au WebMuseum**: Probably one of the most famous home pages on the World Wide Web. The next best thing to a real visit to the Louvre. Its URL is *http://www.cnam.fr/louvre*, but there are mirror sites available, too.

- **Welcome to thomson.com**: The home page of Thomson Publishing. You'll find a lot of interesting information here (does this sound like a commercial or not?), like the ***WebExtra*** available for this book. A ***WebExtra***, a Thomson exclusive, contains additional information that either didn't make it into this book, or wasn't available when this book went to print. The URL for the Thomson Home Page is *http://www.thomson.com.*

- **Online Service Industry Weekly Update**: If you work in the information service industry, or if you have more than a passing interest in what's going on there, be sure to pay a visit to this home page, created by Robert D. Seidman. Robert's newsletter is one of the best available! The URL is *http:/www.clark.net/pub/robert/.*

Save your bookmarks file!
If you would like to temporarily replace your own Bookmarks menu with this one, exit Netscape and rename the *bookmark.htm* file (you'll find it in your Netscape directory). This file contains the items that are listed in the Bookmarks menu.

To create this bookmark file, either add the items manually, or download the file from the ***WebExtra*** page that belongs to this book. (See this book's Preface for more information.)

Figure 4.13 shows the Bookmarks menu with these entries.

Select the View Bookmarks option and press the Edit button. Your screen should now look like the one shown in Figure 4.14.

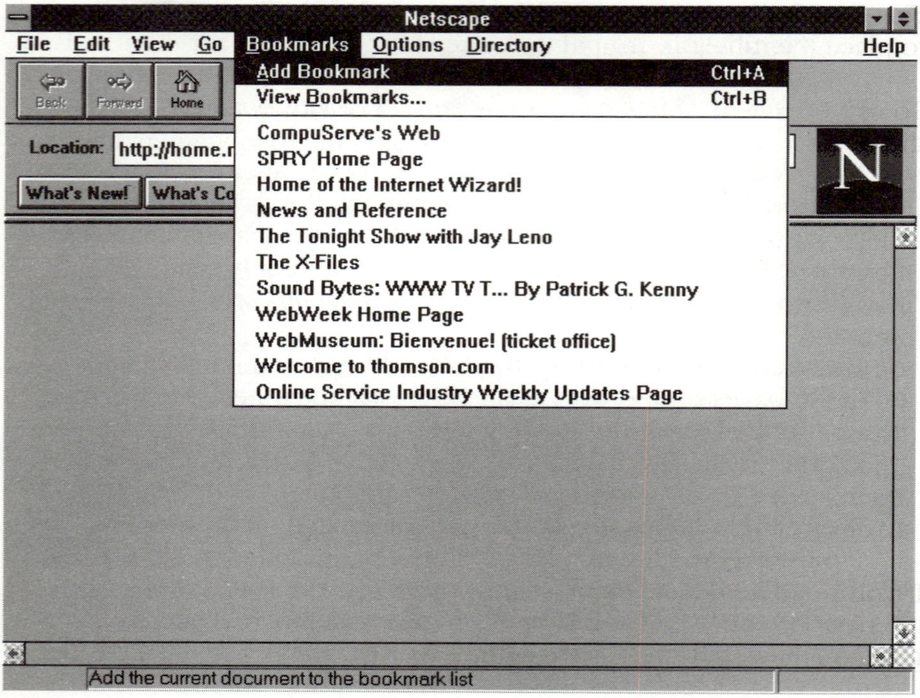

Figure 4.13 An extract from my personal Bookmarks menu

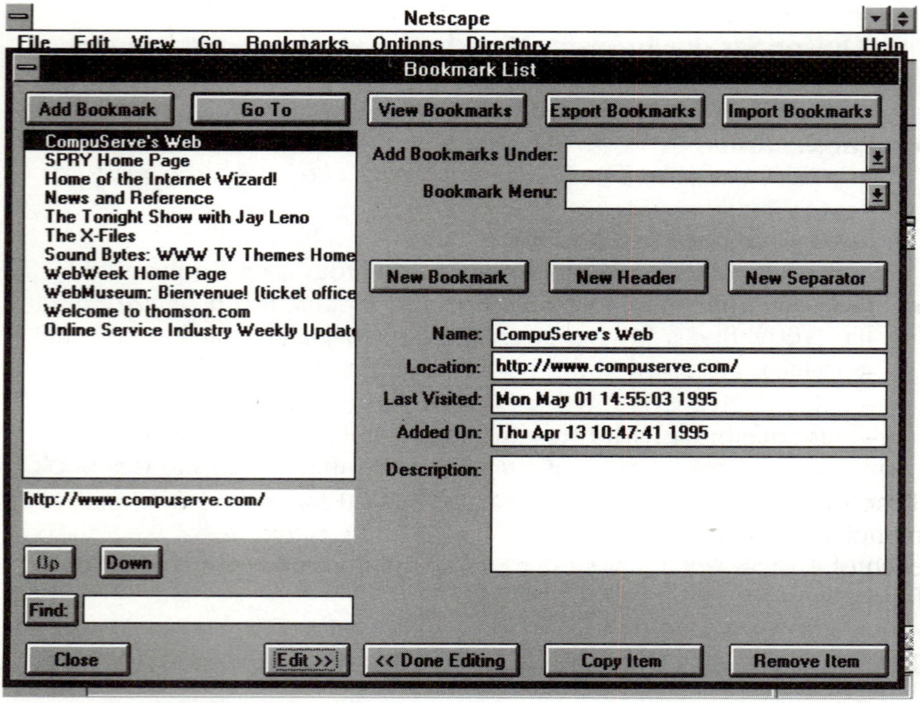

Figure 4.14 Use this dialog to edit the Bookmarks menu

First, we'll change the order of the items a bit; we'll move some items to place them next to related items.

To move an item, select it and press the Up or Down button. Change the order in which the items appear to match the following layout:

```
CompuServe's Web Page
SPRY Home Page
Home of the Internet Wizard
News and reference
WebWeek Home Page
Online Service Industry Weekly Update
Welcome to thomson.com
The Tonight Show with Jay Leno
The X-Files
Sound Bytes: The WWW TV Themes Home Page
Bienvenue au WebMuseum
```

If you wish, you can now close the Bookmark List dialog and look at the new Bookmarks menu. If you look closely, you'll see we have grouped the items into three categories:

- **Web and Internet information**:
  - SPRY Home Page
  - Home of the Internet Wizard
  - News and reference
- **Publications**:
  - WebWeek Home Page
  - Online Service Industry Weekly Update
  - Welcome to thomson.com
- **Entertainment**:
  - The Tonight Show with Jay Leno
  - The X-Files
  - Sound Bytes: The WWW TV Themes Home Page
  - Bienvenue au WebMuseum

Time for our next step. We'll add some **submenus** to the Bookmarks menu: *Web/Net Info*, *Publications* and *Entertainment*. Next, we'll move each of our current 11 entries to its appropriate submenu. Proceed as follows:

1 Press Ctrl-B and the Edit button to display the expanded Bookmark List dialog.

2 Press the New Header button. The text - *New Header* will now appear in the item list: we've created a submenu. In the Name field, replace the text *New Header* with *Web/Net Info*. You can see that the text in the item list is updated as you type.

3 Now, move the - *Web/Net Info* item to the first place in the items list. Since the item is already selected, press the Up button until it has become the first item (the Up button will become grey, as well).

4 We're almost done with the first series of items. The only thing we need to do is to **indent** them, to indicate that they actually belong to the *Web/Net Info* header. To do this, select the first link (*CompuServe's Web*) and press the Up button *once*. As you can see in Figure 4.15, Netscape will indent the item, indicating that it is now part of the *Web/Net Info* submenu. If you press the Up button again, you see that the item now moves to the first row of the item list; simply press the Down button to move it back in place.

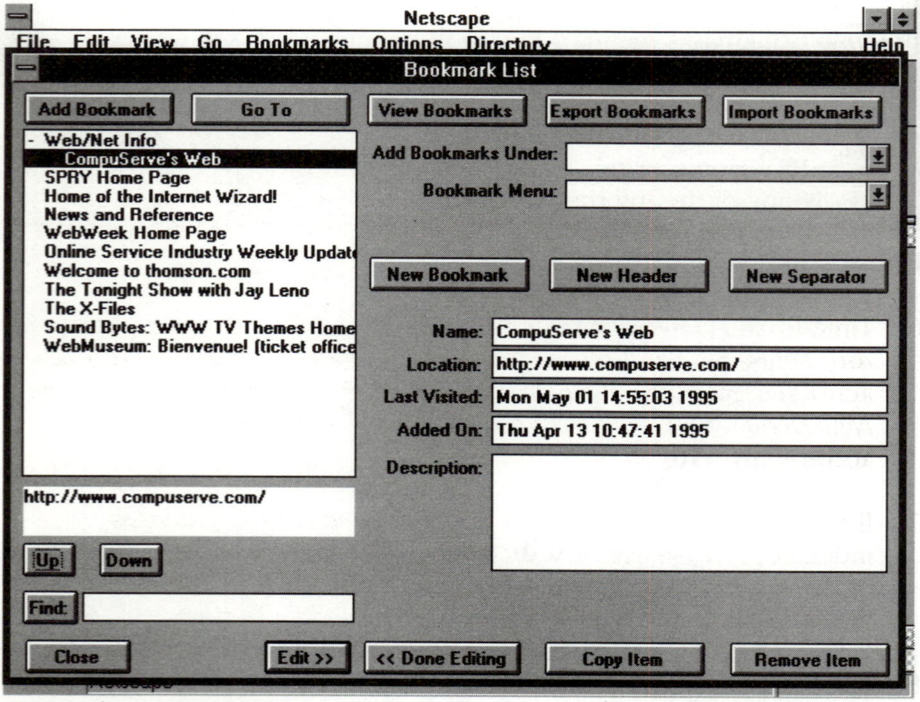

Figure 4.15 The CompuServe's Web item is indented, to show that it is part of a submenu

5 Repeat this for the next three items: *SPRY Home Page*, *Home of the Internet Wizard* and *News and Reference*. Your item list should now look like the one displayed in Figure 4.16.

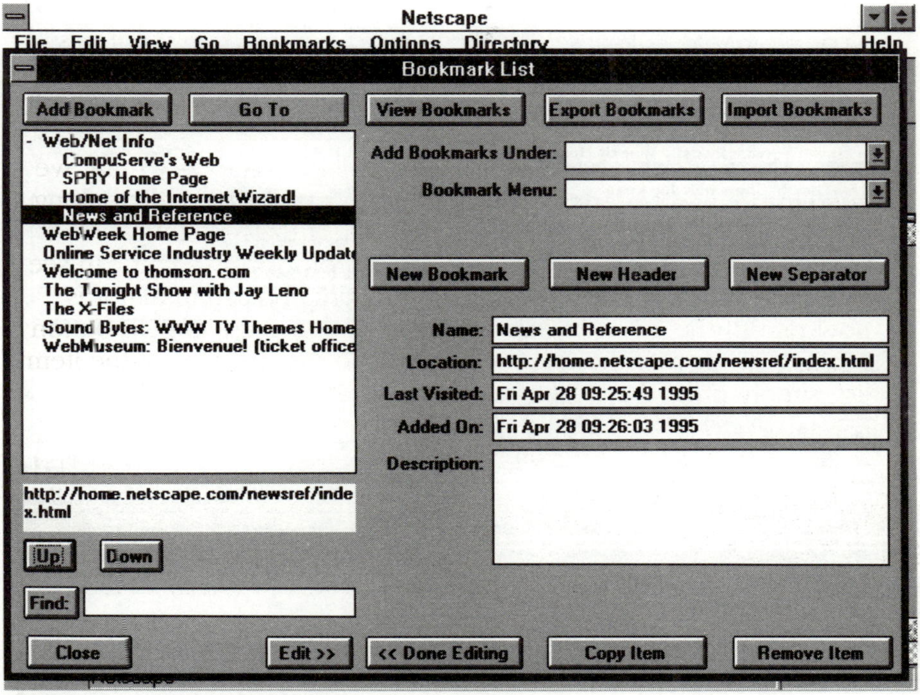

Figure 4.16 Our first submenu is completed

6 Time to add our second submenu, *Publications*. Select the *News and Reference* item (the new item will be added after the current item) and press the New Header button. In the Name field, replace *New Header* with *Publications*. The item list will be updated accordingly.

7 If you look closely, you'll see that the *Publications* header is indented, too. This means that it itself has now become a submenu of the *Web/Net Info* submenu. To bring the *Publications* menu on the same level as *Web/Net Info*, press the Down button.

8 Now select the *Web Week Home Page* item and press the Up button once. It will now become indented, to indicate that it is part of the *Publications* submenu. Repeat this for *Online Service Industry Weekly Update* and *Welcome to thomson.com*. Your item list should now look like the one shown in Figure 4.17.

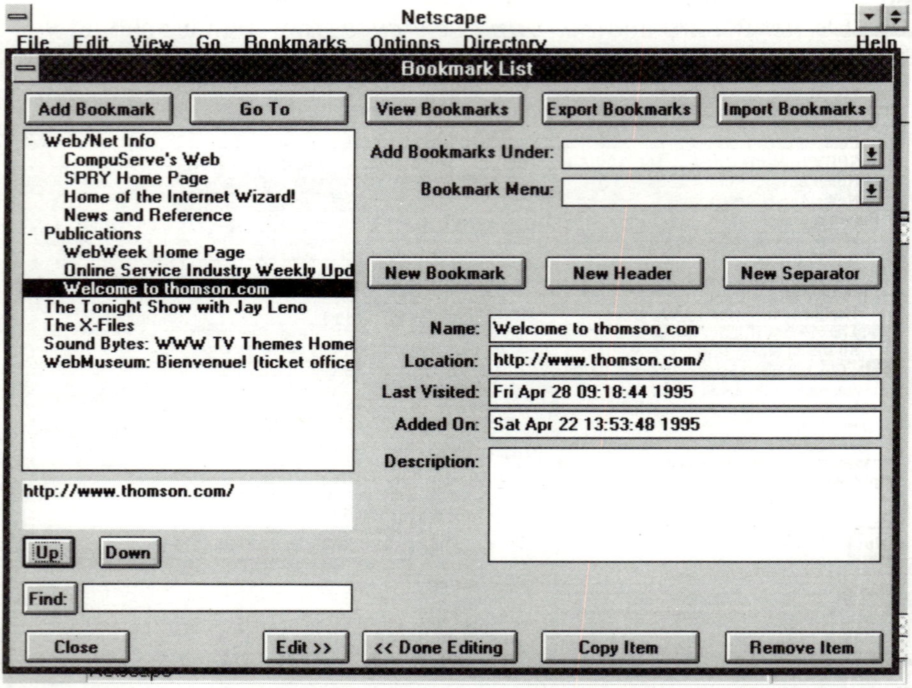

Figure 4.17 A second submenu is added to the list

9 You're almost there! Select the *Welcome to thomson.com* item and press the New Header button to create an *Entertainment* header. Press the down button once to outdent. Time to add items to our *Entertainment* submenu: select *The Tonight Show with Jay Leno* and press the Up button; repeat this for the remaining entries in the item list. If all went well, your item list should now be similar to the one shown in Figure 4.18.

That's it! You can now close the Bookmark List window. Take a look at the Bookmarks menu; quite a change, isn't it? (See Figure 4.19).

Your bookmarks as a World Wide Web document

Since Netscape stores its bookmarks in an HTML file, you actually create a World Wide Web document while you add, delete and/or edit bookmarks. To see this World Wide Web document, select the Open File option on the File menu and open the *bookmark.htm* file. Look at Figure 4.20 for the impressive results!

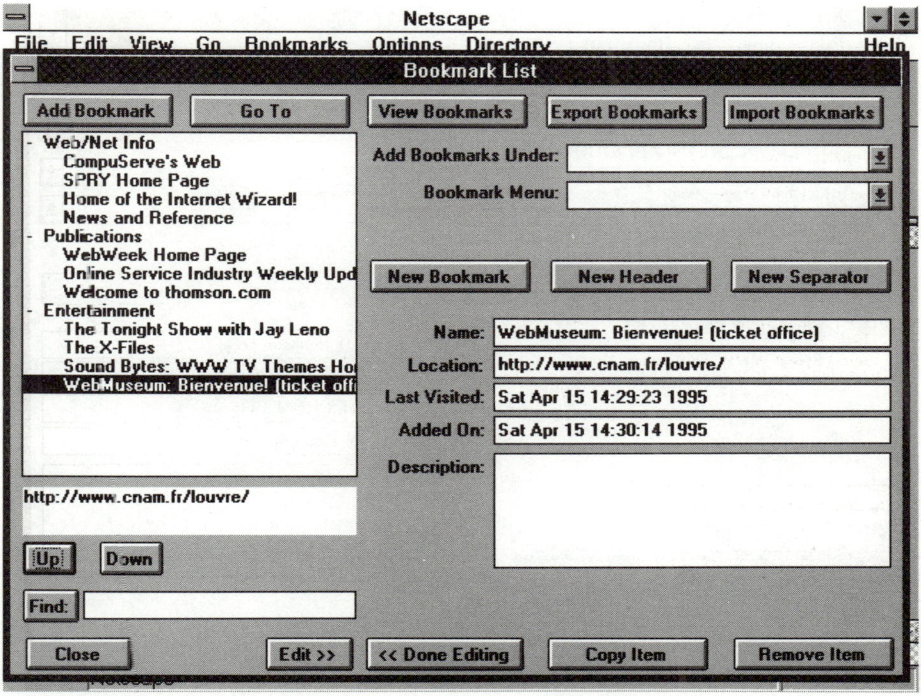

Figure 4.18 The layout for our new Bookmarks menu

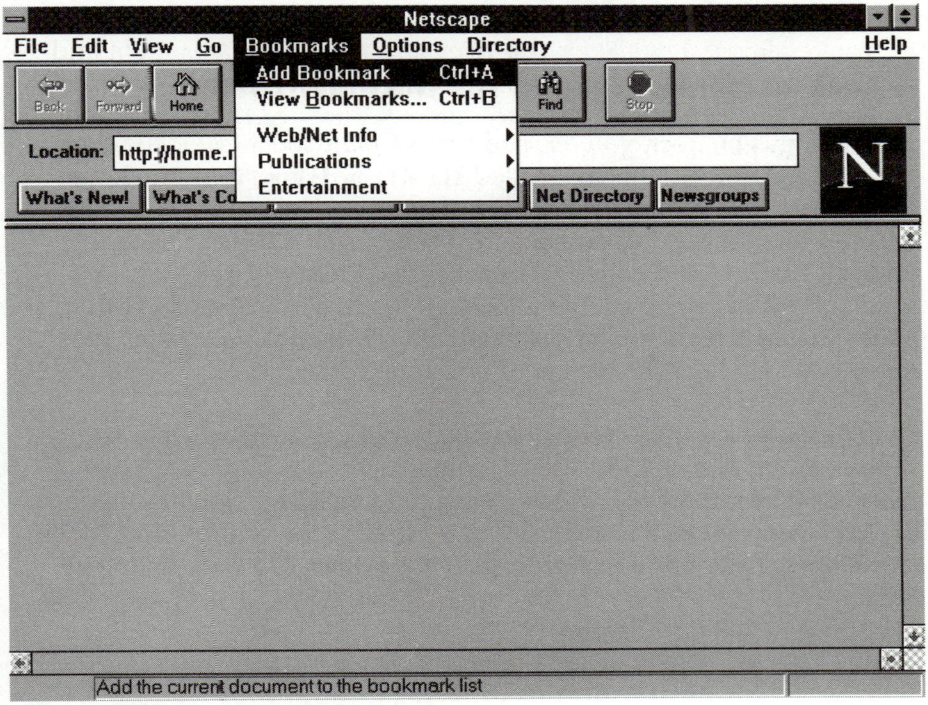

Figure 4.19 The new Bookmarks menu

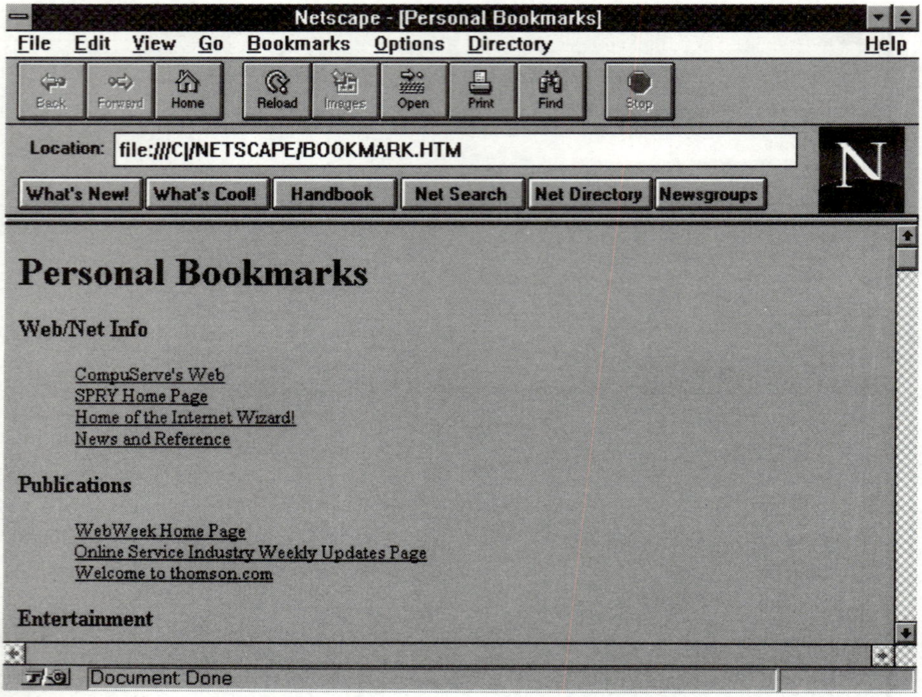

Figure 4.20 The Bookmarks menu displayed as an HTML document

A peek at HTML: viewing the document source

Earlier in this chapter, you learned that World Wide Web documents are created using a language called **HTML**, or **Hypertext Mark-Up Language**. Basically, HTML consist of a number of codes, which are inserted into an ANSI document. You can create HTML documents yourself easily, using either an editor (like Windows Notepad), or a special HTML writer containing features that make inserting HTML codes easier. For a summary of available HTML tools, see page 19, under the heading 'The Internet Publishing Forum'.

Both SPRY Mosaic and Netscape contain options to review the source of the current World Wide Web document. While a particular page is being displayed on your screen, select the Document Source option on the File menu (SPRY Mosaic), or the Source option on the View menu (Netscape). As you see in Figure 4.21, the results can look quite impressive...

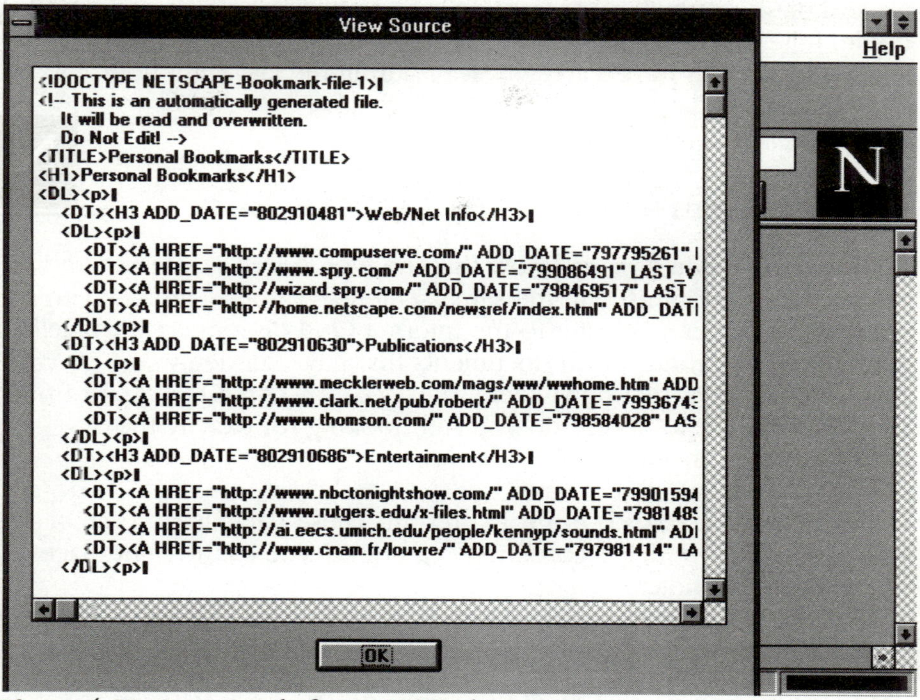

```
<!DOCTYPE NETSCAPE-Bookmark-file-1>
<!-- This is an automatically generated file.
   It will be read and overwritten.
   Do Not Edit! -->
<TITLE>Personal Bookmarks</TITLE>
<H1>Personal Bookmarks</H1>
<DL><p>
   <DT><H3 ADD_DATE="802910481">Web/Net Info</H3>
   <DL><p>
      <DT><A HREF="http://www.compuserve.com/" ADD_DATE="797795261" I
      <DT><A HREF="http://www.spry.com/" ADD_DATE="799086491" LAST_V
      <DT><A HREF="http://wizard.spry.com/" ADD_DATE="798469517" LAST_
      <DT><A HREF="http://home.netscape.com/newsref/index.html" ADD_DATI
   </DL><p>
   <DT><H3 ADD_DATE="802910630">Publications</H3>
   <DL><p>
      <DT><A HREF="http://www.mecklerweb.com/mags/ww/wwhome.htm" ADD
      <DT><A HREF="http://www.clark.net/pub/robert/" ADD_DATE="7993674:
      <DT><A HREF="http://www.thomson.com/" ADD_DATE="798584028" LAS
   </DL><p>
   <DT><H3 ADD_DATE="802910686">Entertainment</H3>
   <DL><p>
      <DT><A HREF="http://www.nbctonightshow.com/" ADD_DATE="79901594
      <DT><A HREF="http://www.rutgers.edu/x-files.html" ADD_DATE="798148
      <DT><A HREF="http://ai.eecs.umich.edu/people/kennyp/sounds.html" ADI
      <DT><A HREF="http://www.cnam.fr/louvre/" ADD_DATE="797981414" LA
   </DL><p>
```

Figure 4.21 Source code for an HTML document

Actually, HTML falls beyond the scope of this book. That's the bad news. The good news is that I simply couldn't resist the temptation to write something about it anyway. You'll find some introductory information about HTML on page 223, under the heading 'HTML: The language of the Web'. It is by no means complete, but it will give you a good introduction about this versatile, yet surprisingly easy to master, language.

Finding your way around the World Wide Web

Once you start exploring the World Wide Web, lots and lots of documents will find their way to your computer screen. Some of them are beautiful, others are filled with useful information, many are absolutely fantastic – or downright outrageous.

Nevertheless, you will want to bring some structure to what you are doing, unless you want to end up thinking 'Look! The sun's rising again – now what have I actually *seen* during the last eight hours?'

Search engines

By now, you might already know that the words *well-structured* and *Internet* are seldom used in the same sentence. Because anyone can connect his or her computer to the Internet (and disconnect it as well), you will be confronted with documents that have suddenly disappeared, URLs that don't seem to exist and so on. Quite apart from problems like these, where do you start looking for exactly the information you need?

Here's where the **search engines** step in. These databases, some of which are being updated constantly, can direct you to the right places in a matter of minutes.

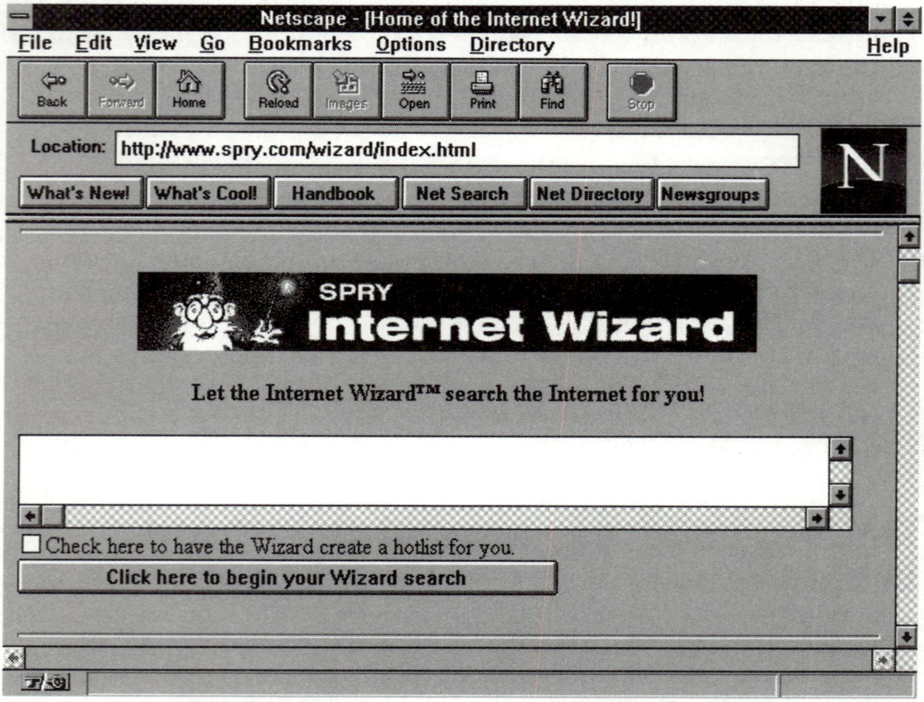

Figure 4.22 A World Wide Web search engine: the Internet Wizard

A nice place to start is the **Home of the Internet Wizard** (see Figure 4.22). It is amazingly easy to use: just enter one or more keywords in the text box, press the Search button and review the results. And naturally, since we're talking about the World Wide Web, the results are by themselves hyperlinks. Once a list of search results is displayed on your screen, you're only a mouse click away from the information you're looking for! If you use SPRY Mosaic, you can even have the Wizard make a hotlist with the search results.

Tips and guidelines

As stated before, you can easily spend hours, days and even months on the World Wide Web. You will certainly have a great time 'surfing the Web' during the first few days, but in the end, you will probably want to use the World Wide Web as an valuable information retrieval tool. In that case, consider the following tips and guidelines:

- **Save documents often**. If you spend a considerable amount of time browsing through World Wide Web documents, you will want to read the information in your own time, without the meter running. (Especially when you have to pay telephone charges, or when you have used up your free Internet hours for that month.) Just collect all documents you need and save them to your hard disk. If you use SPRY Mosaic, see page 80 for more information. Netscape users can look up page 96.

- **Disable images**: although they are often pretty, they take quite some time to download. Mosaic Users don't have to wait until they are downloaded though; the software will initially show icons and download the real images in the background, while you are reading the document. If you use Netscape, you might want to press the Images button or select the Auto Load Images option on the Options menu.

- **Use search engines**. Resist the temptation to search for information by just browsing through some World Wide Web documents. Although you will undoubtedly see great documents and learn a lot, you may not get to the information you were looking for in the first place!

- **Use hotlists or bookmarks**. Make a few hotlists or bookmark 'categories': 'fun', 'work' and 'others', for instance. Whenever you see an interesting document, just add it to your hotlist or

Bookmarks menu. Don't worry about editing your hotlists or bookmarks; you can do that later, once you are disconnected.

- `GO INETFORUM` to look for interesting tips about new World Wide Web sites, search techniques etc.

- **Ask around!** With more and more people getting access to the World Wide Web, you might benefit from their experiences as well. Don't hesitate to leave a message in the Internet Forum, asking for particular information and where to find it.

Chapter 5

Internet Mail

- **More about electronic mail**
- **Mail costs**
- **Your mail address**
- **Sending a mail message to another Internet user**
- **Receiving messages from the Internet**
- **Mailing lists**
- **Mail: Frequently Asked Questions**
- **Abbreviations and emoticons**

COMPUSERVE Internet Services

More about electronic mail

Electronic mail is simple to use, inexpensive and, above all, fast. Normally, it takes about three to five minutes for mail to arrive at its destination, regardless of whether it has been sent to London, New York, or Sydney. A few examples where electronic mail can be useful are:

- To keep in touch with the office, while you're on the road. Journalists send their articles via electronic mail to their editor. Managers call meetings via electronic mail.

- To do business. Electronic mail gets your message across, often quicker and more efficiently than a telephone call. And because electronic mail is informal by nature, it's often not necessary to ponder for hours at a time on the contents of your message, as you might do with a fax or letter.

- To keep in contact with friends. A letter with only three lines of text looks silly, but electronic mail messages don't suffer from that problem. Electronic mail is the perfect way to let someone know that you haven't forgotten about him or her, even if you don't have the time to write long epistles.

The main advantages of electronic mail are:

- It's fast. Typically, an electronic mail message to an Internet address is delivered within an hour at the most.

- It's inexpensive. CIS charges $0.10 for a three-page message (containing up to 7,500 bytes). Every 7,500 bytes more cost $0.02. And the first $9 per month is free for members of the Standard Pricing Plan, which means that the first 90 or so three-page messages don't cost you anything at all. Try to get a deal like that with your local post office! Distance doesn't apply: sending a message to someone in Budapest costs precisely as little as sending a message to someone at the front desk of your office building.

- It's informal. Electronic mail messages are almost always exchanged on a first-name basis.

- It can be 'to the point'. The best example of this is a reaction I once received from a CompuServe product manager: 'Electronic mail allows me to just say "yes" or "no". It takes away a lot of the formality that comes with letters and faxes. I get a lot more work done that way.'

- Time and place are of no account. Anyone can check his or her mailbox any time of the day. And from any place in the world! This is a very important aspect when it comes to 'teleworking'. You're always within reach, even if you are in one of the far corners of the world.

Naturally, there are some drawbacks too, especially when you compare Internet mail messages with messages sent via CompuServe Mail:

- Unlike messages to a CompuServe Mail address, where you can ask for a **receipt notice** (a confirmation from CompuServe that your message has either been read or deleted by the addressee), there is no way to check if an Internet mail message has arrived at its destination. Although in most cases you will receive a message - mostly automated, sent by a 'mailbot' ('mail-robot') named POSTMASTER - when your mail can't be delivered, there is absolutely no way to be assured that the addressee has actually read your message. It might therefore be a good idea to ask him or her to confirm receipt of your mail, especially when the message is important.

- The Internet is by no means a closed system. There are lots of clever people around who have the knowledge to intercept your Internet messages! Whether or not this is done is another matter, but be careful when sending confidential information like credit card numbers etc. as Internet mail messages. You might want to encrypt your message using a protocol like **Pretty Good Privacy** (PGP). More about such protocols can be found on page 124, under the heading 'Protecting your information'.

Mail costs

Before you start to send mail messages to the Internet, it is a good idea to look at the costs. You will see that the charges for sending and receiving Internet messages are very reasonable; many CompuServe members end up paying nothing at all!

As a member of the Standard Pricing Plan, you get a $9 monthly mail allowance. This means that you can incur up to $9 in mail costs before CompuServe charges you for your mail activities. And no, you can't take your allowance with you to the next month: at the start of a new billing month, any remaining allowance will be discarded. You therefore start with a new $9 mail allowance, every month.

With regular CompuServe Mail, you normally pay only for messages you send. Receiving CompuServe Mail messages is free, with some exceptions (you can send a message **Postage Due** to someone else, or you and the receiver could decide to 'go Dutch' and split the mail charges).

Internet mail messages are another story, however. You pay for every Internet mail message you either send or receive; incoming Internet mail messages will be flagged as **Postage Due**, to indicate that there is a charge to read them.

For every Internet mail message, either incoming or outgoing, you will be charged a minimum of $0.10. If the message is not longer than 7,500 characters (about five typewritten pages), that's all you have to pay. For every additional 7,500 characters in the same message, you pay $0.02 extra. The following table shows some examples:

Message size	**Mail charges**
2,500 characters	$0.10
5,000 characters	$0.10
7,500 characters	$0.10
10,000 characters	$0.12
15,000 characters	$0.12
25,000 characters	$0.16
100,000 characters	$0.36
500,000 characters	$1.42
1,000,000 characters	$2.76

As the first $9 are 'on the house' (thanks to your monthly mail allowance), you actually start paying after either 90 mail messages or a little more than 3 Megabytes, whichever comes first.

The hidden danger: mailing lists

Participating in one or more mailing lists (see also page 144) is the way to boost up your mail charges. Some mailing lists result in Megabytes of text per day! If you are not sure about the amount of traffic to expect, consider putting your incoming mail 'on hold': on the Special menu, select Preferences, followed by Mail. In the resulting dialog (see Figure 5.1), check the Do not retrieve radio button. When you next use the Send/Receive All Mail option on the Mail menu, only the messages that are not Postage Due will be retrieved automatically.

Figure 5.1 Use this dialog to decide what WinCIM should do with incoming mail that is Postage Due

Your mail address

Do you have a business card? When you order new ones, don't forget to have your CompuServe and/or Internet mail address printed on them! If your CompuServe User ID is 100123,456, you have the following mail addresses:

```
CompuServe: 100123,456
Internet: 100123.456@compuserve.com
```

Look at the dot instead of the comma, used in the Internet address. No typos here: when you convert a CompuServe Mail address into an Internet mail address, the comma has to be changed into a dot.

Sending a mail message to another Internet user

The process of sending a mail message consists of three steps:

1 Specifying the address of the person you want to send the message to.

2 Writing the actual message.

3 Sending the message.

Finding Internet mail addresses

If you have ever sent a mail message to another CompuServe member, chances are that you have used the CompuServe Member Directory (select the Member Directory option on the Mail menu). This directory contains the User IDs of all CompuServe members, except those who prefer not to be listed.

The Internet is another story. First, the bad news: there is no Internet Member Directory. Being the largely unstructured network that it is, with users moving to other networks (and therefore getting other mail addresses) all the time, this isn't too surprising. Therefore, the best way to obtain the mail address of someone you want to write to is to give him or her a call and ask for it!

But there is some relatively good news too. There are a few options that you can use if you are really desperate. The best routes currently are listed in the following sections.

The USENET address database

If you have reason to believe that the person you want to write to has participated in USENET newsgroup postings, you could use the USENET address database. To search the database, send a mail message to *INTERNET:mail-server@rtfm.mit.edu*. The subject is not important. The message text should contain one or more of the following lines:

```
send usenet-addresses/name
```

In this query, replace *name* with one or more words (this is a so-called OR search: it will return results if one or more of the words match) that you think are appropriate for the person you are looking for (like his or her user name, company/institution, address information, etc.).

If the search is successful, you will receive one mail message per query. In each mail message, up to 40 matches are displayed.

If you want to know more about this database, you can send a mail message to *INTERNET:mail-server@rtfm.mit.edu.* The subject field is not important; include the following line in the message:

```
send usenet-addresses/help
```

'whois' databases

Some sites have so-called **whois** databases, which contain information about everyone who has a mail address on that site. Often, the only way for CompuServe members to access such a database is via telnet. A good example is **RIPE**, a growing group of Internet access providers in Europe. When you telnet to *info.ripe.net*, you will be able to access RIPE's database.

Another option is telnetting to *nic.ddn.mil* and selecting the **whois** option on the menu. If you don't want to telnet, you can use CompuServe Mail: send a message to *INTERNET:whois@whois.nic.ddn.mil.* The subject field is not important; place a line with the text **help** in the message. You will receive instructions through electronic mail.

If you need more information about sites that have **whois** servers, you can use FTP to retrieve */pub/whois/whois-servers.list* from *sipb.mit.edu.* See Chapter 7 for more information about FTP.

Sending a message

Once you have retrieved the Internet mail address of the person you want to send your message to, you can start writing the actual message.

A few guidelines

- Keep your messages short and simple. Don't use long paragraphs, and try to be brief and clear. And an important one: don't shout.

That's right: you can actually shout while writing messages. But be assured: the addressee of your message will almost certainly give you a 'reprimand' that shouting is not a nice thing to do.
So how do you shout digitally? Well, in a very simple way: just write everything IN CAPITALS. BUT AS YOU CAN SEE FROM THIS TEXT, IT MAKES YOUR MESSAGE SIGNIFICANTLY HARDER TO READ, especially on computer screens. So do not shout.

- Electronic mail messages are composed and sent in plain ASCII, leaving no room for special characteristics like bold text, underlining, etc. You can't even use accented characters! Therefore, you will have to resort to other means of accentuating your text. A few of the most often used methods are:
  - Use asterisks to surround your text, as is done with the *following* word. Experienced users of online services (and you will be one shortly!) know that the text is meant to be in *italics*.
  - In a similar way, you can <u>underline</u> your text by enclosing it between underscores, as is done with the _following_ word.
  - Another method you can use (but sparingly, for the reason mentioned above): put important text in CAPITALS.

  Regardless which one of the above methods you use: take care not to 'clutter' your message by overusing these attributes.

- If you want to indicate that a certain character needs to have an accent, follow the character by a single or double quote. A few examples:

```
e'   (é)
o"   (ö)
a'   (à)
```

- Be careful when making jokes! Don't forget that the recipient, when reading your message, won't see the expression on your face at the moment you wrote it. Something that you intended to be witty could come across as being too sarcastic, or even offensive. When in doubt, use special characters or abbreviations, like the so-called **emoticons**. A list of commonly used abbreviations and symbols can be found on page 153.

- Avoid 'flaming': a too often used practice to 'punish' people you do not agree with by sending rude messages. Always picture yourself as the recipient of the mail message you are about to send. Would you yourself be offended by it? If you cannot help but answer that question with 'yes': back to the keyboard!

Writing the message

When writing mail messages with WinCIM, you use one or more of the following elements:

- The WinCIM Address Book. This is a personal database, kept on disk, that contains mail addresses.
- The built-in WinCIM editor. This is a standard Windows editor, which has all the key commands that you find in edit boxes, and in applications like Notepad. Because the WinCIM editor supports cutting and pasting of text via hot keys, it is actually possible to use your favourite word processing program to write electronic mail messages: when you have finished, a simple copy-and-paste action is enough to transfer the message text to WinCIM.
- The WinCIM Out-Basket: an archive that contains all mail messages that you have written and that are waiting to be sent off. Because the Out-Basket can contain a virtually unlimited number of messages, you can write all messages offline before sending them. After you have finished, one command suffices to send and receive all your mail.

To write and send a mail message using WinCIM, you do the following:

1 Select the Create Mail option on the Mail menu. WinCIM shows the Recipient List dialog (see Figure 5.2). This dialog allows you to specify the destination address, or addresses, for your mail message. (You can actually send a message to several addresses at the same time.) Take some time to study the Recipient List dialog: there are several ways to fill in the respective fields. The fields and command buttons include the following:
   - **Name** and **Address**
     In the Name field, you type the name of the person you want to write to. Both the Name field and the Address field are connected to the contents of the Address Book: as soon as you type a few characters, WinCIM will scan through the Address Book for the entry that corresponds to the information you typed. If an appropriate entry is found, the Address field is updated automatically. If you want to specify a combination of a name and address not listed in the Address Book, you just type them in the respective Name and Address fields.

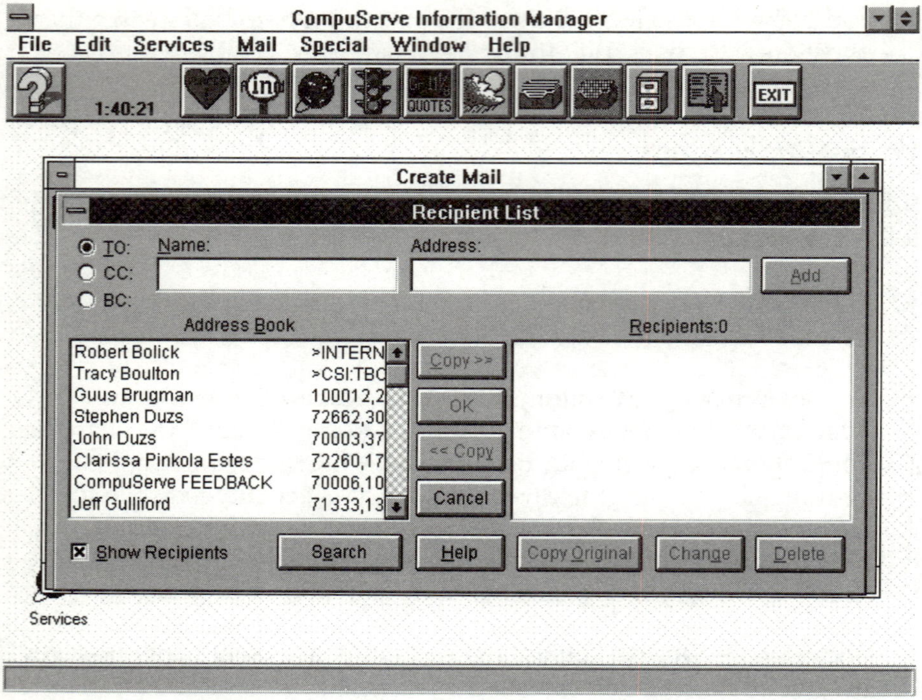

Figure 5.2 WinCIM's Recipient List dialog

Important: Note that you will have to insert the text *INTERNET:* in the address field. The following address is invalid:

```
roelf@novalink.com
```

The correct address is:

```
INTERNET:roelf@novalink.com
```

- **Add**
  Press this button to add a new name and address to the list of recipients of your message.
- **Address Book**
  In this box, the contents of your WinCIM Address Book are shown. After selecting an address (either with the keyboard or with the mouse), you can copy it to the Recipients box by double-clicking on it, or by choosing the Copy option.
- **Recipients**
  This box contains the future addressees of your mail message.
- **TO, CC and BC**
  These option buttons refer to the status of the recipient of your message. If there is only one recipient, you do not have to

bother with these options. But if you are about to send a message to several people at the same time, you could consider marking recipients for 'carbon copies' or 'blank copies', just as you would when sending a company memo. There is a small difference between carbon copies and blank copies: addressees who receive a blank copy are not shown in the list with recipients.

– **Show Recipients**
This field determines whether or not all recipients of a message are shown in a special Recipients list, which is attached to each mail message to more than one addressee. When you do not want the addressee of your message to know who else received the same message, you can uncheck this option box.

2 After you have decided to whom you are going to send your message, it's time to actually start writing: press OK to display the Create Mail window. The name of the (first) recipient is displayed after the Address button (see Figure 5.3). As we learned earlier, an electronic mail message consists of three parts: an address, a subject and the actual message text. Now look again at Figure 5.3. Do you notice that both the Out-Basket and the Send Now button are greyed-out? The reason for this: WinCIM detects that one or

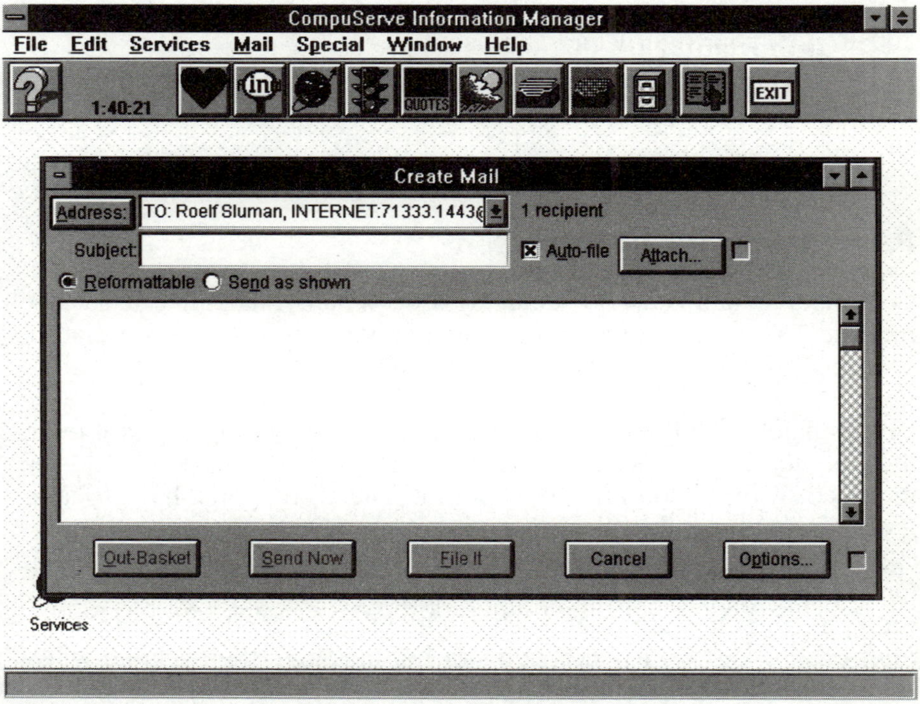

Figure 5.3 This is where you write your message: the Create Mail dialog

more of the obligatory parts are missing. Write a small subject header that summarizes the contents of your message. Then enter the actual message text into the large text box. You will see that, as soon as you have typed the first character, both the Out-Basket and the Send Now button can be selected. WinCIM has noticed that your message meets all requirements.

3 When you have finished your mail message, you have two options:
   - You can put the message into your Out-Basket: a practical option when you want to compose more messages and send them all out in one session. Press the Out-Basket button. When you have finished writing all messages, you can choose either the Send/Receive All Mail option (the mail contents of your Out-Basket will be sent, and your In-Basket will be filled with new mail messages sent to you), or the Out-Basket option. In the latter case, WinCIM shows a list of all the messages stored in your Out-Basket.
   - You can send it out right away by pressing the Send Now button. If you are offline, WinCIM will connect to CompuServe. Note that you have to disconnect manually after WinCIM has sent the message.

Tip: If you want to practice sending messages to the Internet, use the 'Internet version' of your own CompuServe User ID. If your User ID is 100567,123, your Internet address is *INTERNET:100567.123@compuserve.com* (note the dot instead of the comma).

Protecting your information

CompuServe Mail is a very secure system. When you send a mail message to another CompuServe member, you can rest assured that the contents can be read by the addressee only.

Unfortunately, the Internet is a different case. Everything is possible on the Net; your mail message could be intercepted by a hacker, and even modified, without you knowing about it! Therefore, you'll have to take great care with confidential messages.

One of the ways to ensure confidentiality is to use a special **encryption schedule**. With such a schedule, the sender uses an **encoding program** to encrypt his or her message (the message will still consist of ASCII characters, but it will look completely different from the original one (to be honest, an encoded text message looks like complete chaos)). To be able to read the message, the receiver uses a **decoding program**, in combination with a secret code that is only known to the sender and receiver of the message, to **decrypt** the message.

There are several encryption schemes. One of the most popular is **PGP** (**Pretty Good Privacy**), developed by Philip Zimmermann. Unfortunately, the latest version of this program cannot be distributed outside the United States. When you try to download the program (via FTP), you will have to go through a series of questions that you have to answer correctly to prove that you actually live in the United States. Only when you have passed the exam will you receive the name of the (hidden) FTP site where you can download the PGP software.

You probably won't be surprised to learn that PGP has actually made its way outside the USA as well. There are already plenty of FTP sites in Europe where PGP 2.6 and PGP 2.6ui (a compatible version) are available. Note that the encryption algorithm used in PGP has been changed to prevent copyright infringements: it is therefore not possible to use older versions of PGP to decode messages encoded with version 2.6.

If you want to know more about PGP, download the following file from the Internet New Users Forum (`GO INETFOR`):

- *[73727,545] Lib: 2*
  UPDATE.003/Text Bytes: 44199

  Title : Everybody's Internet Update
  Keywords: INTERNET PGP PRIVACY ANON GOPHER FTP. WWW

  Everybody's Internet Update 3 (formerly the Big Dummy's Update). This month features articles on privacy and anonymity on the Internet, downloading mail and more.

A good place to start looking for the PGP software, as well as additional information, is *ftp.demon.co.uk*, in the *pub/pgp* directory.

Sending and receiving binary files over the Internet

Electronic mail access to the Internet is limited to ASCII files only, with a maximum size of 2,000,000 bytes per message. Therefore theoretically, it is not possible to send and receive binary messages to and from the Internet via mail.

But there is a solution for this problem. Via special utility programs that convert binary files into ASCII format and vice versa, you can 'encode' your file, split it into parts (there are still Internet sites that only allow mail messages up to 50,000 characters in length), and send it off. All the receiver has to do is decode the ASCII text into the original file.

Believe me, this all sounds much more complicated than it actually is. After you have encoded and decoded a few files, it will become second nature.

The two protocols that are most often used for this purpose are UUENCODE/UUDECODE and MIME. UUENCODE/UUDECODE is one of the first standards; MIME is one of the last. In all cases, three bytes of binary information are converted into four bytes of ASCII text. Therefore, you will have to send and receive 33% more compared to binary transfers via CompuServe Mail.

To encode and decode files, a number of programs are available, for all common platforms. The following list of files, present in the Internet New Users Forum (`GO INETFORUM`), show versions for DOS, Windows and the Apple Macintosh:

- *[76703,407]   Lib: 5*
  UU520.ZIP/Bin   Bytes: 32672

  Title   : UUENCODE/DECODE Utility for PCs (Zipped)
  Keywords: UUENCODE UUDECODE PC

  UUENCODE/DECODE Utility for PCs (Zipped). This utility can be used to convert a binary file into an ASCII file for mailing to an Internet address. (Sending binary files via mail over the Internet does not work otherwise.) The utility is required by users at both ends of the electronic mail link, first to encode and then to decode and convert the file back to binary.

- *[70740,2337] Lib: 7*
  UUD13.ZIP/Bin Bytes: 48966

  Title : Batch UUDecoder (UUD) Version 1.3
  Keywords: UUD UUDECODE UUENCODE USENET INTERNET BATCH DECODE NEWSGROUP NEWSGROUPS

  *Have you ever been stuck UUDecoding one file at a time? Now with UUD, you don't have to anymore. UUDecoding now is as easy as using the DOS "Dir" command! By typing UUD *.*, UUD will decode ALL files in a directory. UUD *.uue will decode all files with extension .UUE. Other features include an advanced parsing system to correctly piece together split files by analyzing information in the header, a "virtual" file system to seamlessly handle appended files, and now support for XXEncoded files!*

- *[100273,1562] Lib: 6*
  WNCODE.ZIP/Bin Bytes: 56277

  Title : Windows UUEncode & Decode
  Keywords: UUENCODE UUDECODE WINDOWS INTERNET FTP MAIL

  *** FreeWare ** Wincode is a Windows 3.1 program (written in Turbo Pascal for Windows) which converts ASCII files to BINARY files (and vice versa) through a process known as uucoding. This allows a user to transmit binary files through mail (or any other ASCII-based communications system) by first converting the files to ASCII and then having the receiver of the files reconvert them to binary. Many NewsGroups (on the Internet) utilize this practice (it is common on UNIX-based systems).*

- *[100065,2636]   Lib: 5*
  XFERP1.ZIP/Bin   Bytes: 134025

  Title   : XFERPRO v1.0
  Keywords: UNIX WINDOWS INTERNET UUENCODE UUDECODE MIME

  XFERPRO is a Windows-based software tool which allows users to send text, application data, messages, images, audio, video, executable files and other data types via electronic mail using the latest MIME 1.0 standards according to RFC1341. Supports UU and XX encoding/decoding. From the author of UUCODE. Shareware. Upl. with the author's consent. Use PKUNZIP v2.04g or similar to unpack.

- *[100065,2636]   Lib: 5*
  UUCOD3.ZIP/Bin   Bytes: 177030

  Title   : UUCODE 3.1.4
  Keywords: UNIX WINDOWS INTERNET UUENCODE UUDECODE MAIL

  This file contains version 3.1.4 of the Windows 3.1 uuencoder/decoder program. This supersedes version 3.1.0 of the software currently located in the Telecommunications forum library #14. See file WHATS.NEW for changes between v3.1.0 and v3.1.4. Shareware. Upl. with the author's consent. Use PKUNZIP v2.04g to unpack.

- *[71663,215]   Lib: 6*
  WNCOD2.ZIP/Bin   Bytes: 256546

  Title   : Wincode V2.3
  Keywords: WINCODE UUENCODER UUDECODER DECODE

  Wincode Version 2.3. A Windows smart UUencoder/UUdecoder program.

  Freeware - uploaded here with permission of the author.

- ```
  [76703,407]     Lib:17
  UUT232.SEA/Bin  Bytes:  43008

  Title    : UUTool 232 - uuencode/uudecode for Macintosh
  Keywords: UUTOOL UUENCODE UUDECODE MACINTOSH

  UUTool 232 - uuencode/uudecode for Macintosh. Uuencode
  is used to convert a binary file into an ASCII text
  file form which can be sent over the Internet using
  standard electronic mail. Uudecode is used at the other
  end to convert the text file back to a binary file.
  Self-extracting archive.
  ```

- ```
  [73072,1413]    Lib:17
  UULITE.SEA/Bin  Bytes: 112128

  Title    : UULite 1.5 (Unregistered)
  Keywords: MAC UUENCODE UUDECODE

  This is an unregistered copy of a Macintosh shareware
  program that can uuencode/decode files from UNIX or PC
  platforms. Automatically types many kinds of graphics
  files: JPEG, GIF, etc...
  ```

Of the above programs, Information Transfer Professional (XFERPRO) is very popular with Windows users. Because it supports almost all binary-to-ASCII formats available, you can use it to encode and decode almost any file you'll ever receive via Internet mail.

In the following example, you'll learn how to encode a file using XFERPRO. Next, you'll send the encoded file via CompuServe mail to your own Internet address – on CompuServe! Finally, you'll retrieve the file and decode it, using the same XFERPRO program. To keep matters understandable, this example contains four parts:

- Encoding the file;
- Sending the file;
- Receiving the file;
- Decoding the file.

Before you try this example, download XFERP1.ZIP from the Internet New Users Forum (`GO INETFORUM`) and install the program.

Part one : encoding a file

In this example, we make matters a little more complicated than necessary: we will split the file into so-called **chunks**. In most cases, you don't need to do this (most Internet sites accept mail messages that are several million bytes long), but there are a few sites that have severe limitations (a maximum message size of 50,000 characters is no exception).

Please note: if you perform all the steps listed in this example, you will incur $0.56 in CompuServe Mail charges. These will be deducted from your $9 monthly allowance.

1 Make a new directory. You might want to call it *\TEMP*, for instance.

2 In your *\CSERVE\ WINCIM* directory, you will find a file named *CTL3D.DLL*. Copy this file to the *\TEMP* directory. This is the file we are about to encode.

3 Start XFERPRO. On XFERPRO's Configure menu, select the Encode option. The dialog shown in Figure 5.4 appears.

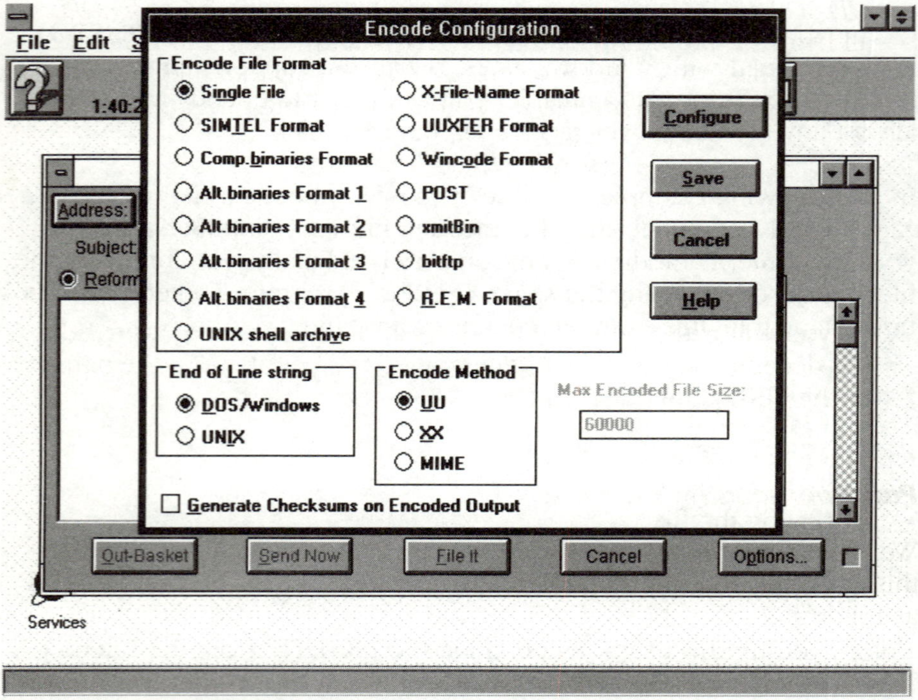

Figure 5.4 XFERPRO's Encode Configuration dialog

4 Make sure that the options Single File, DOS/Windows and UU are selected. These options mean that XFERPRO will encode the information in one single file (as opposed to breaking it into several 'chunks'). Use the DOS/Windows code to indicate the 'End of line' character and use one of three encode methods: UU (still the most frequently used around the Internet, immediately followed by XX, whereas MIME is quickly becoming the new standard).

5 Press the Configure button to close the dialog. You are now ready to convert the *CTL3D.DLL* file, located in the *\TEMP* directory. Press F2, or select the Encode option on the File menu. This results in the Encode dialog being displayed, one of the common dialog boxes in Windows. After you have selected the *\TEMP* directory and indicated that you want to encode the file CTL3D.DLL, press the OK button.

6 XFERPRO will now ask for a filename. Press the OK button to accept the default: *CTL3D.UUE* (the UUE extension indicates that the file is encoded using the UU protocol).

7 XFERPRO will now encode the file. This doesn't take long; after a few moments, the program finishes and a new file is created: *CTL3D.UUE*. This file contains an encoded version of *CTL3D.DLL*; all bytes from the original file have been converted into general ASCII. This is what the first lines of *CTL3D.UUE* look like when you import the file into an editor or word processing program:

```
begin 644 CTL3D.DLL
M35H9'0(''''$''''__\''+@'''''''''''0''''
'''''''''''''''''''''''M''''''''''''''
''''''@'''''X?N@X'M'G-(;@!3,TA5&AI!P]G
```

As you will gather, the first line is of major importance. It provides the decoding software with a vital piece of information: the name of the destination file.

Part two: sending the file

We are now ready to send our file as an electronic mail message. In this example, simply send the file to yourself, via the Internet! Proceed as follows:

1 If you haven't done so already, start WinCIM. Select the Create Mail option on the Mail menu. After a few moments, the Recipient List

dialog appears. Fill in your name in the Name field. In the Address field, type your own Internet mail address. If your CompuServe User ID is 100512,345, mail the message to:

```
INTERNET:100512.345@compuserve.com
```

2 After you have filled in the name and the address, press the Add button, followed by the OK button. After a few moments, the Create Mail dialog is displayed, shown in Figure 5.5.

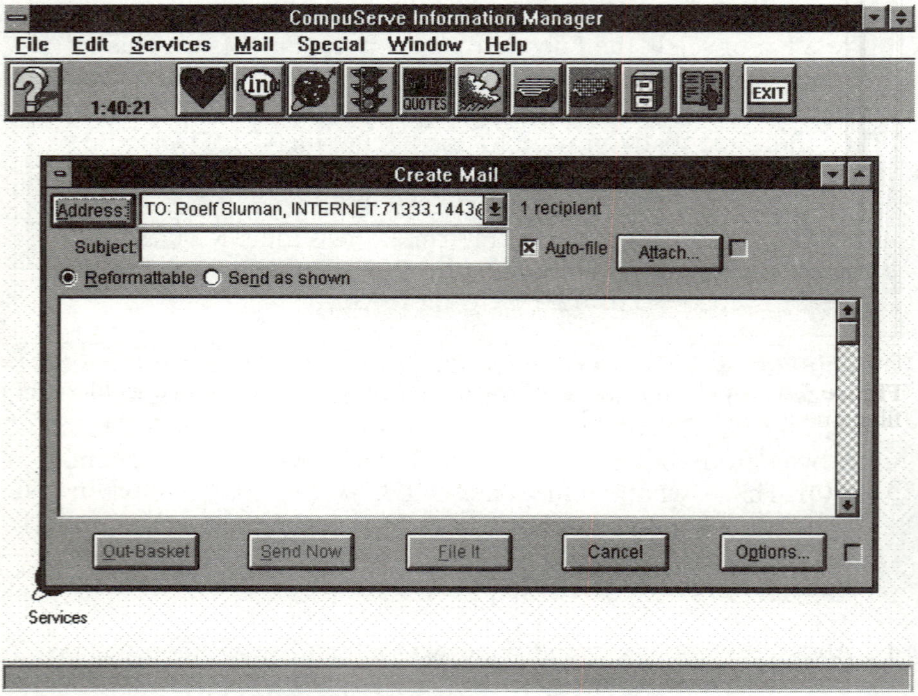

Figure 5.5 The Create Mail dialog

Although the name of the file is encoded in the message text, it might help the receiver if you include it in the Subject field, too. Something like 'Message contains file: CTL3D.DLL', for instance (see Figure 5.6).

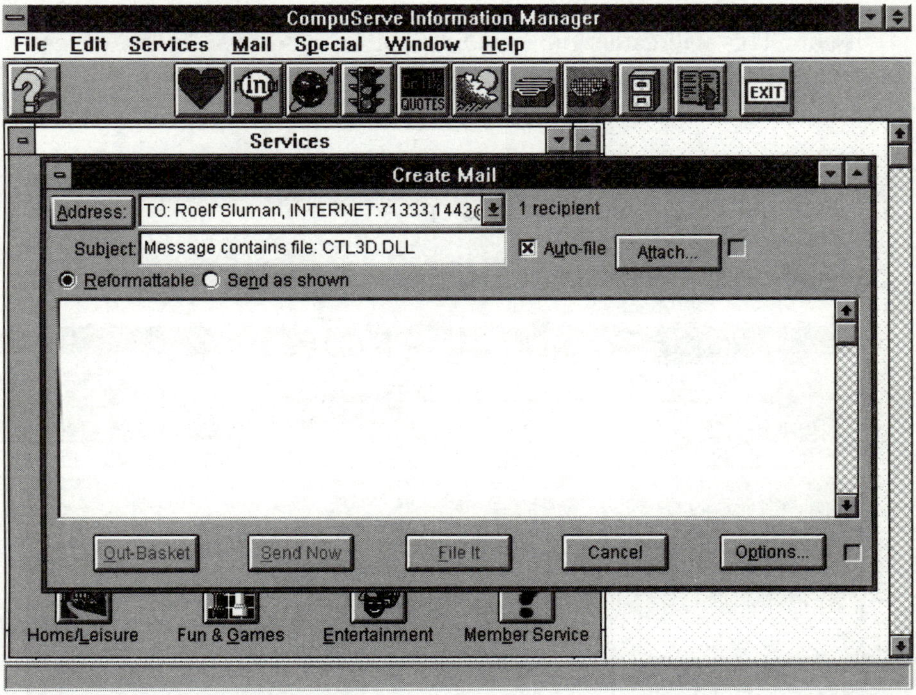

Figure 5.6 An elegant way to show the receiver what to expect: include the filename in the Subject field

3 Now, select the Open option on the File menu. This causes the Open dialog to appear. Enter *.* in the Filename field. Next, select the file *CTL3D.DLL*, located in the *\TEMP* directory. Press the OK button.

4 After a few moments, the Windows Notepad application will be launched. It will contain the contents of the *CTL3D.UUE* file. Select the Select All option on the Edit menu, followed by the Copy option, also on the Edit menu. You can now close the Notepad application; a copy of the encoded file is placed on the Windows Clipboard.

Tip: Don't use the Paste From option on the Edit menu for this purpose. It will only copy the first 32,768 bytes from a text file. Although it wouldn't hurt in this case, you could be faced with a nasty surprise if you use that option when sending larger files over the Internet.

5 In the Create Mail dialog, select the message entry field (the large white square), either by clicking in it once, or by pressing the Tab

key one or more times. Next, select the Paste option on the Edit menu. This will cause the contents of the Windows Clipboard (our *CTL3D.DLL* file) to be placed in the message entry field. (See Figure 5.7.)

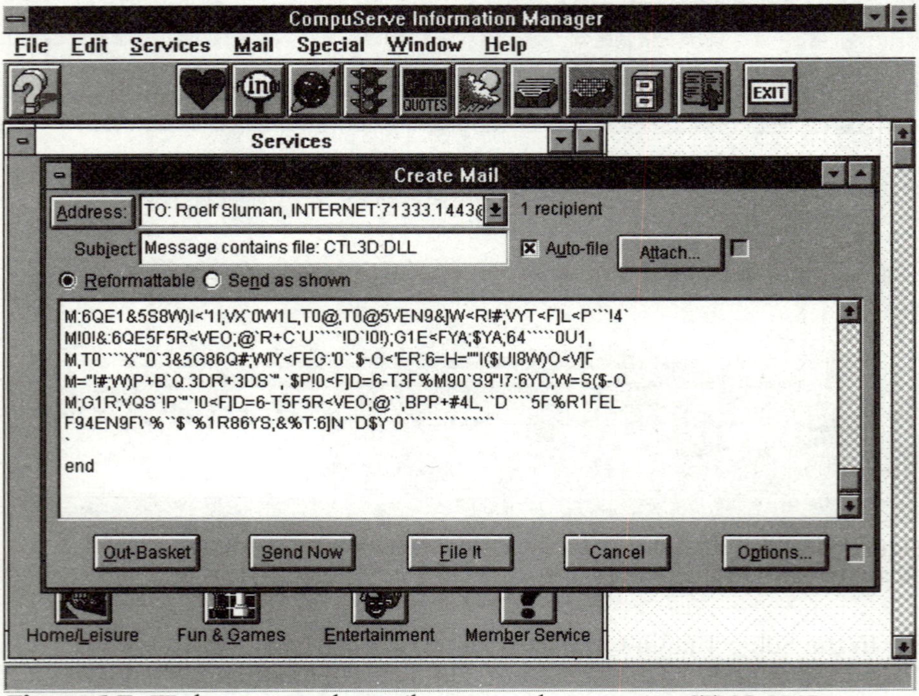

Figure 5.7 We have created a mail message that contains CTL3D.UUE

6 You might like to scroll to the first line of the message, for instance if you wish to include some commentary remarks to the receiver. When you've finished, press the Out-Basket button to place this message in your Out-Basket.

7 That's all! But we've not finished with this example yet. We are going to send the file twice. If you don't need to include any commentary remarks in the message, there is a quicker way to get the mail message into your Out-Basket.

Select the Send File option on the Mail menu. The Recipient List dialog appears again. In the Name and Address fields, enter your name and your Internet address, just like you did in step 1 of this example. Press Add, followed by OK to display the Send File Message dialog (see Figure 5.8).

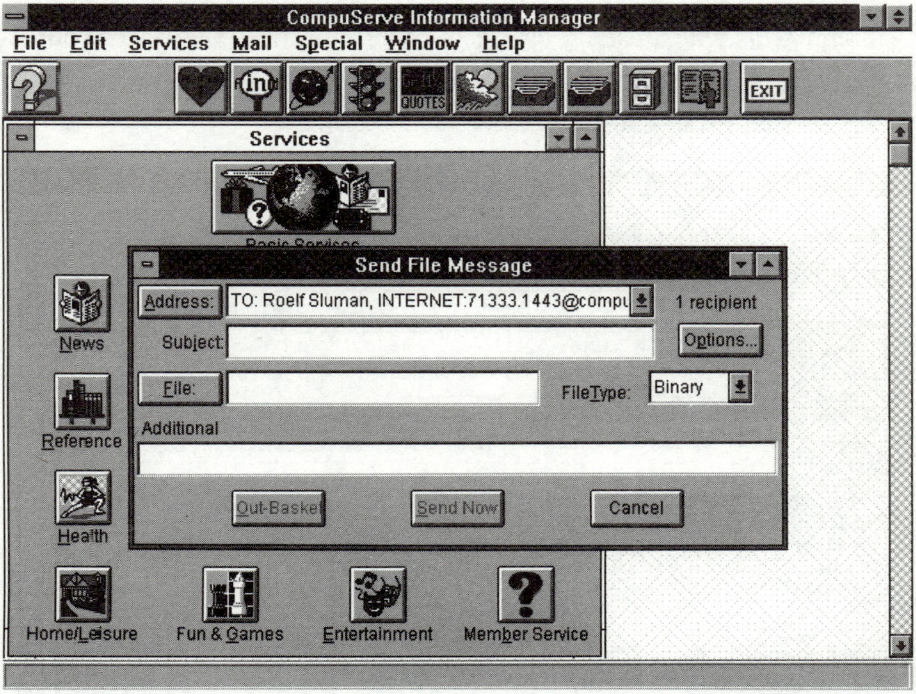

Figure 5.8 The Send File Message dialog, used to send complete files as binary or text messages

8 In the Subject field, type 'File: CTL3D.DLL'. Next, press the File button to select the *CTL3D.UUE* file, located in the *\TEMP* directory.

9 **Important**: In the FileType drop-down box, select the Text option. (Remember: you can't send binary files over the Internet.) The Send File Message dialog should now look like the one shown in Figure 5.9. Don't bother to fill in the Additional field: its contents will be discarded when the message is sent to an Internet mail address.

10 Press the Out-Basket button to place the file into your Out-Basket. Next, press the Out-Basket button on the WinCIM Ribbon, or select the Out-Basket option on the Mail menu. If you have performed all previous steps correctly, your Out-Basket should look like the one shown in Figure 5.10. If you want to review or change one of the messages, select it and press the Open button.

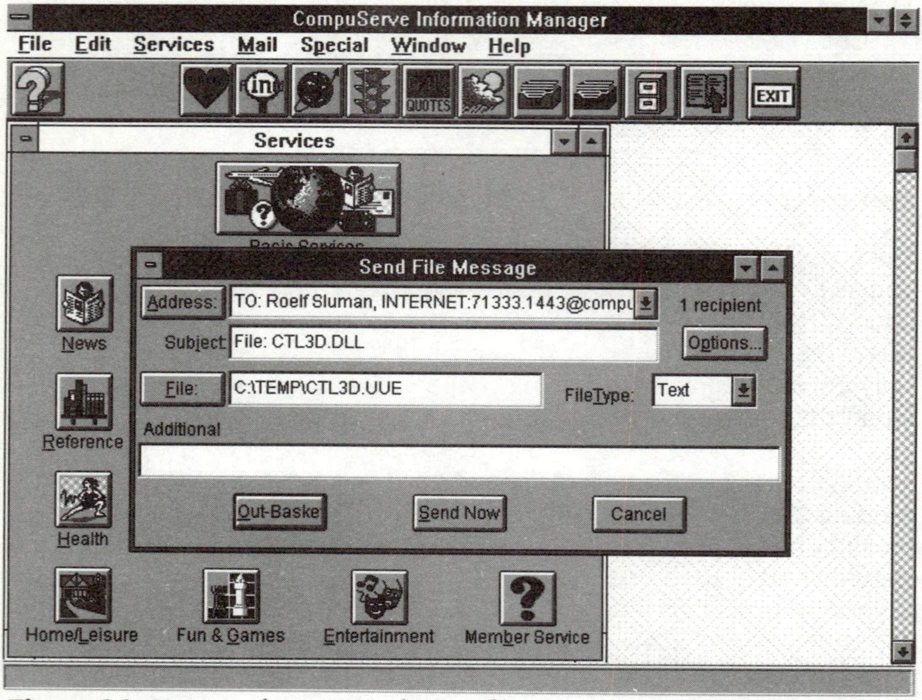

Figure 5.9 You are about to send a text file to an Internet address

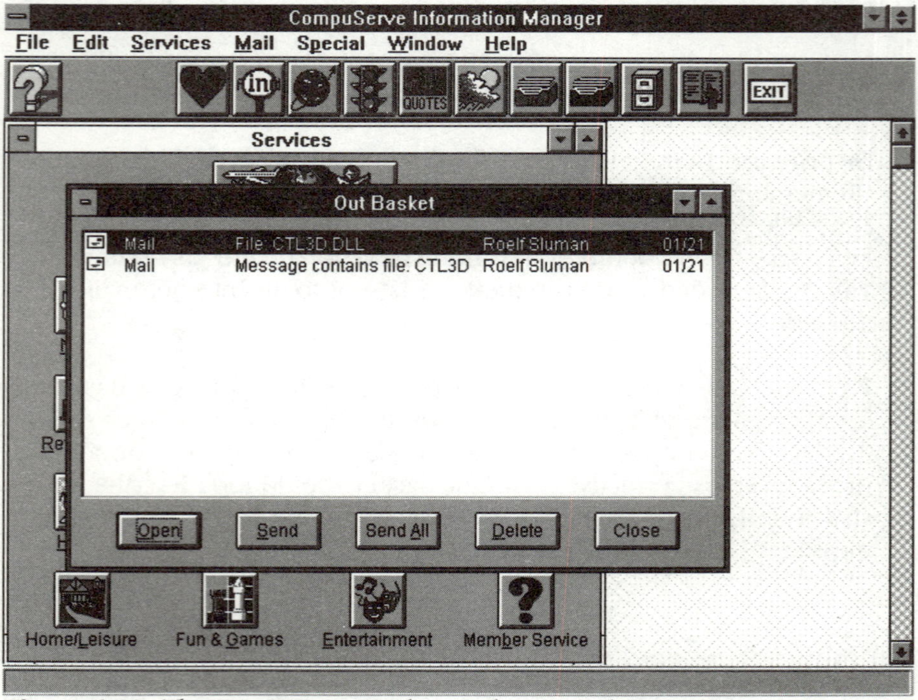

Figure 5.10 The WinCIM Out-Basket, with two mail messages

11 Now, press the Send All button. WinCIM will now connect to CompuServe and send the two mail messages. This will take a few minutes, depending on your modem speed. Don't forget to disconnect after the files have been sent.

Part three: receiving a file from the Internet

Once you have sent the two files (or actually, two ASCII messages) to yourself, you might want to rename the *CTL3D.UUE* file, located in your *\TEMP* directory, to *CHECK.UUE* or whatever name you like. That way, you will be able to see if the files that you will receive shortly are truly equal to the original file. You might also want to rename another file in the *\TEMP* directory, *CTL3D.DLL*, to *CHECK.DLL*.

Sending messages through the Internet takes a little more time than sending them to another CompuServe Mail address. So take a short break before selecting the Get New Mail option on the Mail menu. (It shouldn't take more than about 30 minutes for the messages to arrive.) If your messages have arrived, the Get New Mail dialog will contain the same information as the one shown in Figure 5.11.

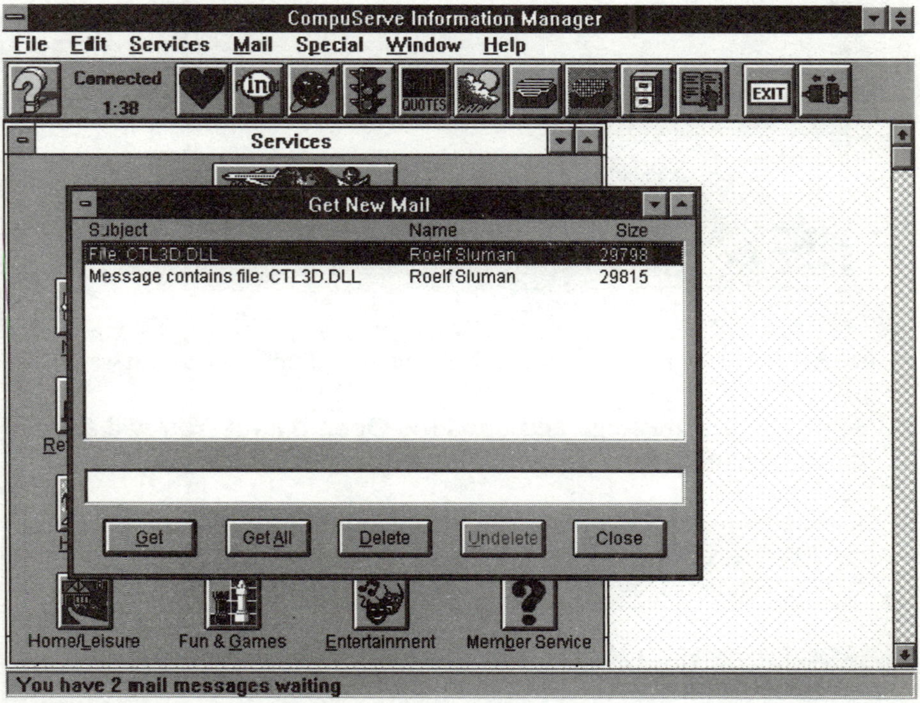

Figure 5.11 The Get New Mail dialog: the files have arrived – from the Internet

Press the Get All button to retrieve both messages. Again, this will take a few minutes, depending on your modem speed. When all messages have been retrieved, disconnect from CompuServe.

Now comes the hard part. You will have to convert the two messages into two files. In both cases, the procedure is identical:

1 Press the In-Basket button on the WinCIM Ribbon, or select the In-Basket option on the Mail menu. This causes the In-Basket to appear (see Figure 5.12).

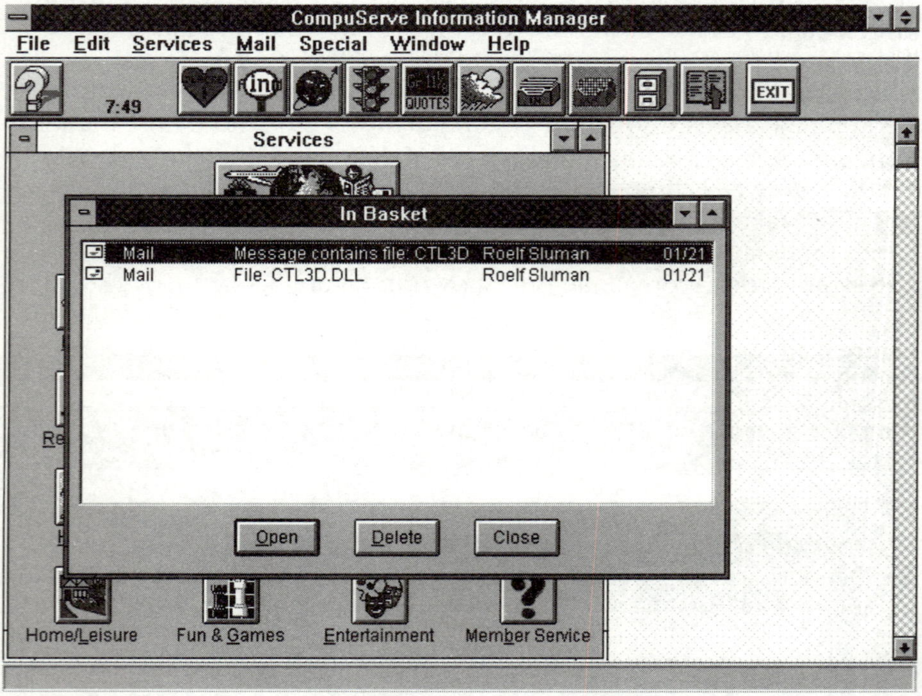

Figure 5.12 The WinCIM In-Basket, containing two unread mail messages

2 Select the first message and press the Open button. You will see a message like the one shown in Figure 5.13.

3 As you can see, the Subject field is included in the message. Using the Save As option on the File menu, save this message in the *TEMP* directory, as *FIRST UUE*. You can now close the window.

4 Repeat these steps for the second message in the In-Basket, but save it as *SECOND.UUE*, also in the *TEMP* directory.

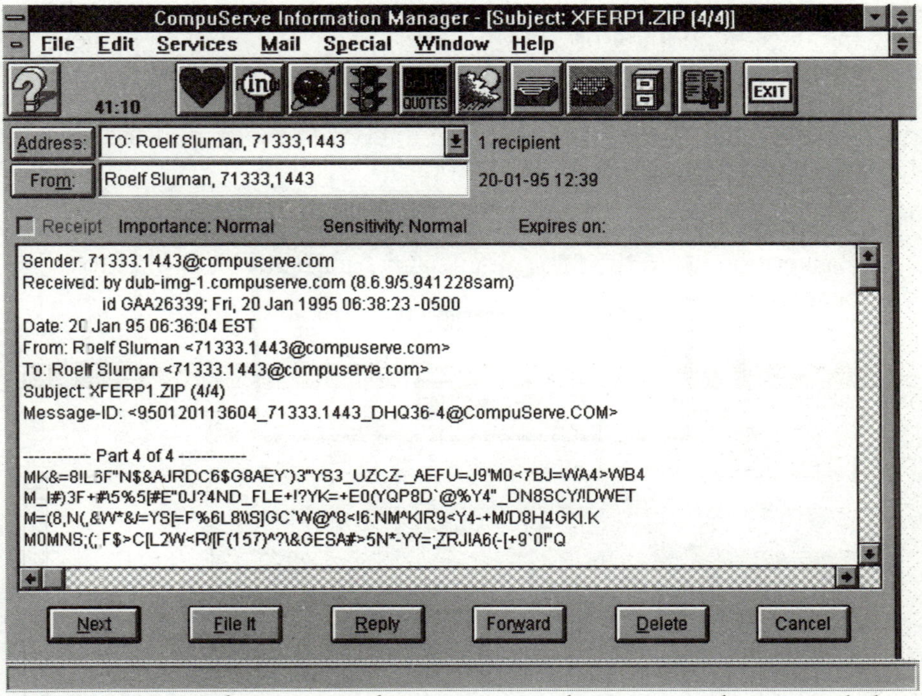

Figure 5.13 We have received an Internet mail message with an encoded version of the CTL3D.DLL file. Note the Internet header in front of the message. In some cases, the header could be as long as two or more computer screens

5 Using XFERPRO, we will now decode both files, to give them their original binary form. Start XFERPRO and press F3, or select the Decode option on the File menu. Select the *\TEMP* directory. You will see at least two UUE files: *FIRST.UUE* and *SECOND.UUE.*

6 Select *FIRST.UUE* and press the OK button. XFERPRO will recognize the UU header and even suggest a filename (*CTL3D.DLL*, the name of the original file). Change the suggested filename into *FIRST.DLL* and press the OK button. XFERPRO will now decode the file. After a few moments, the dialog shown in Figure 5.14 appears: the decoding process was successful.

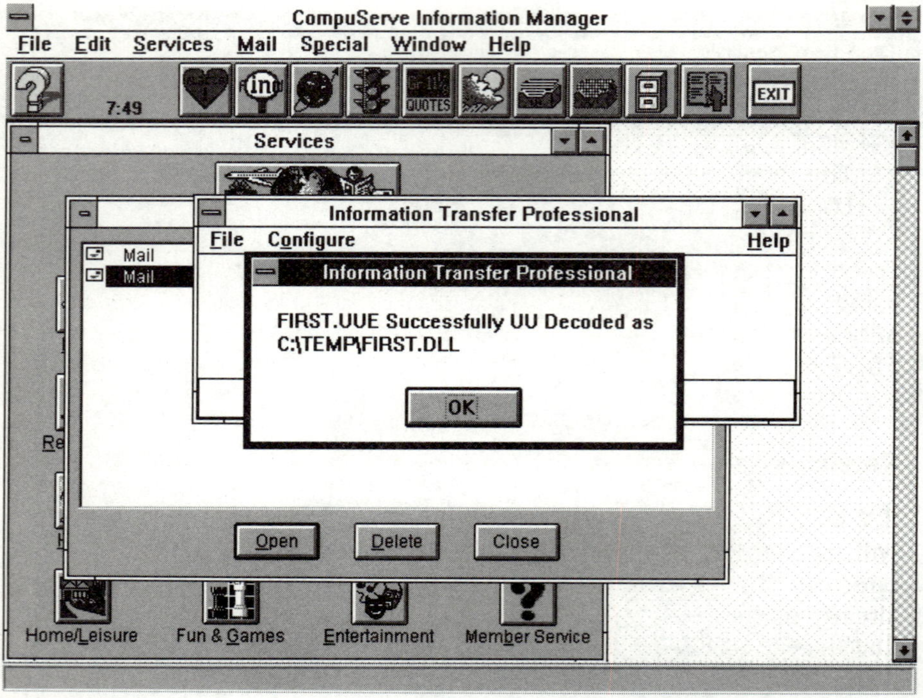

Figure 5.14 Our ASCII message has successfully been decoded into a file: FIRST.DLL

7 Repeat step 6 for the *SECOND.UUE* file. When XFERPRO suggests a filename, enter *SECOND.DLL*. After a few moments, this message will be decoded as well.

You've finished! Your *\TEMP* directory will now contain the following files:

- *CTL3D.DLL*: the original file.

- *CTL3D.UUE*: the original file, UUencoded.

- *FIRST.UUE*: the first message we received, an encoded version of *CTL3D.DLL*. Note that *CTL3D.UUE* and *FIRST.UUE* have different file sizes, even though they contain the same binary file! The reason is that the *FIRST.UUE* file, which was actually transferred via electronic mail, contains Internet mail header information.

- *FIRST.DLL*: a copy of *CTL3D.DLL*, derived from the *FIRST.UUE* file. Note that *CTL3D.DLL* and *FIRST.DLL* have the same file sizes – the first indication that all went well.

- *SECOND.UUE*: the second message we have received, another encoded version of *CTL3D.DLL*. Again, the file size differs from the other two UUE files.

- SECOND.DLL: a copy of *CTL3D.DLL*, derived from *SECOND.DLL*. The file size is identical to those of *FIRST.DLL* and *CTL3D.DLL*. Looks like we've made it!

To be perfectly sure, you might want to perform a file comparison, using the DOS utility *FC.EXE*. First, compare the files *FIRST.DLL* and *SECOND.DLL* – they will prove to be identical. Now, compare *FIRST.DLL* with the original: *CTL3D.DLL*. Identical, too. Congratulations!

Receiving large files as ASCII messages: the DOWNLOAD directory

If WinCIM retrieves an ASCII message larger than 50,000 characters, it will place the message as a **text file** in your *\CSERVE\DOWNLOAD* directory. The file will be named *NONAME.DAT* or, if such a file already exists, *NONAME.001*, *NONAME.002*, etc. You will be notified that the file has been stored via a message in your In-Basket.

To decode a message that has been stored in such a way, just decode the appropriate *NONAME.???* file.

Compressing

In many cases, files are **compressed** before they are transferred electronically. You might have heard of popular compression programs like PKZIP, ARJ and ARC. But actually, there are scores of compression tools in use. A few examples of filename extensions that are used to indicate compressed files are:

```
.arc, .arj, .bck, .cpt, .gif, .gz, .z
.ha, .hqx, .lha, .lzh, .pak, .pit, .pp
.sea, .sdn, .shar, .sit, .?q?, .sqz, .tar
.tar.Z, .tar-z, .taz, .tar.gz, tar.z, .tgz
.uc2, .z, .zip, .zoo, .F, .Y, .Z
```

For most compression formats, utilities are available on CompuServe, spread throughout a number of forums. The PC File Finder and Mac File Finder are useful tools in finding them. You can read more about the CompuServe File Finders on page 198, under the heading 'The CompuServe File Finders'. The following listing contains (part of) the results of a search in PC File Finder, using the keywords COMPRESS and UTILITY:

```
AIN Archiver v2.2
     BCPPDOS/Non-Tech General  AIN22.EXE
ARC.EXE 6.01 to make, extract *.ARC files  MS-DOS
     AIEXPERT/Utility Room  ARC.EXE
ARC utility for Mac
     AIEXPERT/Utility Room  ARCMAC.BIN
ARC v 6.01 for OS2
     IBMSYS/File Utilities [S]  ARC2.EXE
ARJ v2.41a File Compression Utility
     PWOFORUM/New Uploads  ARJ241.EXE
CRUSH v1.2 File Compressor
     PWOFORUM/DOS Apps/Utilities  CRUSH.ZIP
GZIP Executables for SCO UNIX
     PCVEND/Magma Systems  GZSCO.Z
GZIP Executables for Sun Solaris 2.3
     PCVEND/Magma Systems  GZSOL.Z
JRchive - file archiving and compression software
     IBMSYS/File Utilities [S]  JRC101.ZIP
LHA (2.13) compresses better than PKZIP: free
     ZENITH/DOS Utilities  LHA213.EXE
Lharc LHA version 2.11 File Compression Utility
     MIDIFORUM/IBM/PC Compatible  LHA211.EXE
PKWare's PKZIP and PKUNZIP (2.04G) for DOS
     ZENITH/DOS Utilities  PK204G.EXE
SEA ARC version 6.02 for MSDOS computers
     MUSICARTS/Forum Info/Misc  ARC602.EXE
SHEZ v10.5
     PEARL/Utilities/Tools  SHZ5-N.EXE
Squish: File Compression with redirection & pipes
     IBMSYS/File Utilities [S]  SQUI10.ZIP
UNSTUFF (1.0) extracts Mac StuffIt and other SIT
     ZENITH/DOS Utilities  UNSIT.EXE
WinUnzip 4.0
     TAPCIS/Scripts and Tools  WUZIP.EXE
Ten kinds of compression, including ARC and ZIP
     ZENITH/DOS Utilities  XCH103.EXE
```

If you are a Macintosh user, you can GO MACFF to use the Macintosh File Finder.

A very useful file, with lots of information about file compressing, can be found in the Internet New Users Forum (GO INETFORUM):

- ```
  [73710,1430]     Lib: 6
  COMPRS.ZIP/Bin  Bytes:  73738

  Title    : File Compression FAQ
  Keywords: COMPRESS FAQ ZIP TAR ARCHIVE JPEG TIFF

  Frequently Asked Questions about file compression.
  Many files retrieved from various Internet sites will
  be compressed in some manner. This FAQ will describe
  the various types of compression, theory behind
  compression, and  also describe some hardware
  compression.
  ```

This file also contains information about FTP sites where a particular file can be downloaded.

Receiving messages from the Internet

Important: To be able to retrieve messages from the Internet, you will have to change your **online mail settings**. (Note that these settings have nothing to do with your WinCIM mail preferences.) You will only need to do this once. Proceed as follows:

1 Start WinCIM. Select the GO option on the Special menu and enter ASCIIMAIL. Press the OK button.

2 After a few moments, the Terminal Emulation window will be displayed. After the *Mail!* prompt, type **set receive yes**.

3 A few moments later, another *Mail!* prompt will be displayed. Press Enter to close the Terminal Emulation window.

As you learned in the previous section, receiving messages from the Internet works in almost the same way as receiving normal CompuServe Mail messages. There is one difference, however: all mail messages coming in from the Internet are Postage Due. That means that you have to pay for them, just like you pay for sending mail. The rates for sending and receiving Internet mail are identical.

So when do you pay for an Internet message? Not until you start reading it. If you decide to delete an Internet message before taking a
  ```

look at its contents (that is, before you press the Get or Get All button), you don't pay anything.

Mailing lists

As a CompuServe member, you know that forums are the ultimate way to exchange messages about a particular subject. On the Internet, discussions are held in three different ways:

- **Private mail**. In some cases, discussions between a small group of people are held by 'carbon copying' everyone in the group on each message sent.
- **USENET newsgroups**. A USENET newsgroup is actually a large collection of messages that were all mailed to one address: the address of the newsgroup. Everyone who subscribes to that particular newsgroup can read all messages posted. More about USENET newsgroups can be found in Chapter 6.
- **Mailing lists**. Mailing lists can be compared to USENET newsgroups. Everyone can post a message to a particular mailing list. All new messages are, either piece by piece or in one big chunk, distributed (through electronic mail) to anyone who has **subscribed** to that particular mailing list.

Background information

The big difference between USENET newsgroups and mailing lists is the amount of interactivity involved. To read messages that were posted in a USENET newsgroup, you actually have to 'visit' the newsgroup and either read those messages online or store them on your hard disk for later processing. If you don't visit the newsgroup, you will not be able to read the messages posted in it. The messages posted in mailing lists however are 'dropped at your front door': your CompuServe Mailbox.

Participating in mailing list discussions, or simply reading mailing list messages pertaining to a topic that you are interested in, can be a very rewarding experience. A few basic facts:

- To receive messages posted in a certain mailing list, you will have to **subscribe** to that mailing list. Subscriptions are free; apart from the mail costs (normal CompuServe rates apply), you won't be charged anything. Subscribing is easy: it involves nothing more than sending a mail message to a so-called **mailing list manager**. This can be either a real person or an automated computer program. In most cases, subscription is entirely automatic, including the confirmation messages.

- As a part of the subscription process, you will often receive an (automated) electronic mail message explaining more about the mailing list, covering topics like cancelling your subscription, posting messages, replying to other messages, etc. **Important**: save this message in a secure place. The commands to cancel a mailing list subscription differ slightly, and it is a good thing to have them handy when you decide to stop participating. Keep in mind that participating in a mailing list discussion could involve receiving anywhere from a few messages per week to thousands of messages per day!

- Not all mailing lists allow active participation. Some mailing lists are nothing more than news bulletins, while others involve heavy debates. Some mailing list discussions are moderated (a **moderator** looks at every message posted to the mailing list and decides whether or not it will be included in the mailing list), others aren't. Once again, read the subscription information for more information.

Finding the right mailing list(s) for you

So now you want to see what mailing lists are available. Where to start?

A good place, as always, is the Internet New Users Forum (`GO INETFORUM`). In the libraries, search for files with keywords such as MAILING and MAILLIST. Look at the following list for some of the files found in the Internet New Users Forum:

- *[76703,407]   Lib: 8*
  BPRLST.TXT/Text Bytes: 6291

  Title   : Business Process Redesign Mailing List
  Keywords: BUSINESS PROCESS REDESIGN

  Business Process Redesign Mailing List

- *[76703,407]   Lib: 8*
  CIS-L.TXT/Text Bytes: 3081

  Title   : Careers in Information Systems Mailing List
  Keywords: CAREERS INFORMATION SYSTEMS

  Careers in Information Systems Mailing List

- *[72640,3053]   Lib: 8*
  EXPLOR.TXT/Text Bytes: 2097

  Title   : Ford Explorer Mailing List
  Keywords: FORD EXPLORER MAILING LISTS INTERNET

  This is a mailing list for owners of or those interested in the Ford Explorer. Areas of discussion are expected to focus on problems, warranty service, costs, performance, operation, and 3rd party or after-market add-ons. There are also discussions on other topics relating to the Ford Explorer. If interested, read this file and subscribe!

- *[73177,3346]   Lib: 8*
  EZOO30.EXE/Bin Bytes: 134462

  Title   : Electronic Zoo - Version 3.0
  Keywords: ANIMAL COMPUTER RESOURCES INTERNET BBS

  The Electronic Zoo is a list of animal-related computer resources on the Internet and beyond, including mailing lists, telnet and FTP sites, Gophers, WWW, online services and BBSs. Current as of 5/94. Uploaded by the author.

- *[76703,407] Lib: 8*
  EDI-L.TXT/Text Bytes: 1670

  Title : Info on the EDI-L EDI Mailing List/Archives
  Keywords: EDI-L EDI MAILING LIST

  Info on the EDI-L EDI Mailing List/Archives

- *[76703,407] Lib: 8*
  EFJAPN.TXT/Text Bytes: 5907

  Title : Electronic Frontiers - Japan Mailing List
  Keywords: ELECTRONIC FRONTIERS JAPAN

  Electronic Frontiers - Japan Mailing List

- *[76702,1127] Lib: 8*
  HERP-L.TXT/Text Bytes: 1744

  Title : Details for HERP-L mailing list [reptiles, etc.]
  Keywords: REPTILE AMPHIBIAN HERPETOLOGY BIOLOGY ZOOLOGY ANIMALS ECOLOGY

  Announcement and sub details for Herp-L - a mail list for the scientific study of reptiles or amphibians.

- *[76703,407] Lib: 8*
  HTMKTG.TXT/Text Bytes: 1724

  Title : Info on High Tech Marketing mailing list
  Keywords: HIGH TECH MARKETING MAILING LIST

  Info on High Tech Marketing mailing list

- *[73710,1430] Lib: 5*
  MLARCH.ZIP/Bin Bytes: 12750

  Title : Mail Archive Software Summary
  Keywords: MAIL ARCHIVE MAILING LIST LISTSERV

  Summary of known mail archive servers. Mail archive servers receive requests and act upon them. Most often, they manage mailing lists or return information to requesters.

- ```
  [76703,407]       Lib:14
  MNGOVT.TXT/Text Bytes:    2165

  Title    : Info on Minnesota Government Mailing List
  Keywords: MINNESOTA MN GOVT

  Info on Minnesota Government Mailing List
  ```

- ```
  [74431,2303]     Lib: 8
  PERULI.TXT/Text Bytes:   11839

  Title    : Peru List of lists
  Keywords: MAILING LISTS PERU

  A guide to the names and types of mailing lists found
  in and dealing with Peru.
  ```

- ```
  [100265,2423]    Lib: 8
  ROTLIS.TXT/Text Bytes:     731

  Title    : Info on Rotary/Rotaract Mailing List
  Keywords: MAILING LIST ROTARY ROTARACT

  Mailing list info for Rotary/Rotaract
  ```

- ```
  [100272,1660]    Lib: 8
  YORKU.LST/Text   Bytes:    1960

  Title    : 19 Mail-lists available on
  LISTSERV@vm1.yorku.ca
  Keywords: MAIL LISTS CANADA YORKUNIV SUBSCRIBE

  List of 19 mailing lists available on
  LISTSERV@vm1.yorku.ca Instructions on how to subscribe.
  Wide range of subjects covered. Uploaded by
  [100272,1660]
  ```

You might also want to try the new Internet Resources Forum (GO INETRESOURCES), which has a special Mailing Lists library.

Tip: If you would like to receive a summary of most of the available public mailing lists in your CompuServe Mailbox, send a mail message to *INTERNET:mail-server@rtfm.mit.edu*. It doesn't matter what you put in the Subject field. Include the following lines in the actual message text:

```
size 0
send usenet/news.answers/mail/mailing-lists/*
```

Note that this mailing list is huge (it currently exceeds 500 kB). This means that you will incur about $1.50 in mail charges (which will be deducted from your monthly allowance). It is very useful, however, especially since the mailing lists are sorted by topic.

Another tip: if you need even more information, you can request an even larger file to be sent to your mailbox (more than 1.3 MB): the *SRI NISC 'interest-groups' list of lists.* To receive a copy in your CompuServe Mailbox, send a mail message to *INTERNET:mail-server@sri.com.* Again, the contents of the Subject field are not important. In the message text, include the following line:

```
send interest-groups
```

Subscribing to a mailing list

Once you have found a mailing list you are interested in, you have to **subscribe** to it, in order to receive messages posted in the mailing list. This is done by means of a mail message to the so-called **request address**. Typically, you will subscribe in one of the following two ways:

- If the mailing list manager is a live person: send him or her a mail message, asking to be put on the mailing list. Don't forget to specify the name of the mailing list, as some mailing list managers are responsible for several different mailing lists.

  Courtesy helps. If you know that the mailing list manager is a live person, refrain from using 'cold' programming language commands like *subscribe formula-1 John Smith.* A message like *I'd like to subscribe to your formula-1 mailing list. My mail address is 100567.123@compuserve.com* is little work to write, and much more friendly to receive.

- If the mailing list manager is automated, like **listserv**, **majordomo** and **listproc**, place whatever you like in the Subject field. In the message text, include the standard subscription line for that list server (this information will be included in the standard mailing list information you have received), for instance:

```
subscribe hungarian-food John Smith
```

Note that you don't have to include your electronic mail address in the message text; it is already present in the message header. In most cases, you can send a message with commands like **help** or **info** (use a separate line for each command) to get additional information should you need it.

Reading and posting messages

Once you have subscribed to a mailing list, the messages will start to come in on a frequent basis. Some mailing lists send all messages in one big chunk, once per day for instance, while others simply send all contributions as separate mail messages.

Saving costs!

As a CompuServe member, you pay $0.10 for every mail message that you receive from the Internet, regardless of whether it is only 500 bytes or 7,500 bytes. When receiving longer mail messages, you pay only $0.02 for each additional chunk of 7,500 bytes. Therefore, mailing lists that compile all contributions are much less expensive than mailing lists that forward all contributions as they come in.

For example, let's say that you have subscribed to a mailing list that forwards each message as soon as it is posted. Fifty messages are posted per day, with an average length of 2,000 characters. Per month, you would incur no less than $150 in mail charges!

Figures look entirely different when all contributions are sent out as one large chunk, every day. In that case, you would end up paying no more than $10.80 for the same number of messages... Quite a difference.

Knowing this, it might help to be selective in the mailing lists you subscribe to. Consult the mailing list info (see page 145, under the heading 'Finding the right mailing list(s) for you', for more details before subscribing – it might help to save you a lot of money.

You've had enough: cancelling your subscription

If you would like to cancel your subscription to a mailing list, send a message to the request address, following the guidelines you received when you subscribed earlier.

Tip: Have you forgotten how to cancel your subscription? Send a message to the request address, with the text **help** or **info**.

As it can take a few days before your mailing list subscription is cancelled, you will likely receive some more messages in the meantime. Remember that you don't incur any mail charges for messages that you haven't read. It might therefore be a good idea to change the WinCIM settings so that you don't receive Internet mail (that is, Postage Due mail) automatically. To do this, select the Preferences option on the Special menu, followed by Mail. The Mail Preferences dialog will be displayed. In the Postage Due Messages box, select the Do not retrieve option. That way, your Postage Due mail will not be collected when you retrieve your mail automatically (by selecting the Send/Receive All Mail option, for instance).

Mail: Frequently Asked Questions

- **Do I have an Internet Address?**
  Yes. Take your CompuServe User ID and replace the comma by a dot. Add the text *@compuserve.com.* That's all. For instance, if your CompuServe User ID is 100234,123, your Internet address is *100234.123@compuserve.com.*

- **How do I send a message to my friend, who has a CIX account?**
  Just like you, your friend has an Internet address as well. Suppose her CIX login name is *susan.* In that case, send your mail message to *INTERNET:susan@cix.compulink.co.uk.*

- **Do other online services have Internet mailboxes, too?**
  Most of them have. A few examples (replace *user* by the login name of the member you want to send a message to) are:

America Online	*INTERNET:user@aol.com*
BIX	*INTERNET:user@bix.com*

CIX	*INTERNET:user@cix.compulink.co.uk*
GENIE	*INTERNET:user@genie.com*
Prodigy	*INTERNET:user@prodigy.com*

- **Can I send Internet mail with a Receipt Notice?**
  No. Or rather: yes, but the Receipt Notice doesn't mean a thing. Unlike a CompuServe Mail message sent to a CompuServe User ID, where you receive the Notice as soon as the addressee either reads or deletes the message (whichever comes first), you will receive the Notice as soon as CompuServe transfers the mail message to the Internet, giving it no value whatsoever. The only way to be sure that the addressee has received your message is ask him or her to confirm it – by means of another message.

- **I don't receive any Internet mail. And my In-Basket is cluttered with error messages. What's happening?**
  In your WinCIM settings, you have indicated that you don't want to retrieve Postage Due Mail (that is, mail for which you have to pay to read, like mail from the Internet) when you use one of WinCIM's automated actions (like Send/Receive All Mail on the Mail menu). Select the Preferences option on the Special menu, followed by Mail. The Mail Preferences dialog will be displayed. In the Postage Due Messages box, select the Always retrieve option.

- **Can I use the Internet to send a message to someone with a FIDOnet address?**
  Yes, although the addressing protocol is a little complicated. To send mail to someone with a FIDOnet address, use the following format:

  ```
  INTERNET:first name.last
  name@ppoint.fnode.nnet.zzone
  ```

  An example of a FIDOnet address is:

  ```
  INTERNET:john.simpson@p4.f3.n2.z1
  ```

  As a CompuServe member, you can be reached from any FIDOnet address as follows:

  ```
  id@compuserve.com ON 1:1/31
  ```

  where *id* is your CompuServe User ID, with the comma replaced by a dot.

Abbreviations and emoticons

To keep messages short and to the point, and often out of habit, many electronic mail writers use a comprehensive range of abbreviations. Although some of these abbreviations are rather far-fetched, there are others that are hard to do without, once you are accustomed to using them.

The following list contains most of the abbreviations that you will encounter in electronic mail messages. And if you should see an abbreviation that is not included in this list: don't hesitate to ask the sender what it means!

0.02	Throwing in your two cents' worth
AFAIK	As far as I know
AWHFY	Are we having fun yet?
B4	Before
B4N	Bye for now
BAD	Broken as designed
BBR	Burnt beyond repair
BBS	Bulletin Board System
BCNU	Be seein' you!
BFN	Bye For Now
BION	Believe it or not
BMTIPG	Brilliant minds think in parallel gutters
BRB	Be right back (during conferences, and on CB)
BRS	Big red switch
BTA	But then again
BTAIM	Be that as it may
BTOBD	Be there or be dead
BTSOOM	Beats the s**t out of me
BTW	By the way
BWQ	Buzz word quotient
CAD	Control-Alt-Delete
CADET	Can't add, doesn't even try
CIM	CompuServe Information Manager
CIS	CompuServe Information System
CI$	CompuServe Information System
CO	Conference
CU	See you
CUL8R	See you later
DIIK	Darn if I know
DL	Download
DOSCIM	CompuServe Information Manager for DOS
DTRT	Do the right thing

DWIMC	Do what I mean, correctly
ENS	Executive News Service (one of CompuServe's services)
FCFS	First come, first served
FISH	First in, still here
FOAF	Friend of a friend
FTF	Face to face
FUBAR	Fouled up beyond all recognition
FUD	Fear, uncertainty, and doubt
FWIW	For what it's worth
FYI	For your information
g,d&r	grinning, ducking, and running
g,d&rf	grinning, ducking and running FAST!
g,d&rvvf	grinning, ducking and running VERY VERY FAST
GA	Go ahead
GDW	Grin, duck and weave
GIGO	Garbage in, garbage out
GLGH	Good luck and good hunting
GMTA	Great minds think alike
GOWI	Get on with it
GPF	General Protection Fault
GP,F	Go puke, fast!
HSIK	How should I know
IAAA	I am an accountant
IAAL	I am a lawyer
IANAA	I am not an accountant
IANAL	I am not a lawyer
IAC	In any case
IAE	In any event
IMO	In my opinion
IMHO	In my humble opinion
IMCO	In my considered opinion
IMAO	In my arrogant opinion
IME	In my experience
IMPOV	In my point of view
IOW	In other words
ITFA	In the final analysis
IWBNI	If would be nice if
IYFEG	Insert your favourite ethnic group
JAM	Just a moment
JAS	Just a second
JAWS	Just another Windows shell
JIC	Just in case
LMAO	Laughing my arm off
LOL	Laughing out loud
MOF	Matter of fact

MOTAS	Member of the appropriate sex
MOTOS	Member of the opposite sex
MOTSS	Member of the same sex
MOTM	Member of the month
NBD	No big deal
NFW	No f***ing way
NINO	Nothing in, nothing out
NOYB	None of your business
NQA	No questions asked
NTIM	Not that it matters
NTIMM	Not that it matters much
NUI	Network user identification
OBTW	Oh, by the way
OIC	Oh, I see
OTF	On the floor
OTL	Out to lunch
OTOH	On the other hand
OTTH	On the third hand
OTTOMH	Off the top of my head
PABG	Pack a big gun
PDN	Public data network
PITA	Pain in the anatomy
PLOKTA	Press lots of keys to abort
PMBI	Pardon my butting in
PMFBI	Pardon me for butting in
PMFJI	Pardon me for jumping in
POSSLQ	Person of opposite sex sharing living quarters
POV	Point of view
PPN	Programmer Project Number: old term for User-ID
RFD	Request for discussion
RHIP	Rank has its privileges
RLCO	Real Life COnference
RNA	Ring, no answer
ROFL	Rolling on floor, laughing
RPG	Role playing games
RSN	Real soon now (release date of software ...)
RTFM	Read the "friendly" manual
SMOP	Small matter of programming
SNAFU	Situation normal, all fouled up
SO	Significant other (cybertalk for "partner")
SUFID	Screwing up face in disgust
SWMBO	She who must be obeyed
Sysop	System Operator
TAFN	Thats all for now
TANJ	There ain't no justice

TANSTAAFL	There ain't no such thing as a free lunch
TBYB	Try before you buy
TFTT	Thanks for the thought
TGIF	Thank god its friday
TIA	Thanks in advance
TIC	Tongue in cheek
TM	Thread mangler
TPTB	The powers that be
TSR	Totally stupid rules
TTFN	Ta ta for now
TTL4N	Thats the lot for now
UAE	Unrecoverable application error
UL or U/L	Upload
WAEF	When all else fails
WizOp	Wizard Sysop (the "chief" sysop of a forum)
WOA	Work of art
WYSIWYG	What you see is what you get
WYSBYGI	What you see before you get it
WYGIWYPF	What you get is what you pay for
YADS	Yet another DOS shell
ZNT	ZiffNet

Digital sign language: emoticons

Remember the 'smileys' that people used to wear some years ago? Well, they are back! The smileys of the digital age, called **emoticons**, have invaded the electronic SuperHighway. By far the most popular one is :). If you don't see what this symbol represents, just tilt your head to the left!

Take a look at the following list, which contains an overview of the creatures that might invade your messages too, sooner or later...

:-)	Smiling
:-|	Grim
:-(	Frowning
:-c	Real unhappy
:-[	Pouting
'-)	Wink
:-,	"Hmmmm "
:-o	Wow!
:-C	Just totally unbelieving
:= |	Baboon
:-B	Drooling
:-v	Speaking

:-,	Smirk
:-V	Shout
:-||	Anger
:-w	Speak with forked tongue
:-r	Sticking tongue out
:-*	Oops!
:-T	Keeping a straight face
;-)	Sardonic incredulity
:-D	Said with a smile
%->	Drunk with laughter
:-x	Kiss kiss
:-"	Pursing lips
:-#	My lips are sealed
|-{	"Good Grief!"
:-}	"Thish wine tashted pretty good"
8-]	"wow, maaan"
:^D	"Great! I like it!"
B-D	"Serves you right, dummy!!"

Chapter 6

USENET newsgroups

- Background information
- Accessing USENET newsgroups with WinCIM
- Accessing USENET newsgroups through Dial PPP
- Useful files
- Frequently Asked Questions

CompuServe Internet Services

Background information

Just like CompuServe has its **forums**, digital meeting places that cover a broad range of topics, the Internet has a series of **USENET newsgroups**. USENET is the name of a series of computers that exchange articles about a wealth of subjects, divided into seven categories. Each category contains a large number of **newsgroups**: a collection of messages pertaining to a particular subject, or **articles** in USENET jargon.

Currently, there are seven official newsgroup categories. In addition, there are lots of non-official newsgroups in existence. Although these newsgroups are not officially part of USENET, they use the same structure as the official newsgroups. Not all of these newsgroups apply to a large audience; some of them are only available on one or more local Internet sites, while others are almost as widespread as the official USENET newsgroups.

The seven official newsgroup categories, which are normally available on any Internet site, are:

- **news**: this category covers subjects that are related to the newsgroups phenomenon. One of the most important newsgroups in this category is *news.newusers.questions*, in which questions are posted about usage of the newsgroups, **netiquette** (the way to 'behave' when you post messages to newsgroups), and so on.

- **sci**: this category contains newsgroups with scientific topics.

- **comp**: in this category, newsgroups about a broad range of computing topics can be found.

- **rec**: the newsgroups in this category cover topics like hobbies and recreation.

- **soc**: the **social** newsgroups, in which people get together, discuss topics pertaining to a particular country or culture, etc.

- **talk**: typical discussion newsgroups, about a broad range of issues.

- **misc**: if a newsgroup doesn't fit in any of the other six categories, it is placed here.

The seven official USENET categories contain lots and lots of newsgroups (several thousands). But that's not all: there is also a large range of non-official newsgroup categories. These categories came into existence because the founders didn't want to deal with the official, 'bureaucratic' USENET approach. One of the most famous categories is **alt** (alternative), where you find things that you're even afraid to dream of...

Note that there is no such thing as an official 'USENET administration': in principle, anyone who feels like it can start his or her own USENET newsgroup. However, your newsgroup will only become successful if many Internet sites decide to 'carry it', that is, to pass it through to their users. Most site administrators are fairly critical when it comes to accepting a new newsgroup that belongs to one of the seven main categories.

As a CompuServe member, you will be tempted to approach newsgroups the same way you approach forums. However, don't expect the structure and elegance of CompuServe's forums, with their sections, conference rooms and libraries, to apply to newsgroups as well. A newsgroup is, in fact, nothing more than a series of mail messages, so-called **articles**. In other words: every time you read newsgroup articles, you effectively read a bunch of mail messages. Articles that are posted in newsgroups contain subject and sender fields, but there is no recipient field! (Actually, there is: the newsgroup itself is the recipient.) If you wish to respond to the author of an article directly, you will have to send him or her your reply via mail. If you post your reaction in a newsgroup, it is effectively addressed to all its **subscribers**, and you have absolutely no guarantee that the addressee will read it.

The main differences between forums and newsgroups are listed in the following table.

Forums	**Newsgroups**
Forums contain **sections**. In each section, messages about a particular subject or range of subjects are posted.	A newsgroup is, in fact, a section: it is part of a newsgroup **category**. If you look at it from a distance, a newsgroup category is, in fact, a kind of forum, often with several thousands of sections. In other words: there are seven 'forums', each with numerous 'sections'.

A section contains one or more **threads**: messages that are linked together.	A newsgroup contains separate articles: mail messages that were posted to the newsgroup.
All messages in a thread share the same subject. If you **reply** to a message, you don't have to specify a subject: your reply becomes part of the thread.	There is no way to reply to an article, other than via e-mail. To indicate that an article mailed by you to a newsgroup is a reaction to a previous article, you use the original article subject.
When you start a thread, you specify a **subject** or **topic**, as well as a recipient. You can also send a message to *sysop* or to *all* forum members.	There are no threads: you simply write articles and mail them to the newsgroup. There is no way to specify a recipient: the newsgroup is the recipient of your article.
You post a message in a forum.	You post an article to a newsgroup.
Every forum has room for a certain number of messages. Once that number is reached, the message that was posted first will 'scroll off' the message board. If you have written a message to a particular forum member, it will be delivered to that member's mailbox if it scrolls off before he or she reads it on the forum.	The number of articles that are visible when you look into a newsgroup depends on the capacity of your Internet access provider. Because articles are mailed to the newsgroup and not to a particular person, there are no 'unread' articles.
Forums are managed by sysops.	A number of newsgroups are 'unmoderated': there is no 'sysop'. As you can imagine, this can lead to total anarchy, 'flaming' and other effects that are rare events on CompuServe forums. Be prepared for the worst!

Forums are, without exception, friendly places. New members are always welcome to post a message, and you will almost certainly get a nice reply.	If you are a 'newbie', watch out where you mail your articles to. Some newsgroup members can react very, let us say, 'aggressively' to new and inexperienced people. Don't expect your 'Hi, I'm here too!' messages to be responded to nicely; you are likely to receive a lot of 'flames' in your mailbox. The same applies if you post a message that is considered to be wrong, or in the wrong newsgroup. It can be a jungle out there!
Forums have conference rooms.	Newsgroups are nothing more than series of mail messages. Internet members 'conference' via a feature called Internet Relay Chat, or IRC. This feature has nothing to do with the newsgroups.
Forums have libraries with files that you can download.	Some newsgroups contain binary articles, stored in a special ASCII format. These articles are **UUencoded**: the sender has used a special program to convert the binary file into one or more chunks of regular ASCII articles. When you have retrieved those articles, you can use a decode program to convert the ASCII contents into a binary file. More about UUencoding files and decoding them can be found on page 125, under the heading 'Sending and receiving binary files over the Internet'.

Accessing USENET newsgroups with WinCIM

If you use WinCIM, you have easy access to basic USENET newsgroups, and to a number of non-official newsgroups. Can you guess the GO word? Right: `GO USENET`.

Typically, the process of accessing USENET newsgroups with WinCIM consists of two steps:

1 You subscribe to the newsgroups that interest you. Once you have subscribed to a certain newsgroup, CompuServe will maintain internal information about the last message in that newsgroup that you have read. To you, it will look as if CompuServe stores all messages posted to that newsgroup in a special online 'Newsgroup Basket' (not unlike CompuServe's **Executive News clipping folders**), which can be used to store news pertaining to topics you are interested in.

2 You access the newsgroup and read all articles that you are interested in. CompuServe will maintain information about the articles you have read, so that you won't see them the next time (this can, in a way, be compared to the way CompuServe handles forum messages).

3 When you are no longer interested in a certain newsgroup, you can **unsubscribe**. Although this isn't necessary, unsubscribing to newsgroups that you no longer need will keep your newsgroup summary window clean and nicely arranged.

Selecting and subscribing to newsgroups

Before you can subscribe, you need to find newsgroups that you are interested in. Proceed as follows:

1 `GO USENET`. After a few moments, the USENET Newsgroup entrance menu appears, as shown in Figure 6.1. This entrance menu contains the following options:
  - **About USENET Newsgroups**: select this option to read a little background information about USENET newsgroups.
  - **Newsgroups Disclaimer**: When you read USENET newsgroup articles, you access information that is not controlled by CompuServe. Therefore, CompuServe cannot be held

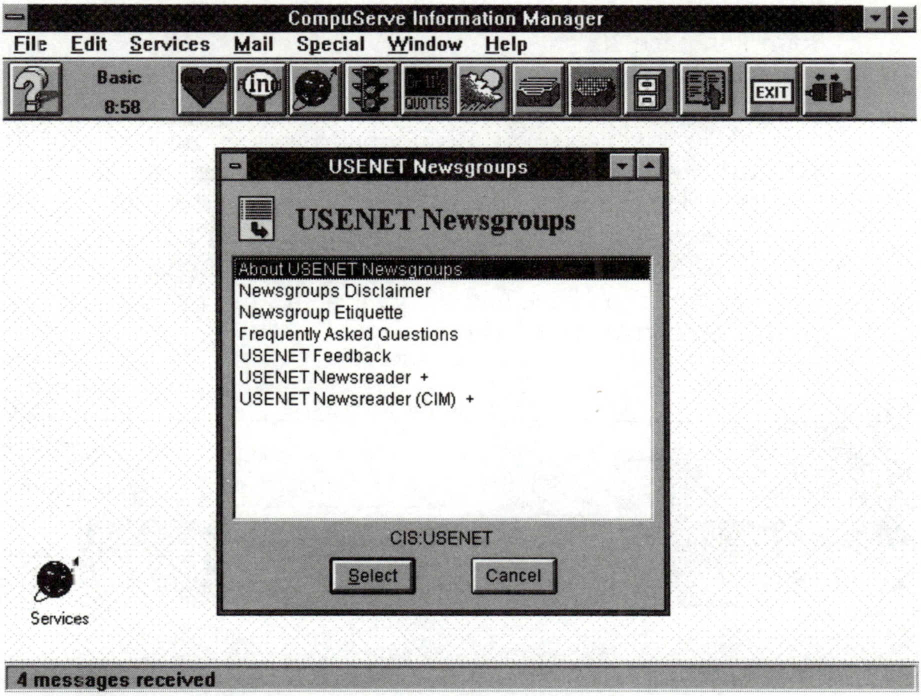

Figure 6.1 The USENET Newsgroup entrance menu

responsible for the content of that information. Because, unlike CompuServe forums, most newsgroups are not moderated at all, you might encounter newsgroups and/or newsgroup articles that you find offensive. The complete CompuServe Newsgroups Disclaimer is available by selecting this option.

Tip: Instead of reading this article online, press the File It button to have it stored into your WinCIM Filing Cabinet. After you have disconnected, you can read it offline without incurring telephone charges.

- **Newsgroup Etiquette**: Just like CompuServe forums, participating in newsgroups demands a certain etiquette, often referred to as 'netiquette'. Over the years, a lot of newsgroups have developed their own style. Before actively participating in newsgroup discussions, you are advised to monitor the articles posted to that newsgroup for a while. This will help you to get a good 'feel' for what is permitted and what is not. Select this option to read an article that contains more information about Netiquette.
- **Frequently Asked Questions**: Select this option to retrieve a summary of questions that are often asked, as well as the

answers to those questions. An extract from this list can be found on page 181.

- **USENET Feedback**: If you experience problems while accessing USENET, or another CompuServe Internet Service for that matter, you can select this option to write a message to the USENET Feedback department. After you have selected this option, a dialog appears, containing the names of available Internet Services. In this dialog, select the USENET News option. After a few moments, the dialog shown in Figure 6.2 appears. After you have entered your name and the message, press the Send Message button.

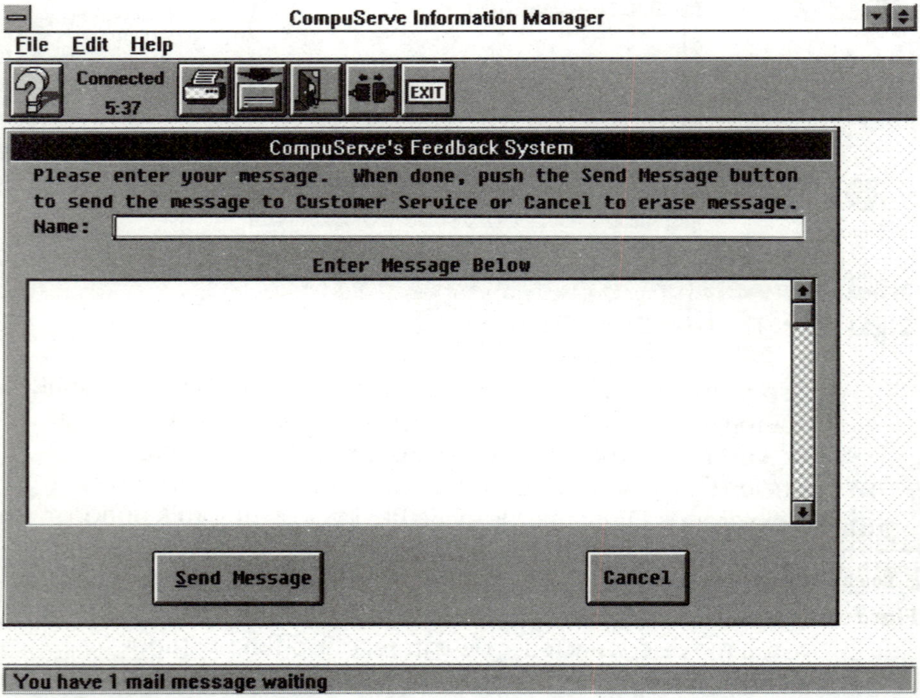

Figure 6.2 Use this dialog to send a message to the CompuServe Feedback department

- **USENET Newsreader**: Select this option to access the USENET Newsreader using CompuServe's ASCII interface. This option is available for CompuServe members who don't use a version of the CompuServe Information Manager (CIM).
- **USENET Newsreader (CIM)**: Select this option to subscribe and unsubscribe to newsgroups and to read articles posted to those newsgroups.

2 Select the USENET Newsreader (CIM) option. You might want to select options Newsgroup Etiquette and Frequently Asked Questions, first; these contain additional information about what's lying ahead of you.

3 After a few moments, the USENET Newsgroups main menu is displayed, as shown in Figure 6.3. This menu contains the following options:

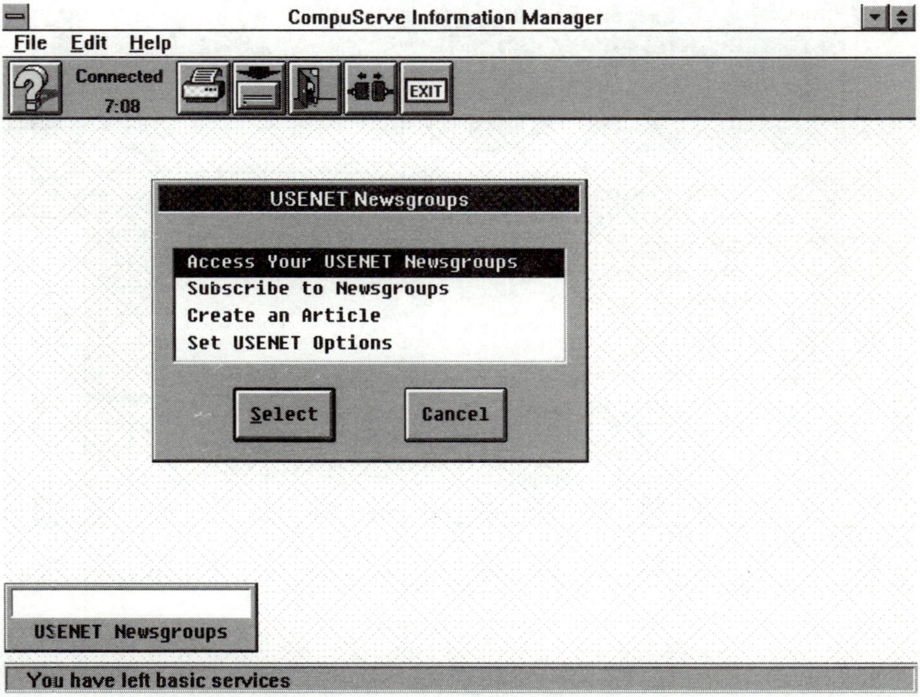

Figure 6.3 The USENET Newsgroups main menu

- **Access your USENET Newsgroups**: This option is available only when you have subscribed to at least one newsgroup.
- **Subscribe to Newsgroups**: This is the option we are about to select.
- **Create an Article**: This option, which will be discussed later, allows you to write newsgroup articles.
- **Set USENET Options**: Use this option to specify information about your name and company, and about the number of articles that you want to be displayed initially. You can also specify your signature: one or more lines with some original quote, or with additional information about yourself. In USENET newsgroups, a signature is a fashion statement. You'll

see no 'Regards, John' over there! If you're curious: just be patient for a few more moments.

4 Select the Subscribe to Newsgroups option. After a few seconds, the Subscribe to Newsgroups dialog appears, shown in Figure 6.4.

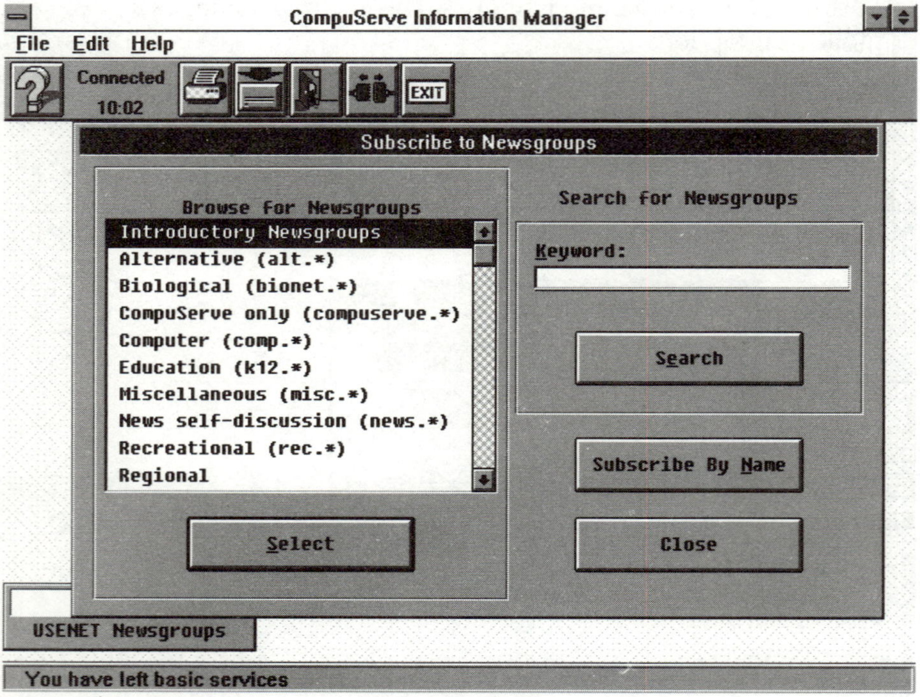

Figure 6.4 Select your newsgroups from this menu

5 On the left side of this dialog, you see a list of newsgroup categories. When you select a category and press the Select button, CompuServe will display a list of available newsgroups for that category. You can try this out for yourself: select a category, for instance Computer, and press the Select button. A possible result (remember: newsgroups are deleted and added all the time!) is displayed in Figure 6.5.

6 If you see a newsgroup that you like, check the box in front of it. If you wish to know more about the contents of a particular newsgroup, press the Preview button. WinCIM will display a list of current articles in that newsgroup, as shown in Figure 6.6. In this window, which is identical to the one you will use when reading messages in newsgroups to which you have subscribed, you have the following options:

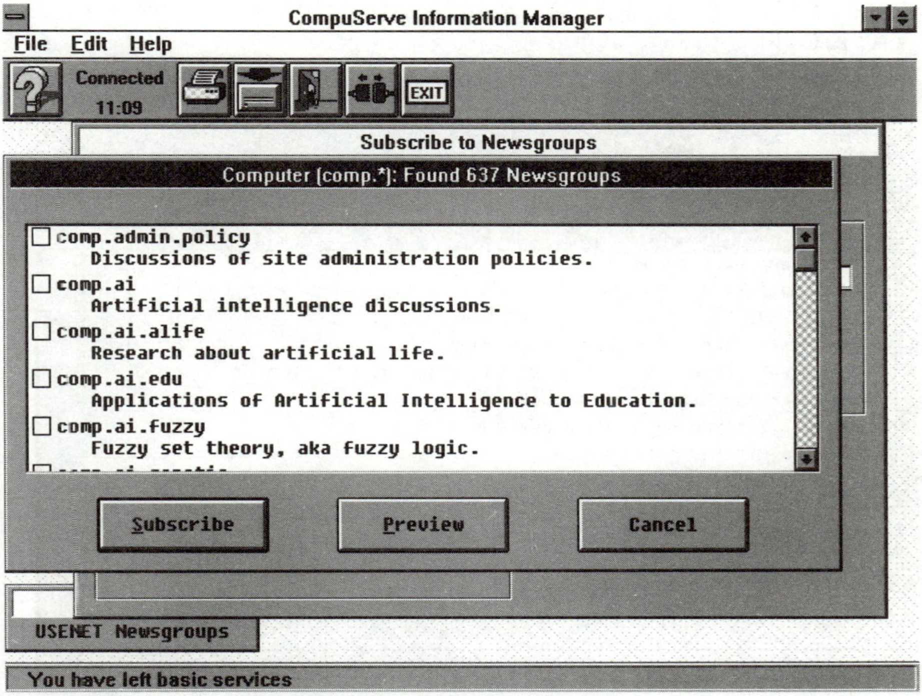

Figure 6.5 A selection of available newsgroups

- **Get**: Select this option to read a selected thread or article. (That's right: you don't have to subscribe to newsgroups to read articles. However, it is much easier to read them once you have subscribed because you don't have to plough your way through several hundred newsgroups.).
  We cover the process of reading newsgroup articles on page 171.
- **Clear**: This option, which is used to erase a selected thread or article from a newsgroup you have subscribed to, is of no use in this dialog. It is discussed more extensively on page 171.
- **Create**: Select this option to create an article for the selected newsgroup. This option is discussed on page 175.
- **Retrieve**: Select this option to capture the selected article into a text file, which will be stored in the *\CSERVE\DOWNLOAD* directory unless you specify otherwise.
  If you wish to **quote** the original article in another article (this is customary in USENET newsgroups), select the Quoted option button. In that case, all message lines will be preceded by a **quote symbol**: >.
- **Cancel**: This will close the Browse dialog. You will now be asked if you want to subscribe to the newsgroup.

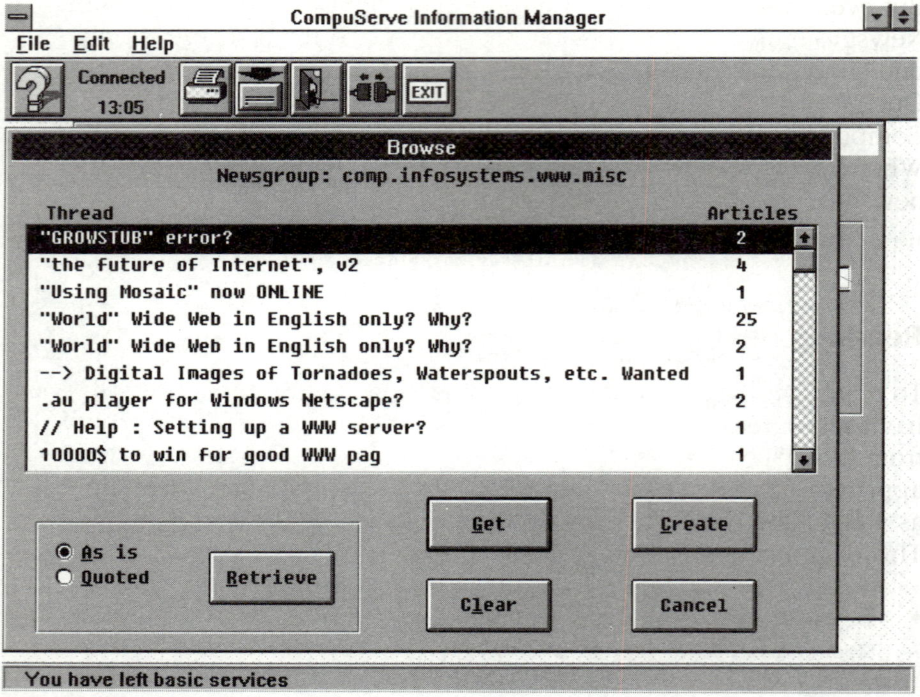

Figure 6.6 A typical list of articles in a newsgroup

After you have subscribed to a newsgroup, it will appear in your list of selected newsgroups. You are now ready to read the articles that were posted in that newsgroup.

Searching for newsgroups

There are several thousand newsgroups available. If you are looking for newsgroups that deal with a certain topic, type a search string in the Keyword field and press the Search button. After a few moments, CompuServe will show the names of all newsgroups that pertain to that topic.

Subscribing to unlisted newsgroups

As you probably know, the number of USENET newsgroups available is larger than the number shown in the Subscribe to Newsgroups windows. The reason for this is that CompuServe tries to avoid members being offended when, browsing through the list, they are confronted with all kinds of newsgroups that are, to put it kindly, provocative.

But even although these newsgroups are not visible in the Subscribe to Newsgroup dialog, it is possible to subscribe to them. There is only one condition: you need to know the exact name of the newsgroup. Once you know the name, press the Subscribe by Name button. CompuServe will ask you to type the exact name of the newsgroup. When you have entered the correct name, CompuServe will add the newsgroup to your subscription list.

Reading newsgroup articles

To read the articles that have been posted in newsgroups to which you have subscribed, select the option Access Your USENET Newsgroups from the USENET Newsgroups menu. The Access Newsgroups dialog appears, showing a list of newsgroups to which you have subscribed, as well as the number of unread articles available for each newsgroup. This dialog contains the following options:

- **Browse**: After you have selected a newsgroup, press this button to start reading the new articles posted to that newsgroup.

- **Search**: Press this button to search for all articles that pertain to a certain topic.

- **Clear**: If you decide to skip all articles posted in a newsgroup, select the newsgroup and press this button. If you change your mind, you can always press the Reread button.

- **Reread**: As soon as you have cleared an article, CompuServe will no longer show it to you. If you want to see it again, press this button. CompuServe will ask you for the number of articles you want to reread. By default, it will show the number of messages you have cleared during the current session.

- **Remove**: Select this option to 'unsubscribe': to remove the selected newsgroup from your subscription list.

- **Cancel**: Select this option to return to the USENET Newsgroups entrance menu.

To read the articles in the selected newsgroup, double-click on the newsgroup, or press the Browse button. After a few moments, the Browse window appears, containing a list of all articles in the newsgroup. (See Figure 6.7.)

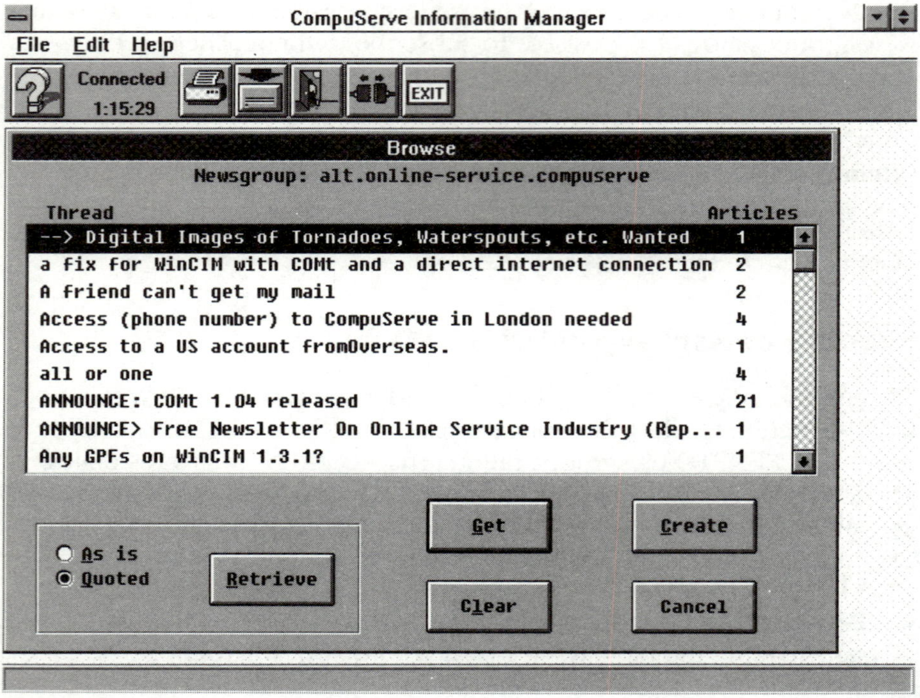

Figure 6.7 The Browse window

The Browse window

The most important part of the Browse window is the list of available **threads**. Unlike a forum thread, a newsgroup thread is nothing more than a group of messages that have the same subject, without any other links. (All newsgroup articles are posted to the same address, remember?)

The Browse window contains the following options:

- **Get**: Select this option to read a selected thread or article. See below, under the heading 'Reading an article', for more information.
  - **Clear**: Select this option to delete the selected thread from the list. It will no longer be visible, unless you choose the Reread option on the Access Newsgroups dialog.
  - **Create**: Select this option to create an article for the selected newsgroup. This option is discussed on page 175.
  - **Retrieve**: Select this option to capture the selected article in a text file. By default, this file will be stored into your *\CSERVE\DOWNLOAD* directory.
    If you wish to **quote** the original article in another article

(customary in USENET newsgroups), select the Quoted option button. In that case, all message lines will be preceded by a **quote symbol**: >.

Reading the article

After you have selected the article you want to read and pressed the Get button, the Display Article Contents dialog appears (see Figure 6.8). Apart from the actual article, this dialog contains the following options:

- **Article, >**: Press this button to see the next article in the same thread.

- **Article, <**: Press this button to see the previous article in the same thread.

- **Thread, >**: Press this button to see the first article in the next thread.

- **Thread, <**: Press this button to see the previous thread in the current newsgroup.

- **Hold**: Press this button if you would like to see this article again the next time you access your USENET newsgroups.

- **Reply**: Press this button if you want to reply to the current article. You can send your reply via e-mail (in that case, only the sender of the original article sees your reply), and/or you can post it to the newsgroup. In the latter case, it is not certain that your reply will be seen by the sender of the original article. If he or she doesn't access that newsgroup for some time, your article will 'scroll'. Therefore, if you want to be sure that the sender reads your reaction, send it via e-mail as well.

  When you select the Reply button, you can **upload** a file that you have prepared offline. Note that this file must be in text format.

- **Forward**: Press this button to forward this article via e-mail. You can either forward it to someone with an e-mail address, or you can post it in another newsgroup.

- **More**: Pressing this button displays additional details about the article.

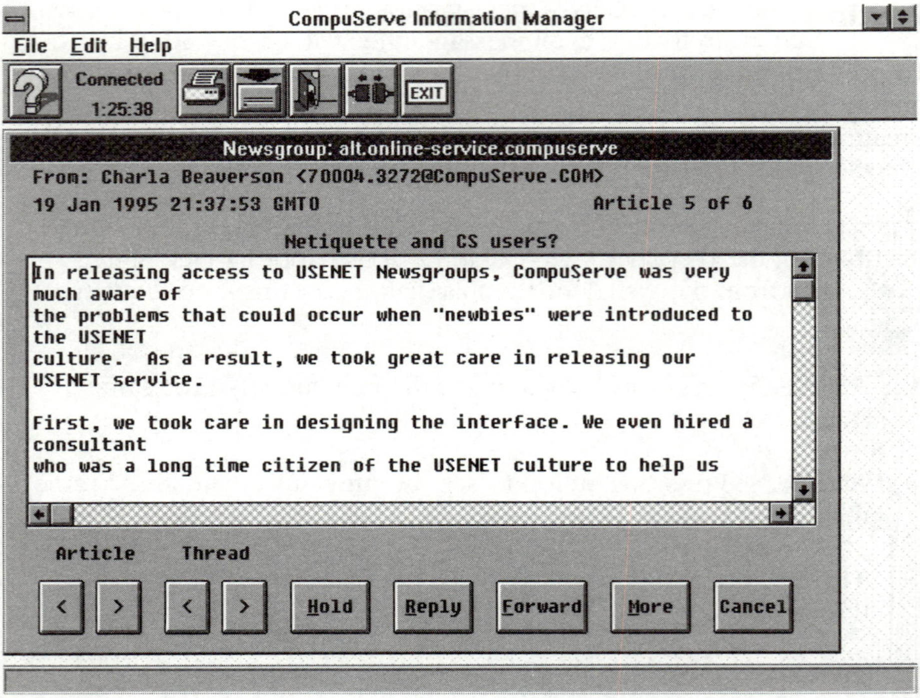

Figure 6.8 Use this dialog to read the available newsgroup articles

Converting encoded files to binary

There are quite a few newsgroups with the word **binaries** in their name, referring to the fact that some or all messages in that group contain actual binary files, **encoded** in such a way that they can be distributed as ASCII messages.

In many cases, a binary file has been not only encoded, but split into **chunks** as well. Every chunk is then posted as a separate message in the newsgroup. Naturally, you will need all the chunks to be able to decode the message text into a useful binary file.

Decoding files is surprisingly easy once you get the hang of it. Just save all parts of the message to separate files, and use a decoding program like XFERPRO, discussed on page 125.

Posting an article to a newsgroup

To post an article to a newsgroup, select it and press the Browse button. In the Browse dialog, press the Create button. This causes the Create USENET Message dialog, displayed in Figure 6.9, to appear.

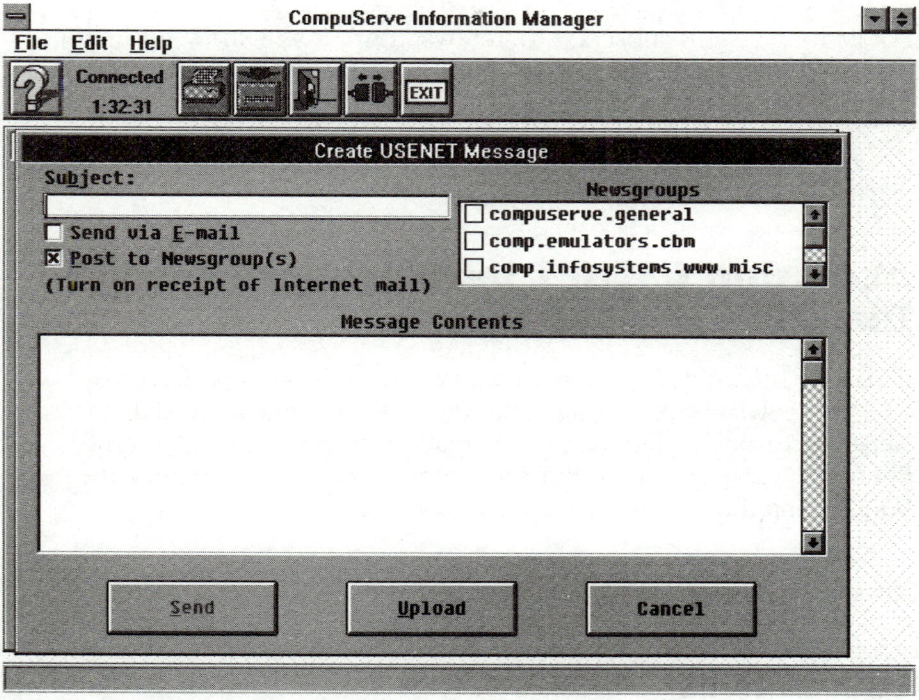

Figure 6.9 Use this dialog to create a USENET article

The most important options in the Create USENET Message dialog are:

- **Subject**: Type the article subject in this field, just like you would do with a regular forum message.
- **Newsgroups**: Select the newsgroup you want to post the message to. Note that you can select more than one newsgroup, provided that you have a subscription to all of them.
- **Message Contents**: Type the actual article in this field. If you have prepared the message offline, you can press the Upload button to copy it to the Message Contents field. Note that you can upload only text messages.

- **Send**: Press this button to send the message to the selected newsgroup(s).

You've had enough: unsubscribing

For as long as you subscribe to a newsgroup, it will show up in your Access Newsgroup dialog. If you no longer need it, you can press the Remove button to get rid of it.

Accessing USENET newsgroups through Dial PPP

If you wish, you can use *news.compuserve.com* as a server to read USENET newsgroups through Dial PPP. Using applications like Netscape or one of the many newsreaders available in the Internet Forum (GO INETFORUM). But for most CompuServe members, the WinCIM interface is by far the best way to go.

Useful files

As always, the Internet New Users Forum (GO INETFOR) is the route to follow when you are looking for updated, in-depth information about USENET newsgroups. The following list shows a few of the numerous files in the forum libraries pertaining to this subject.

- *[73710,1430]   Lib: 7*
  ALTGRP.ZIP/Bin Bytes: 7597

  Title   : How to create an Alt Newsgroup
  Keywords: USENET NEWSGROUP ALT

  How to create an Alt Newsgroup. Describes what one should do to create a newsgroup in the alt. hierarchy that system administrators will wish to carry.*

- *[73710,1430] Lib: 7*
  ANSWER.ZIP/Bin Bytes: 5526

  *Title : FAQ for *.answers newsgroups*
  Keywords: FAQ ANSWERS

  *Frequently Asked Questions file regarding postings to the *.answers Usenet newsgroups. These newsgroups are used to post the answers to the Frequently Asked Questions for various newsgroups.*

- *[76703,407] Lib: 7*
  CREATE.TXT/Text Bytes: 24135

  Title : The Usenet Newsgroup Creation Companion
  Keywords: USENET NEWSGROUP CREATION

  The Usenet Newsgroup Creation Companion

- *[76703,407] Lib:17*
  CWNAV.SIT/Bin Bytes: 11904

  Title : CW's Navigator UseNet Scripts (SIT)
  Keywords: NAVIGATOR USENET MACINTOSH

  "CW's Nav UseNet Scripts" are intended to be used with "CompuServe Navigator" for the Macintosh.

- *[72113,2342] Lib: 7*
  FAQ.TXT/Text Bytes: 122397

  Title : ALT.BINARIES.PICTURES FAQ*
  Keywords: FAQ ALT BINARIES PICTURES USENET INTERNET

  This is the current (as of 9/16/94) FAQ (Frequently Asked Questions) downloaded from the news.answers newsgroup. It explains in detail how to download binary files and what to do with them once you have them. It also touches on netiquette, and explains various platform specific utilities. A must have for any usenetter!

- *[76703,407]   Lib: 7*
  FNDNWS.TXT/Text Bytes: 16826

  Title   : Finding Usenet Newsgroups FAQ
  Keywords: USENET NEWS NEWSGROUPS

  There are thousands of Usenet newsgroups, and it is sometimes difficult to find the right newsgroup to ask a question or start a discussion. This document gives some general methods of finding the right newsgroup or mailing list for a topic.

- *[76703,407]   Lib: 7*
  NEWSGR.TXT/Text Bytes: 7942

  Title   : Info about the news. Usenet newsgroups*
  Keywords: NEWS. NEWS.ANNOUNCE NEWSGROUPS USENET

  This file describes the major Usenet announcement newsgroups. The moderated groups news.admin.technical, news.answers and news.lists are also described, since they are closely related to the announcement newsgroups.

- *[72263,770]   Lib: 7*
  NG-CIS.TXT/Text Bytes: 161920

  Title   : Listing of USENET Newsgroups on CompuServe.
  Keywords: USENET NEWSGROUPS LIST

  A listing of the 2000+ USENET Newsgroups available through CompuServe. Lists group name and one line description. Updated: Aug 19, 1994.

- *[76703,407] Lib: 7*
  PCHWNW.TXT/Text Bytes: 3871

  Title : PC-Clone Hardware Newsgroup Pointer
  Keywords: PC-CLONE PC HARDWARE NEWS NEWSGROUP USENET

  PC-Clone Hardware Newsgroup Pointer, By: John M. Grohol

  This Pointer will help you find the information you need and get your questions answered much quicker than if you were to simply crosspost to every hardware newsgroup in existence. It is provided as a public service.

  Post your article in the most appropriate newsgroup according to its topic.

- *[76703,407] Lib: 7*
  PRIMER.TXT/Text Bytes: 22221

  Title : Primer on Using Usenet
  Keywords: USENET PRIMER

  Primer on Using Usenet. Tips and advice on how to make the best use of Usenet newsgroups, netiquette for postings, etc.

- *[76703,407] Lib: 7*
  PSYNEW.TXT/Text Bytes: 5957

  Title : Psychology & Support Groups Newsgroup Pointer
  Keywords: PSYCHOLOGY SUPPORT GROUPS NEWS NEWSGROUP USENET

  Psychology & Support Groups Newsgroup Pointer, By: John M. Grohol

  This Pointer will help you find the information you need and get your questions answered much quicker than if you were to simply crosspost to every psychology or support newsgroup in existence. It is provided as a public service. Post your article in the most appropriate newsgroup according to its topic.

- *[76703,407] Lib: 7*
  ROMANC.TXT/Text Bytes: 145686

  Title : FAQ for alt.romance Newsgroup
  Keywords: ROMANCE NEWS NEWSGROUP FAQ USENET

  Frequently Asked Questions and Answers from the alt.romance Usenet newsgroup.

- *[73710,1430] Lib: 7*
  UNSITE.ZIP/Bin Bytes: 15245

  Title : How to be a Usenet site FAQ
  Keywords: USENET NEWS FAQ

  FAQ (Frequently Asked Questions) about how to become a usenet site. Summarizes the steps needed to setup a machine to read news.

- *[76703,407] Lib: 7*
  USENET.FAQ/Text Bytes: 42280

  Title : Usenet Frequently Asked Questions/Answers
  Keywords: USENET NEWSGROUPS

  Usenet Frequently Asked Questions/Answers

- *[72662,1335] Lib: 7*
  USENET.ZIP/Bin Bytes: 948248

  Title : Multimedia intro to USENET for Windows
  Keywords: USENET WINDOWS MULTIMEDIA

  This is a multimedia introduction to the Internet USENET newsgroups for MS Windows. Requires PKUNZIP 2.04g to unzip. This presentation is public domain FREEWARE. Has many, many newsgroup addresses. Uploaded by author, copyright 1994.

Frequently Asked Questions

This section contains a summary from the list of **Frequently Asked Questions**, which can also be read online through the USENET Newsgroups Menu (GO USENET).

- **What are USENET Newsgroups?**
  The USENET is a huge, distributed, decentralized, international discussion system, analogous in many ways to the message areas of CompuServe forums. Participants in the USENET exist around the world, reading and writing 'articles' which are posted to a large, hierarchical set of 'newsgroups', where a newsgroup is a name much like a subtopic in a forum. These articles are relayed among the thousands of participating systems using a variety of transport mechanisms. The primary mechanism, and the one from which CompuServe receives USENET feeds, is the Internet. Within USENET, the newsgroup names are given as dot-qualified descriptions, such as comp.unix.wizards, rec.photo, and sci.astro. The basic USENET hierarchies include:

*comp.**	Computer topics
*rec.**	Recreational topics
*sci.**	Scientific topics
*soc.**	Social issues
*talk.**	Conversational topics, often controversial
*news.**	Topics related to operating a USENET system
*misc.**	Groups that don't fit well elsewhere

  In addition to the 'basic seven' which comprise USENET, several other hierarchies of newsgroups exist, often relating to a specific topic or geographical location. Among the most popular relating to specific topics are the alternative (alt.*) newsgroups.

- **Why is the release of this product important?**
  This product facilitates interaction between CompuServe members and Internet users in a discussion format that complements the current Internet e-mail gateway. Even though a copy of USENET Newsgroups is stored on a CompuServe host, the messages originate from and are propagated back into the Internet, and as a result, are reflective of the culture there. The way in which this product is used and viewed will shape our members' acceptance on the Internet. USENET Newsgroups is the first of several products/services designed to give CompuServe members access to information that exists on the Internet.

- **Will access be given to newsgroups with offensive or 'adult' subject matter?**
  CompuServe cannot put itself into a censorship position, yet we are sensitive to the needs of our varied audiences. Monitoring and censoring information that passes through the Internet USENET News feeds would be an enormous task, and we would never be sure if our criteria for censorship fit that of any given member. Therefore, CompuServe accepts full news feeds (even the 'adult' subject items). However, newsgroups that are questionable in their subject matter will not be placed on the subscription or search menus. A user who knows the exact USENET name can still subscribe. This reduces the chances of someone stumbling upon this type of newsgroup accidentally.

- **How will CompuServe ensure that its members mesh with the cultural expectations of the Internet?**
  The culture of the Internet is very strong, and those who fail to abide by the culture are often the recipients of 'flames' (an Internet term for hate mail). CompuServe intends to do its best to ensure that our members are not flamed, and are able to participate amicably in newsgroup discussions. The rules of 'netiquette' (Internet etiquette) will be displayed to a member the first time they access USENET newsgroups. In addition, these rules will be available from a menu item for review at any time. You are encouraged to review them. CompuServe reserves the right to disallow access to USENET newsgroups to any user who fails to abide by these rules.

- **What settings allow for the best use of the USENET Newsgroup CIM interface?**
  - **WinCIM:** In order to create the largest display area for reading USENET Newsgroups, your video display resolution should be at least 640 by 480 pixels. In addition, the size of the window that displays Newsgroup message text is negotiated between the news server and CIM at the beginning of your USENET session. To take advantage of this you should make your WinCIM window as large as possible prior to entering the CIM interface to USENET. You may resize manually or 'maximize' the WinCIM window.
  - **MacCIM**: MacCIM automatically negotiates the size of the window for displaying Newsgroup text based on the size of your monitor. You need not do anything except be aware you will see a sub-optimal display if you are using a Classic, Mac Plus or other machine with a 9" diagonal display.

Chapter 7

FTP (File Transfer Protocol)

- More about FTP
- Finding the file you are looking for
- FTP in action
- The CompuServe File Finders
- Frequently Asked Questions about FTP
- Useful files

CompuServe Internet Services

More about FTP

Many Internet sites give Internet users the opportunity to transfer files over the Net. Any Internet user who is looking for a specific document, a printer driver or a shareware utility can retrieve that file via FTP. FTP is the abbreviation of **File Transfer Protocol**. In the old days (actually, many Internet users still work this way), you had to give a series of special FTP commands to log in to a particular site, search the directory for a particular file, and transfer the file to your local system. And when the file was finally transferred, it needed to be downloaded from the local system to your own computer.

Nowadays, things aren't that complicated. Anyone who has SLIP or PPP access to the Internet can use FTP software to eliminate the hard work. Most FTP software works the same way as the Windows File Manager: you see your own hard disk's directory in one window, and the site's directory in another. Once you have installed the appropriate Internet software, transferring a file from any Internet site to your own computer involves nothing more than a few mouse clicks.

As a CompuServe user, you have complete FTP access to the Internet. Through FTP, there is an unbelievable wealth of information available, on any imaginable subject. And the best part is that using WinCIM, browsing through directories and downloading files is easy and straightforward. If you know how to download a file from a forum library, using FTP will be a breeze!

In fact, establishing an FTP connection with another Internet site works the same way as telnetting to it. (If you don't know what telnetting is, don't worry – we'll discuss telnet in the next chapter.) A site that provides FTP service has simply a second Internet address, often starting with the letters **ftp**.

Anonymous FTP

Most FTP sites allow you to log in **anonymously**, a process often referred to as **anonymous FTP**. For anonymous users, access is usually limited to several directories. Most FTP sites have a directory called *\pub*, containing files for everyone who wants them. If you haven't FTP-ed to a particular site before, always look for this directory first.

Just like with regular logins, you will have to use a login name and a password. For anonymous FTP, the following has more or less become the netiquette:

- **Login name**: *anonymous*
- **Password**: your Internet address (for example *100345.123@compuserve.com*).

As you will see shortly, CompuServe helps you by entering this information for you whenever necessary.

FTP: the drawbacks

Although anonymous FTP is a very powerful means of getting to the file you have been seeking for ages, there are also some drawbacks. The most important ones are listed below:

- FTP can be slow. Depending on the amount of traffic from and to the FTP site, transfer speed can drop to as little as a few hundred bits per second. That's why CompuServe advises using the CompuServe File Finders whenever possible – you will often get a better deal for the same money.
- Whether or not you can access a certain FTP site depends on the **system load**: the number of users currently accessing the system. You will understand that subscribed users are given priority over users that log in anonymously. Each FTP site has a limit on the anonymous FTP connections it accepts. When this limit is reached, you will see a message telling you to come back and try again later.
- Files that you download via FTP are not necessarily virus-free! Unlike CompuServe forums, where sysops do whatever they can to check every file before it is released to the general audience, FTP sites are not always to be trusted. Therefore, use one or more virus checking programs on every file you have retrieved through an FTP connection. Remember: you actually leave CompuServe when you use FTP!

Finding the file you are looking for

If you are used to the structure that forum libraries and the CompuServe File Finders offer, you are bound to be disappointed when you start using FTP. Unless you know exactly where (on what FTP site, and in which directory) a certain file is stored, you will soon lose your way searching through several hundreds of Megabytes of files. Let alone the fact that there are thousands of FTP sites!

Fortunately, there is a way to find out if and where a certain file can be found on the FTP sites available. Some Internet servers have set up a special query system, called **Archie**. The first Archie was created by a group of Canadians (at McGill University), who were looking for a quick way to scan all available FTP sites. Nowadays, Archie can be found on several Internet sites and contains information from a great number of FTP sites. If the file you're looking for is available on one of those sites, it will show up when you let Archie search for it.

Archie

Archie can be reached through telnet as well as through mail. Don't count on an immediate response, however: it can take several minutes, and sometimes even hours, before Archie has finished scanning. If you're not in a hurry, it might therefore be best to perform the search via mail. As soon as it is your turn (sometimes, the queue you're in can be as large as 10,000 or more people), Archie will perform the search. And when the search is completed, the results will be mailed to your CompuServe mailbox.

If you want to use Archie interactively, telnet to an Archie site. A few sites you might want to try are:

- archie.mcgill.ca (the very first Archie server, in Canada)
- archie.au (Australia)
- archie.funet.fi (Finland)
- archie.th-darmstadt.de (Germany)
- archie.sura.net (Maryland, USA)
- archie.unl.edu (Nebraska, USA)

- archie.internic.net (New Jersey, USA)
- archie.rutgers.edu (New Jersey, USA)
- archie.ans.net (New York, USA)
- archie.doc.ic.ac.uk (United Kingdom)
- archie.hensa.ac.uk (United Kingdom)

To log in, enter `archie` at the prompt. You will see a welcome message, followed by the following prompt:

```
archie>
```

Basically, you will use only three commands:

- **set**: Use this command to specify search settings, like case independence, exact word match, etc.
- **find**: With this command, you will initiate the search. On some older systems, the **prog** command is used instead.
- **quit**: This is the command to end the Archie session and to disconnect from the server.

Typically, you will first need additional information about the **set** and **prog** commands. A good way to get that information is to send a mail message to *INTERNET:archie@archie.mcgill.ca*, placing the word **help** either in the subject or the message text.

Using Archie through mail

If you want to use mail to have Archie perform a scan, send a mail message to, in this case, *INTERNET:archie@archie.mcgill.ca*. The subject will be ignored, but place the word **help** in either the subject or, on a single line, in the message text. You will receive a mail message that contains more information on how to use the Archie commands via mail.

Let's say you'd like to see what files related to CompuServe are available. In that case, send a message with the subject **set search sub**, to indicate that you want to search through substrings too, and that the capitals and lower letters don't need to match. In the message text, include the line **find compuserve**. (See Figure 7.1.)

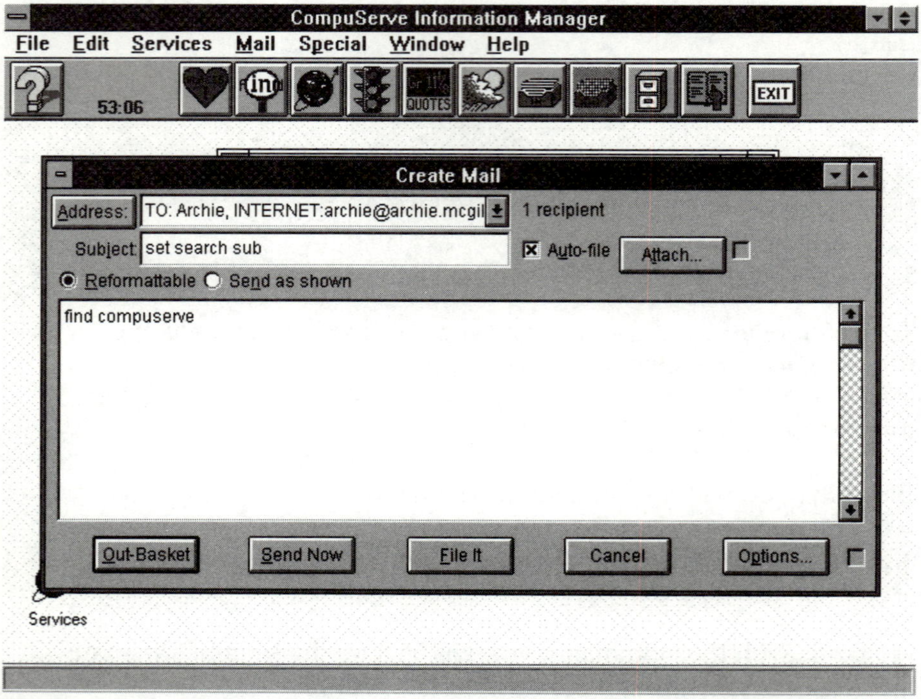

Figure 7.1 Looking for files that have something to do with CompuServe

The following is an example of the reply you might receive in your mailbox:

```
FROM:      INTERNET:archie-errors@bunyip.com,
INTERNET:archie-errors@bunyip.com
TO:        Roelf Sluman, 71333,1443
DATE:      27-01-95 8:44


Re:  archie [find compuserve] part 1 of 1


Sender: archie-errors@bunyip.com
Received: from services.bunyip.com by dub-img-2.compuserve.com
(8.6.9/5.941228sam)
     id CAA26486; Fri, 27 Jan 1995 02:36:18 -0500
Received: (from archie@localhost) by services.bunyip.com (8.6.9/8.6.9)
id CAA03668; Fri, 27 Jan 1995 02:36:17 -0500
Message-Id: <199501270736.CAA03668@services.bunyip.com>
To: Roelf Sluman <71333.1443@compuserve.com>
From:  (Archie Server)archie-errors@bunyip.com
Reply-To:  (Archie Server)archie-errors@bunyip.com
```

```
Date: Fri, 27 Jan 95 02:36 -0500
Subject: archie [find compuserve] part 1 of 1


>> path Roelf Sluman <71333.1443@compuserve.com>

>> set search sub

>> find compuserve
# Search type: sub.

Host ftp.uni-trier.de    (136.199.8.81)
Last updated 14:58 14 Oct 1994

    Location: /pub/tex/fonts/postscript/adobe/Updates
      FILE    -rw-r--r--    1349 bytes  17:00 12 Sep 1993
930913.AcrobatCompuserve.press.Z


Host solomon.technet.sg    (192.169.33.3)
Last updated 11:35 10 Jan 1995

    Location: /pub/NUS/zi/TeX/fonts/postscript/adobe/Updates
      FILE    -r--r--r--    1349 bytes  19:00 12 Sep 1993
930913.AcrobatCompuserve.press.Z



Host dkuug.dk    (193.88.44.89)
Last updated 01:37 26 +Jan 1995

    Location: /mirror/mac/tidbits/tisk/term
      FILE    -rw-r--r--  141943 bytes  20:00 11 Mar 1993
white-knight-compuserve-
scripts.hqx
```

Other ways to find the location of a file

There are a few powerful yet often overlooked ways to see if and where a file is available on the Internet.

- **The Internet New Users Forum (GO** `INETFORUM`): Ask around! In many cases, you are not the only one looking for a particular file, especially when it comes to patches and upgrades. Often, other forum members will talk about interesting FTP sites; it doesn't hurt to follow those discussions. And while you're in the forum, don't forget to take a look in library 6, 'Using FTP & Archie'.
- **The Internet Resources Forum (GO** `INETRES`): This forum contains a 'Where to find' message section, as well as a library with the same name.
- **USENET Newsgroups**: If there is a newsgroup that pertains to the same subject as your file, chances are that someone there can point you to it. To learn more about USENET Newsgroups, see Chapter 6.

Or... Browse!

If you use the FTP Interface that CompuServe has set up for you, you will find that CompuServe has provided some nice starting points. A mouse click is all that it takes to FTP to one of those sites easily (see Figure 7.2).

FTP in action

As stated in the first part of this chapter, WinCIM makes FTP as easy as downloading a file from a forum. To see how easy it is, proceed as follows.

First, `GO FTP`. This will cause the File Transfer Protocol window to appear, as shown in Figure 7.3.

Please note: If you haven't accessed FTP before, it will take a few seconds before this window appears. In this period, WinCIM will download a few icon bitmaps.

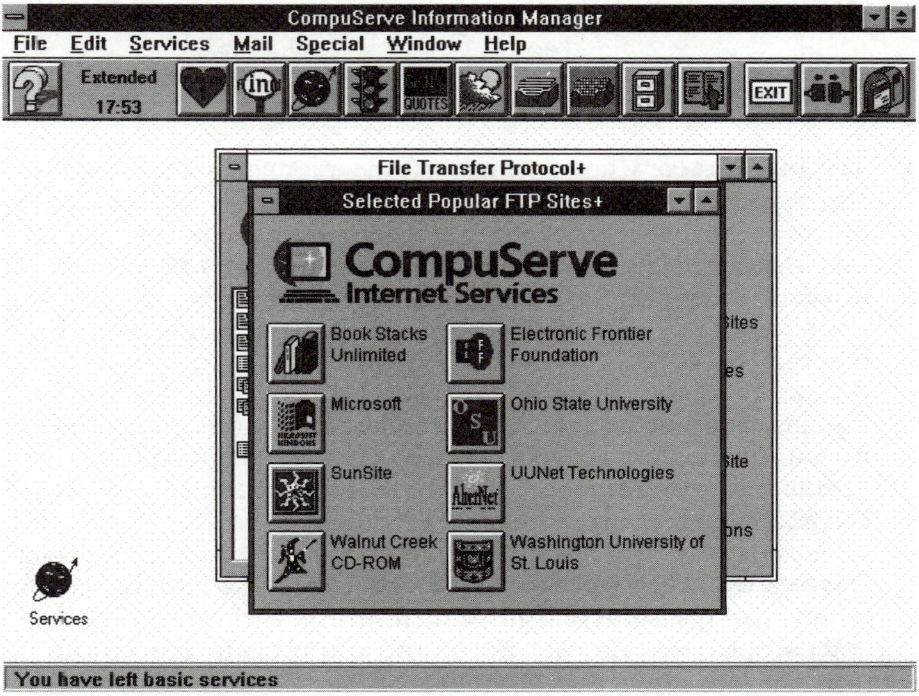

Figure 7.2 Some nice starting points: CompuServe's list of favorite FTP sites

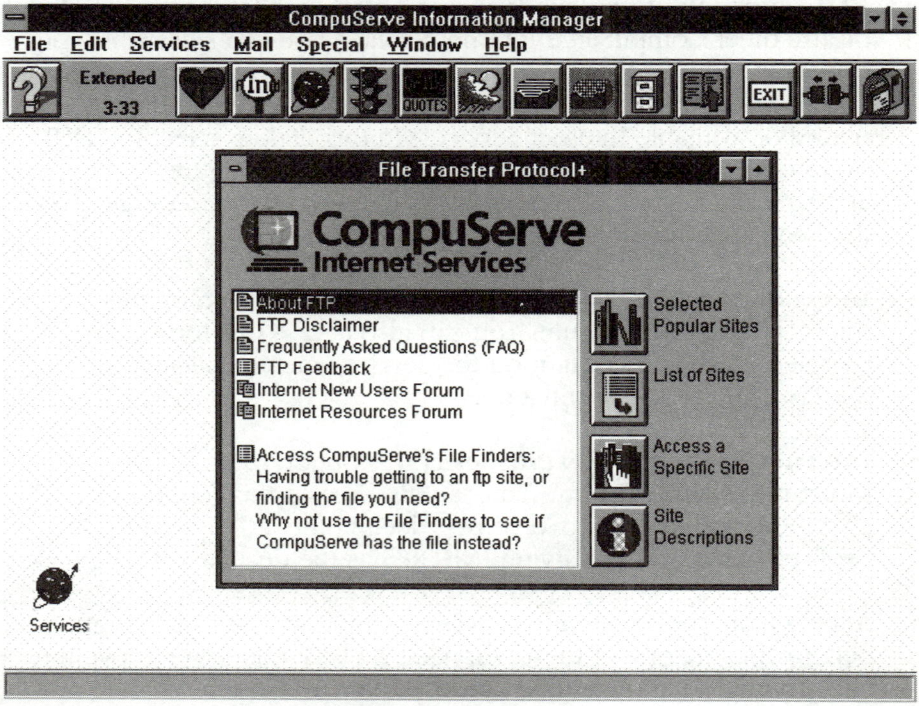

Figure 7.3 The File Transfer Protocol window

The File Transfer Protocol window contains the following options:

- **About FTP**: Select this option to read some background information about the File Transfer Protocol.

- **FTP Disclaimer**: When you use FTP, the information that you retrieve is not controlled by CompuServe. Therefore, CompuServe cannot be held responsible for the content of that information. Note that it is by no means certain that the files you retrieve this way have been checked for viruses.
  The complete CompuServe Newsgroups Disclaimer is available by selecting this option.

  Tip: Instead of reading this article online, press the File It button to have it stored into your WinCIM Filing Cabinet. After you have disconnected, you can read it offline, without incurring telephone charges.

- **Frequently Asked Questions**: Select this option to retrieve a summary of questions that are often asked, as well as the answers to those questions. An extract from this article can be found from page 204 onwards.

- **FTP Feedback**: If you experience problems while accessing FTP, or any other CompuServe Internet Service, you can select this option to write a message to the FTP Feedback department. After you have selected this option, a dialog appears, containing the names of available Internet Services. In this dialog, select the FTP option. After a few seconds, the dialog shown in Figure 7.4 appears. After you have entered your name and the message, press the Send Message button.

- **Internet New Users Forum**: Select this option to go to the Internet New Users Forum. You can also access this forum directly by selecting the GO option on the Services menu, specifying INETFORUM as the destination.

- **Internet Resources Forum**: Select this option to go to the Internet Resources Forum. You can also access this forum from anywhere within CompuServe by selecting the GO option on the Services menu and specifying INETRES as the destination.

- **Access CompuServe's File Finders**: In many cases, you might be better off using one of the CompuServe File Finders to retrieve the file you are looking for. The CompuServe File Finders are safe and

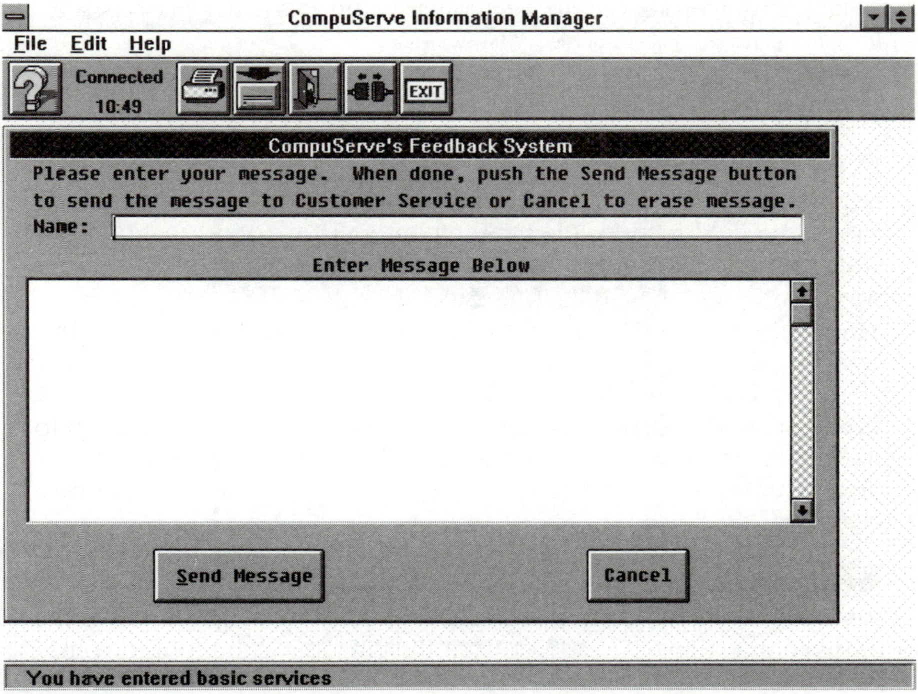

Figure 7.4 If you have a problem using FTP, don't hesitate to send a message to CompuServe's Feedback Department

fast; you are advised to start with the File Finders before resorting to FTP. (See Figure 7.5.)

On the right side of the File Transfer Protocol window, you see four buttons:

- **Selected Popular Sites**: If you're new to FTP, this is the button to press! After a few seconds, you will see a window like the one shown in Figure 7.6.

- **List of Sites**: If you don't know where to start, this is another good place to look. It contains a summary of well-known FTP sites. CompuServe expands this list continuously, so it doesn't hurt to take a look at it now and then.

- **Access a Specific Site**: When you know exactly what you are looking for, press this button. After a few seconds, the dialog shown in Figure 7.7 will appear. Look at the information that has already been placed into the User Name and Password fields: following Netiquette, your Internet address is used as the

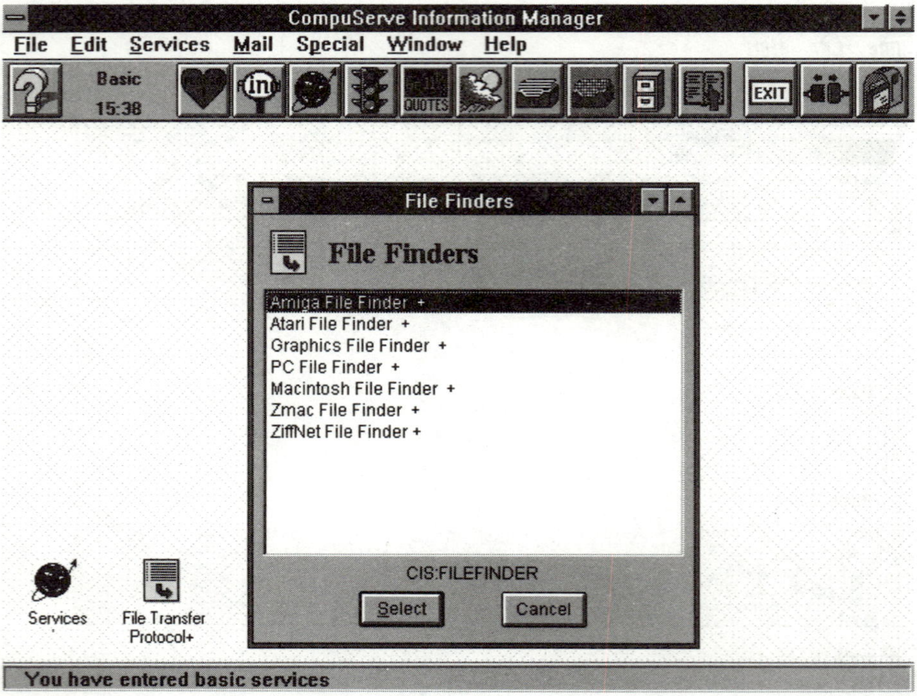

Figure 7.5 A list of CompuServe File Finders

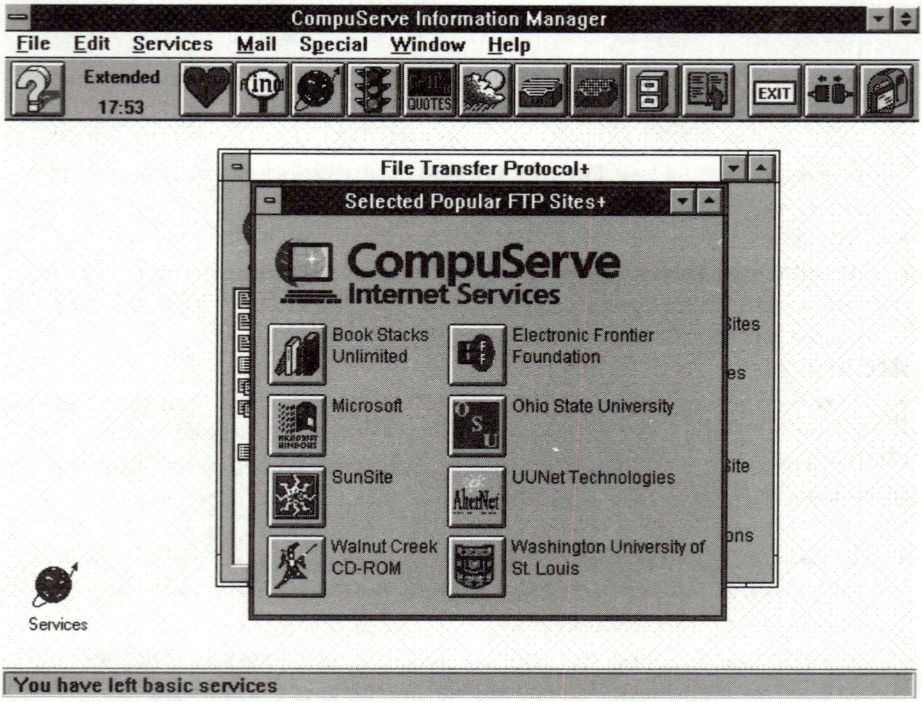

Figure 7.6 The most popular FTP sites are available through a mouse click

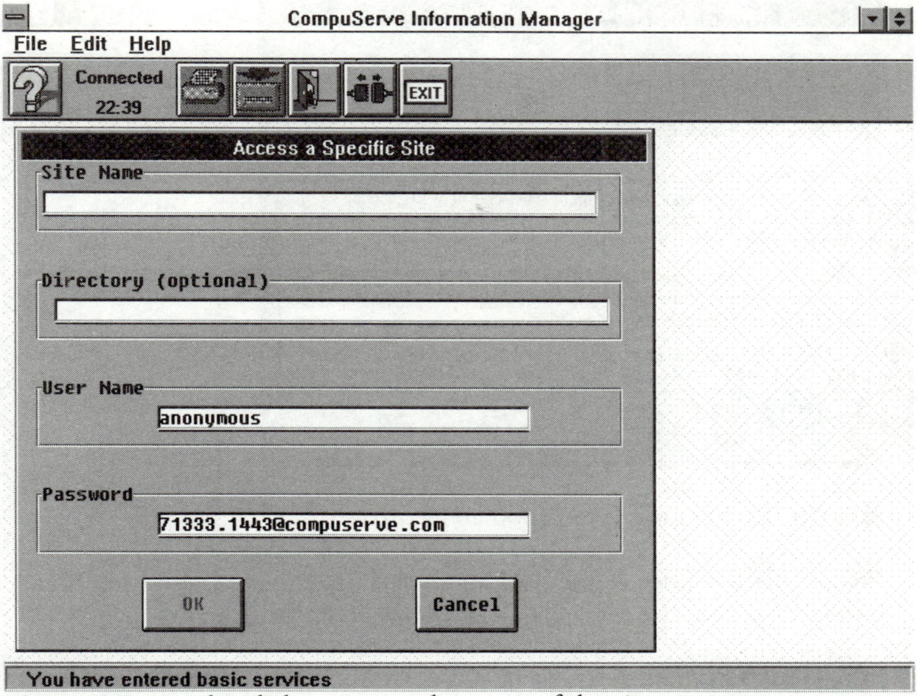

Figure 7.7 Use this dialog to enter the name of the site you want to access

password. However, if you happen to be a registered user of that specific site, you may also enter your login name and password. That way, you will be able to retrieve files to which only registered users have access. After you have entered the name or the Internet address of the site, you can press the OK button to access the site.

- **Site Descriptions**: Select this option if you want to read more about one of the listed sites (see Figure 7.8).

Accessing an FTP site

If you have spent some time browsing through the Site Descriptions, chances are that you can't wait to see what's out there. So here goes: a quick demonstration of what FTP is all about.

1 In the File Transfer Protocol Window, press the Selected Popular Sites button. In the following dialog, press the Book Stacks Unlimited button.

2 After a few seconds, the Access a Specific Site dialog is displayed. The site name, *ftp.books.com*, is displayed in the Site Name field.

Figure 7.8 Background information about a particular FTP site

Note that the User Name and Password fields have been filled in as well.

3 Press the OK button to log in. If you're lucky, your screen will now look like the one in Figure 7.9: you are connected to an FTP site!

4 Take time to read the entire message. It often contains useful information about guidelines, files with useful information etc. In this case, the site advises you to look at the *info.txt* files that can be found in each directory.

5 Once you have read the welcome message, press the OK button. The FTP file list window appears, shown in Figure 7.10. The FTP file list shows the name of the current drive and directory. You also see the names of directories that are present in the current directory, as well as the names of the files in that directory. You can select one or more files by checking the box in front of the filename(s). Furthermore, the window contains the following options:
   - **Select**: Press this button to view the contents of the selected directory.
   - **Top**: Press this button to get back to the top directory. For DOS users: this is the root directory of the current drive.
   - **Back**: Press this button to display the contents of the parent directory; you will move 'one branch up' in the directory structure. If you are in the top directory, pressing this button will result in an error message.

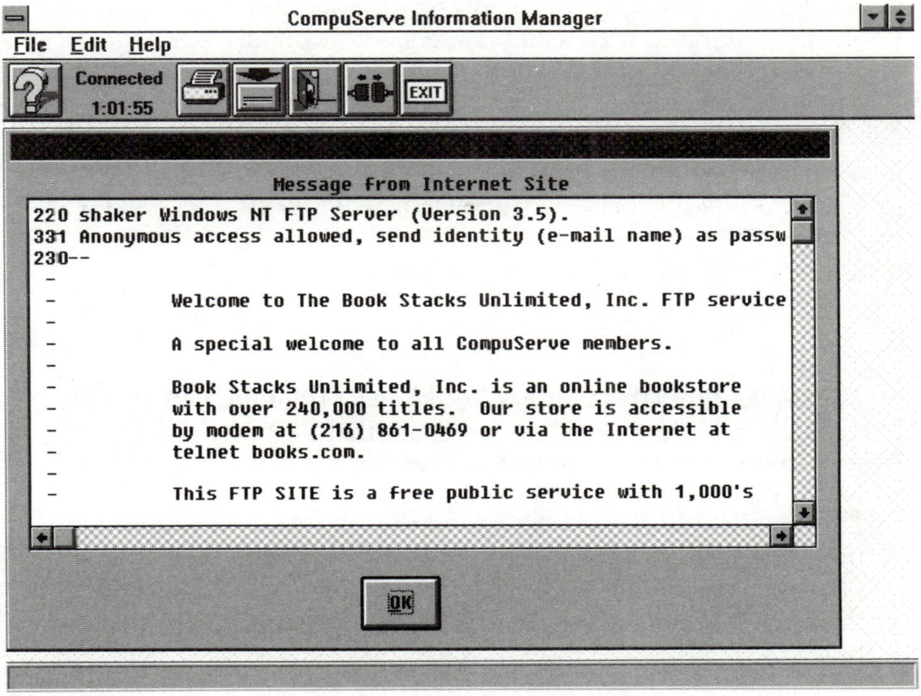

Figure 7.9 The welcome message from *ftp.books.com*

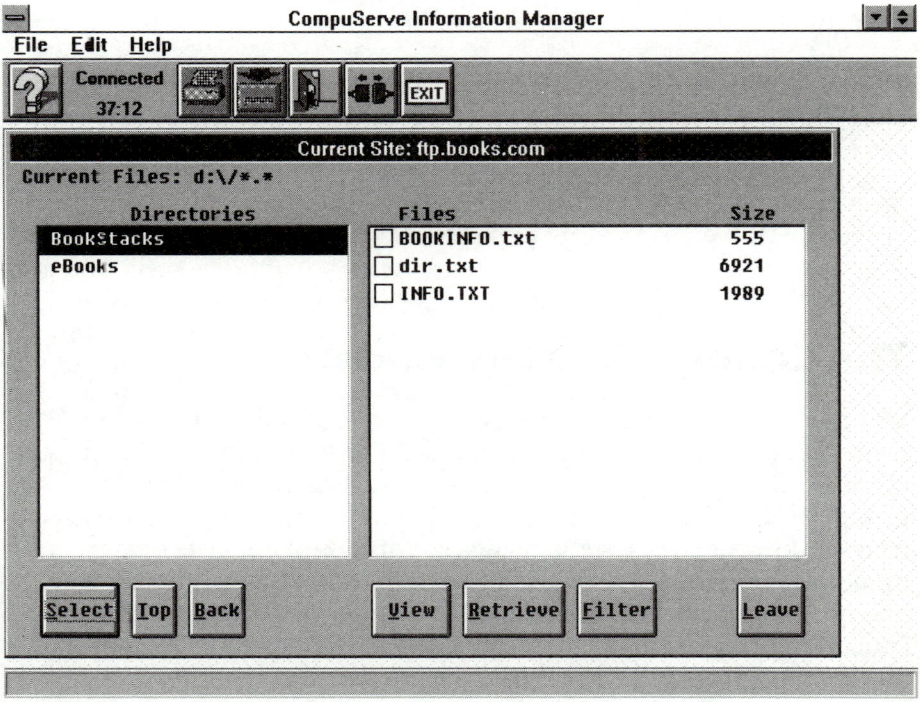

Figure 7.10 Browse through the available directories and files

- **View**: If you have checked one or more files, you can press this button to review the contents of those files one by one.
- **Retrieve**: Press this button to download the selected file(s) to your computer.
- **Filter**: By default, all files in the current directory will be displayed. If you want to display a limited number of files, you can enter a so-called **wildcard specification**. For instance, to display only files with the extension *.txt*, you enter the following file specification:

```
*.txt
```

- **Leave**: Press this button to disconnect from the current FTP site. You can now either select another FTP site, or leave CompuServe's FTP service altogether.

6 For now, check the box in front of the *dir.txt* file (it is located in the top directory). Next, press the Retrieve button. WinCIM will now show the familiar Save As window: after you have confirmed the name of the file that you are about to retrieve, press the OK button.

That's all there is to it! WinCIM will retrieve the file and place it into your download directory (see Figure 7.11).

You might want to stay a little longer, to look around what this fascinating site has to offer. (When I wrote this book, more than 1,000 electronic books were available, covering each and every subject under the sun!)

The CompuServe File Finders

When downloading a file from an FTP server, you are subject to matters that CompuServe can't control. For instance, due to the amount of traffic, file transfer can be painfully slow. Besides, you have no guarantee that files retrieved through FTP are virus-free, so you will have to do your own testing, using one or more virus checking programs. Therefore, it is a good idea to check 'at home' first, using one of CompuServe's File Finders. File Finders are databases that contain information about files uploaded to hundreds of CompuServe forums (not all of them, though!).

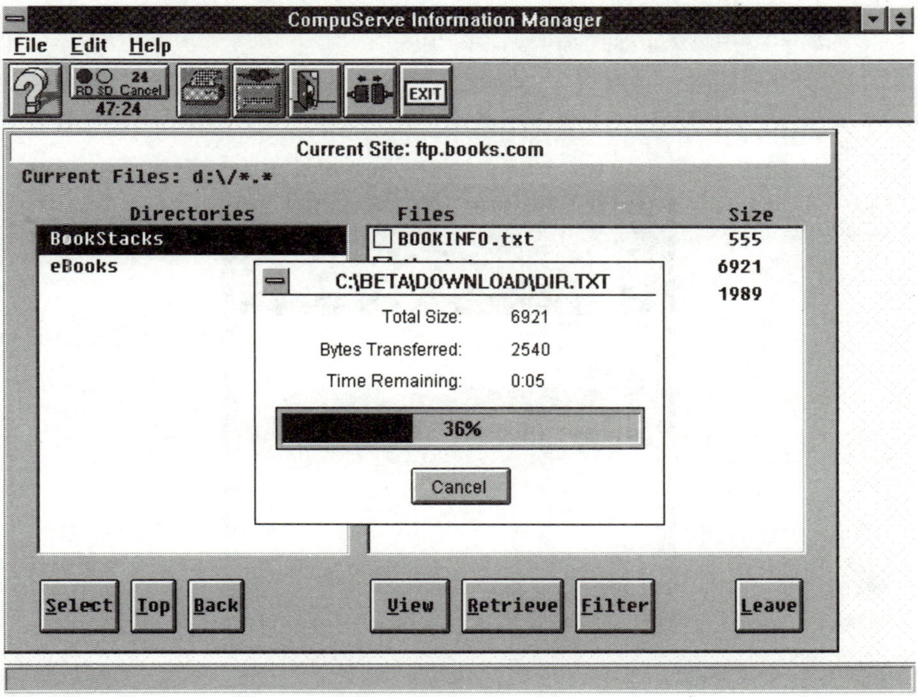

Figure 7.11 Retrieving a file through FTP

To access the CompuServe File Finders, GO FILEFINDER. As you can see from the dialog shown in Figure 7.12, the following File Finders are available:

- **Amiga File Finder**: Contains an index of files for all Amiga computers. GO AMIGAFF to access this File Finder.

- **Atari ST File Finder**: Contains an index of files from the forums devcted to the Atari ST line of computers. GO ATARIFF to use this File Finder.

- **Graphics File Finder**: Contains an index of graphic files, most of them in GIF and JPEG format. GO GRAPHFF to get there.

- **PC File Finder**: Contains an index of files for computers running the MS-DOS and/or Windows operating system. To get there, GO PCFF.

- **Macintosh File Finder**: Contains an index of files for Apple Macintosh computers. GO MACFF will bring you there.

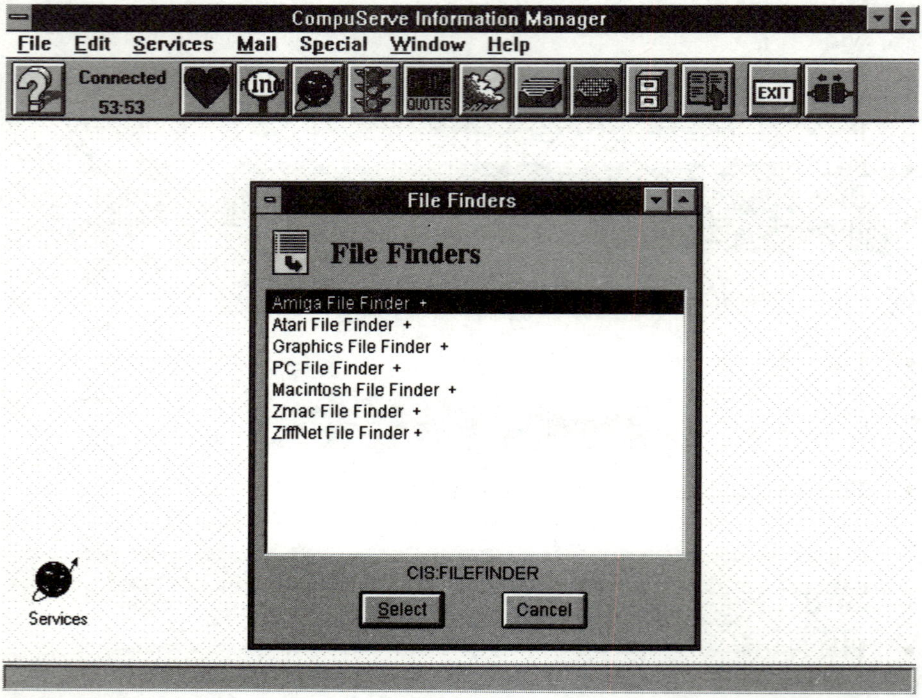

Figure 7.12 The CompuServe File Finders. GO `FILEFINDER` to get to this dialog

If you are a ZiffNet member, you have access to two more File Finders:

- **ZMac File Finder**: Contains an index of all files that can be found in the Macintosh forums on ZiffNet. If you are a ZiffNet Member: `GO ZNT:ZMAC` and follow the instructions to access this File Finder.

- **ZiffNet File Finder**: Contains an index of all MS-DOS and Windows files that can be found in the ZiffNet forums. To access this File Finder, `GO ZNT:ZNTFF`.

When you search for files using the File Finder, you will have to enter information in one or more of the following fields:

- **Keyword**: Select this field to enter one, two, or three keywords. These keywords have to match those that were entered by the person who uploaded the file to one of the forums. Unfortunately, there is no fixed list of keywords. If you don't know where to start, begin with a fairly general keyword and review the results. It is best to 'narrow down' a search (that is, to start with a large number of retrieved items and decrease that number gradually).

- **Submission Date**: If you enter a date in this field, the File Finder will only display information for those files that were uploaded on or after that date. Note that you have to specify the date in MM/DD/YY format.

- **Forum Name**: If you want the search to be limited to one forum, choose this option to select the name of that forum. Note that not all forum libraries are included in the File Finder catalog. When you want to know whether or not a particular forum is included, select this option.

- **File Type**: If you are looking for a specific type of file, you can select this option to narrow your search to ASCII, Binary, Image, Graphics, or JPEG format.

- **File Extension**: If you are looking for files with a specific extension, enter it in this field. Don't include the dot that is normally used to separate filenames from extensions. Note that you can do a **wildcard search** using the File Name field as well.

- **File Name**: If you are looking for a file with a specific name, you can enter that name in this field. Extensions are allowed, and so are wildcards. TEST.DOC, TEST.*, and *.DOC are all valid specifications.

- **File Submitter**: If you want the search to be limited to all files contributed by one member, enter his or her User ID in this field.

- **Display Selected Titles**: Select this option to see the list of titles that the File Finder has retrieved, according to your search specifications.

- **Begin a New Search**: Select this option to reset all search criteria and to start an entirely new search.

Accessing a File Finder

When you access one of CompuServe's File Finders from WinCIM, you see the dialog shown in Figure 7.13. This dialog contains the fields and options discussed in the previous paragraphs. At the top of the dialog, the Current selection field shows the number of files that match your search criteria. If you have just entered the File Finder, the number of available files is shown.

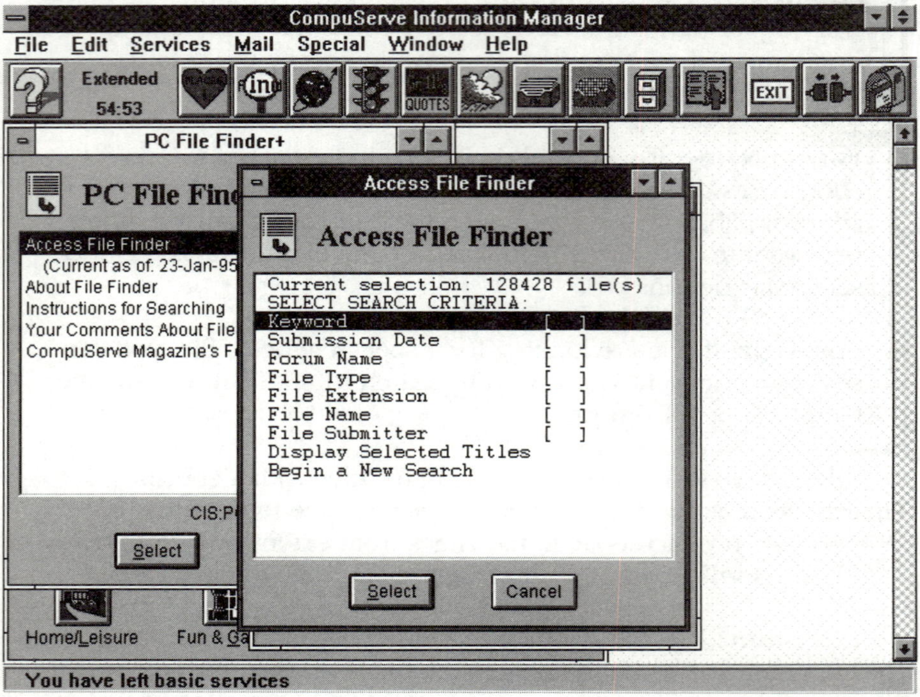

Figure 7.13 WinCIM's File Finder dialog

Normally, you will want to start by entering one or more keywords. If this results in too many files being found, you might like to scan for only the latest files. An example can be seen in Figure 7.14.

When you select the Display Selected Titles option, WinCIM will show a list of files matching your current search criteria. After you select a file, WinCIM shows additional information about it (see Figure 7.15). The dialog contains the following options:

- **Retrieve**: Press this button to download the file to your computer. The File Finder will retrieve the file from the actual forum library. Note that you don't have to be a forum member to do this. After WinCIM has downloaded the file, you return to the File Finder main menu.

- **View**: When you review the information for a file in one of the graphic formats that WinCIM supports, you can select this option to view the graphic.

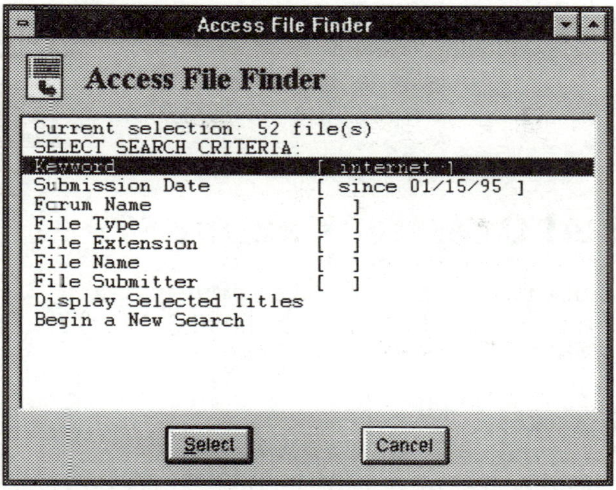

Figure 7.14 Two search specifications have been entered: a keyword (*internet*) and a submission dates (only the files uploaded since 1 January 1995 will be displayed)

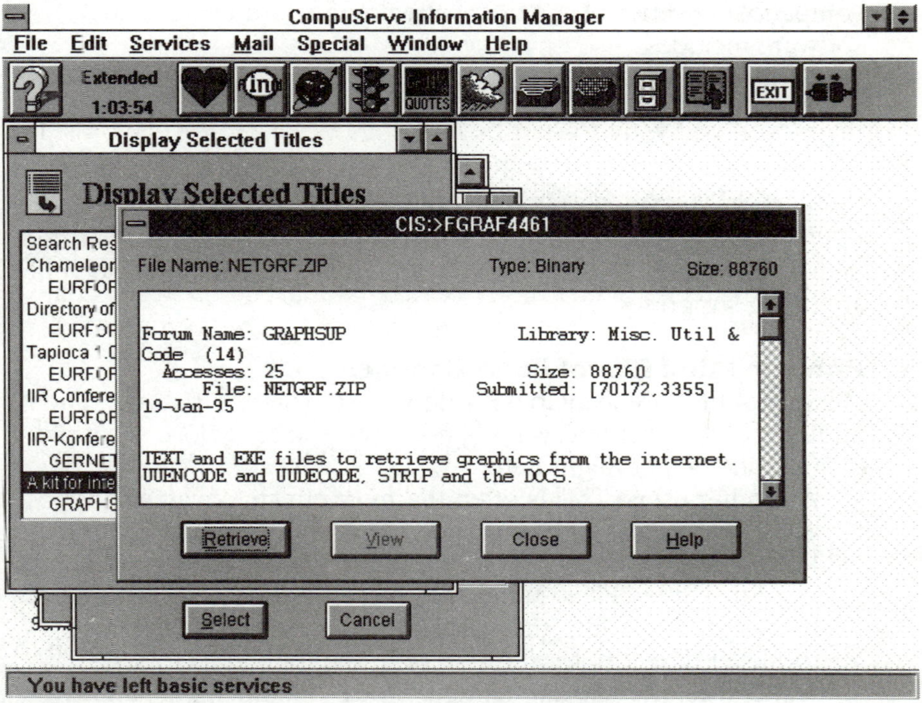

Figure 7.15 Additional information about the selected file

- **Close**: This closes the file description dialog and returns you to the list of matching files.

Frequently Asked Questions about FTP

This section contains a summary from the list of **Frequently Asked Questions**, which can also be read online through the File Transfer Protocol dialog (`GO FTP`).

- **How much does FTP cost?**
  Access to FTP is priced in the same way as forums. These charges will appear on your monthly statement as Extended Services. `GO RATES` for the current Extended Services price.

- **May I access all anonymous sites through CompuServe?**
  Approximately 95% of the FTP sites on the Internet are accessible through the CompuServe FTP interface. Some FTP sites are not compatible with CompuServe's FTP software. These sites are not compatible because of the host software they are using. This software includes:
  - Some Windows NT Servers
  - Macintosh Servers
  - MVS Servers

  If you do find a site that is not compatible, please report this site to FTP Feedback. Also, check the FTP FAQ (list with frequently asked questions – `GO FTP`) from time to time, to see if additional servers are being supported.

- **How can I find files of interest to me?**
  Millions of files are available for download from the Internet, and finding the one that you want is not always an easy job. A couple of suggestions that might help:
  - Ask other users. This is often the most effective way to find things of interest. Others (especially in the Internet forum) may know the exact location of the file for which you are searching.
  - Read the Index Files. Many sites maintain index files listing the names of all the files they provide. These are usually in the top-level directory for the site, or in the 'pub' directory. Sometimes, the files are named 'Index' or something similar. More often, they are named something like 'ls-lR' (because they are the output of the UNIX command 'ls -lR' used to create the

file list). The index files are often compressed, in which case they will have a suffix to indicate the type of compression used (see below). To make use of the index, download it, uncompress it if necessary, view it offline, and then download the files of interest.
- Read the README file. Most sites have a README file containing important information about that site. Often, these files contain valuable information on where to find files of interest.

- **Some of the files I want to download end in a tar extension. What does this mean?**
  Many FTP sites run the UNIX operating system. As a result, files may be archived and stored in a UNIX archive format. One common UNIX archive format is 'Tar'. 'Tar' stands for 'tape archiver', because the tar program was originally used to copy a collection of files to magnetic tape. By convention, files that have been archived using tar usually have a .tar extension.

- **How do I unarchive UNIX tar files?**
  The way in which a 'tarred' file is 'untarred' depends on the operating system you are using. If you are doing this on a UNIX computer, 'untarring' the files from inside a tar archive requires the use of the UNIX tar program itself. If you are running DOS, you need GZIP, a special DOS executable for 'untarring'. This file may be found in the UNIX forum of CompuServe (`GO UNIXFORUM`).

- **Why do some files have no size?**
  Actually, what you are seeing is an alias for the file that is stored at another location on the site. The host gives no information about the actual size of the alias, which is known as a symbolic link on UNIX systems. However, before you download the file, its size is determined so that you can decide whether you want to continue with the download or not.

- **Why do host sites use aliases, or symbolic links?**
  The most common reason is that this allows a single file to be referenced from many different directories. For example, the site may have a README file that it wants to display in every directory. Instead of trying to keep several copies up to date, they simply keep one version of the README file, and place an alias that points to it in each directory.

- **Sometimes when I retrieve a file, I end up in a different directory. Why is this?**
  The reason is again an alias or a symbolic link. To retrieve the file it is necessary for the system to change directories to the directory in which the aliased file resides. Once the retrieve has finished you may find yourself in a different directory than the one in which you started. Likewise, directories can be aliased to point to other directories. When you double-click on a directory, the system will take you to the directory to which the alias points.

- **Sometimes the error box appears when I try to change directories. What does this mean?**
  The most common reason this fails is that the directory is protected. Most of the time you will probably be logging in anonymously (look at the username field in the connect to site window). Many host sites allow different groups of users to have access to some files but not others. As you can guess, anonymous users typically are not allowed into system directories, the private user directories, and any other directory or file the host site wishes to block from the general public.

- **I'm unable to see all of the text in my CIM window. What can I do?**
  - **WinCIM**: In order to create the largest display area for reading textual information, your video display resolution should be larger than 640 by 480 pixels. In addition, the size of the window that displays the message text is negotiated between the FTP server and CIM at the beginning of your FTP session. To take advantage of this you should make your WinCIM window as large as possible prior to entering the CIM interface to FTP. You may resize manually or 'maximize' the WinCIM window.
  - **MacCIM**: MacCIM automatically negotiates the size of the window for displaying text based on the size of your monitor. You need not do anything except be aware you will see a sub-optimal display if you are using a Classic, Mac Plus or other machine with a 9" diagonal display.

Useful files

As always, the Internet New Users Forum (GO INETFOR) is a good place to start when you are looking for more information about FTP. The following section contains a summary of the files you will find in the forum libraries.

- *[73177,3346]   Lib: 8*
  EZOO30.EXE/Bin   Bytes: 134462

  Title   : Electronic Zoo - Version 3.0
  Keywords: ANIMAL COMPUTER RESOURCES INTERNET BBS

  The Electronic Zoo is a list of animal-related computer resources on the Internet and beyond, including mailing lists, telnet and FTP sites, Gophers, WWW, online services and BBSs. Current as of 5/94. Uploaded by the author.

- *[73710,1430]   Lib: 6*
  FTPDOS.ZIP/Bin   Bytes: 27090

  Title   : Recommended MS-DOS shareware/freeware by FTP
  Keywords: MS-DOS DOS FREEWARE SHAREWARE FTP SIMTEL OAK GARBO

  A list of recommended MS-DOS shareware/freeware from major FTP sites.

- *[73710,1430]   Lib: 6*
  FTPFAQ.ZIP/Bin   Bytes: 10351

  Title   : Anonymous FTP FAQ
  Keywords: FTP SITES ANONYMOUS FAQ FTPMAIL

  Frequently Asked Questions about anonymous FTP. Provides introductory information about FTP in general.

- *[76703,407]   Lib: 6*
  FTPHOW.TXT/Text Bytes: 26576

  Title   : How to use anonymous FTP (Internet Draft)
  Keywords: ANONYMOUS FTP HELP

  How to use anonymous FTP (Internet Draft)

- *[73710,1430]   Lib: 6*
  FTPLOC.ZIP/Bin Bytes: 101315

  Title   : Anonymous FTP Site Listing
  Keywords: FTP ANONYMOUS SITES

  A list of many sites accepting anonymous FTP connections. This listing, which unzips to 432K, describes sites, information about the host, and a sample of what can be found there.

- *[74431,2303]   Lib: 6*
  HOWFTP.TXT/Text Bytes: 19095

  Title   : FTP How-To Primer
  Keywords: FTP

  Another file to read before heading off into FTP land with CompuServe.

- *[72130,3557]   Lib: 6*
  MACFTP.SIT/Bin Bytes: 16000

  Title   : Mac FTP List Version 3.8.9
  Keywords: MAC FTP LIST GRUBB GLEASON ANONYMOUS SITES INTERNET

  This is an update {Sept 1,1994} to Mike Gleason's FTP list {He gave me permission to continue it}. It lists a good number of mac anonymous FTP sites with notes on some and a little blurb on how to use anonymous FTP. Must be in Monaco 9 {or PC equivalent} to be readable. Needs StuffIt Expander or equivalent {unsitins.exe} to decompress.

- *[72603,1671]   Lib:13*
  NETGUI.TXT/Text Bytes: 109226

  Title   : Library resources on the Internet
  Keywords: LIBRARIES RESOURCES STRATEGIES GUIDE

  Strategies for selection and use of library resources on the Internet. Includes how to get started, road maps, travel guides, search strategies and information about other library resources.

- *[76703,407] Lib: 3*
  USALST.TXT/Text Bytes: 67906

  Title : InterNIC Internet Access Providers List
  Keywords: INTERNIC INTERNET ACCESS PROVIDERS SERVICE

  InterNIC Internet Access Providers List (United States). Updated 9/9/94. The document contains a list of providers indexed by area code. There is also a main list that is organized alphabetically where more detailed information about each provider is listed. All providers listed offer at least interactive TCP connections (i.e. telnet, FTP).

Chapter 8

Telnet

- More about telnet
- Using telnet
- Capturing data
- Frequently Asked Questions about telnet
- Useful files
- Connecting to CompuServe through telnet

COMPUSERVE
Internet Services

More about telnet

Telnet enables you to access thousands of the computers that are connected to the Internet. Using telnet, you can retrieve information from numerous databases, access computer networks without incurring high telephone charges – even log in to your office computer, provided your company has a correctly set up Internet link.

Basically, telnet does four things for you:

1 It makes a TCP connection with the Internet server you have specified.

2 It converts your input into a standard format that can be sent to the server.

3 It converts the output from the server into a standard format that can be sent to your computer.

4 It reformats the output from the server in such a way that it can be made visible on your computer screen.

There are three ways to use telnet:

1 A lot of computer networks allow so-called **guest logins**. Using the login name **guest**, you will be able to access a limited part of the computer, look around, browse through databases and access other information.

2 If you have a subscription to a particular service (like CIX, one of the larger information services in the United Kingdom), you can use telnet to access CIX when you are in a foreign country, or when you pay lots of money for your interlocal telephone connection to CIX.

3 If you can access CompuServe only through a high-cost interlocal or international call, and if you have local access to the Internet, you can use **inbound telnet** to log in to CompuServe (see page 221). You can even use WinCIM to visit forums, download files etc.!

Please note: When using telnet, you will work in Terminal Mode, also called the **ASCII Interface** of CompuServe, temporarily leaving the menus and dialogs you have become accustomed to. However, most computers that allow for **inbound telnet access** offer a user-friendly menu structure.

To use the telnet service, GO TELNET. After a few seconds, the menu shown in Figure 8.1 appears. This menu contains the following options:

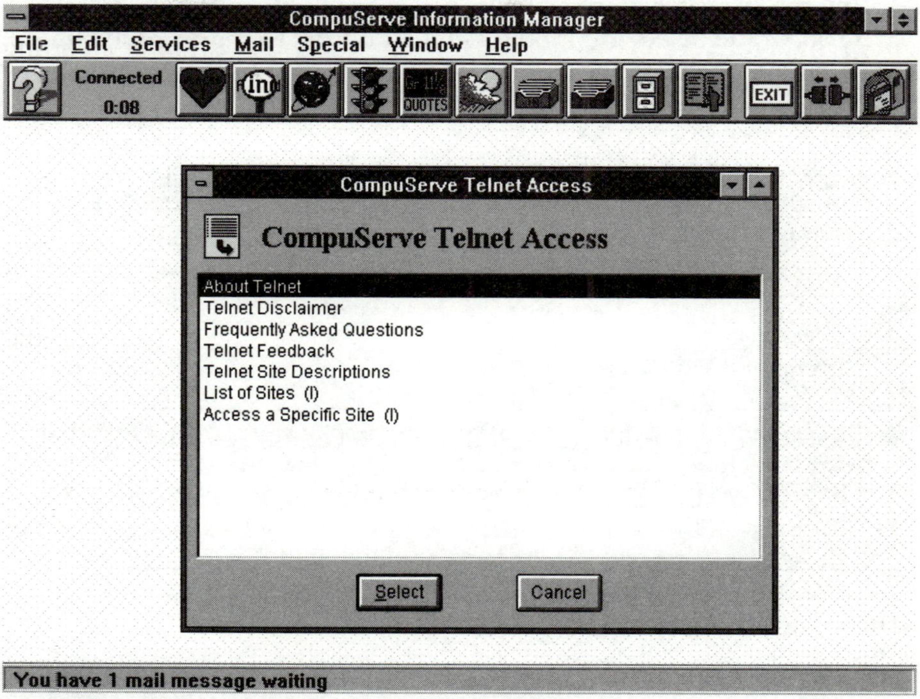

Figure 8.1 The CompuServe Telnet Access menu

- **About telnet**: Select this option to get some background information about telnet.

- **Telnet Disclaimer**: When you use telnet to connect to another computer, you are actually accessing information that is not controlled by CompuServe. Therefore, CompuServe cannot be held responsible for the content of that information. Besides, connections can be slow because of the large amounts of traffic on the Internet. Also, some sites only allow access during specific hours, or for a limited period of time. The complete CompuServe Newsgroups Disclaimer is available by selecting this option.

- **Frequently Asked Questions**: Select this option to retrieve a summary of telnet-related questions that are often asked, as well as the answers to those questions. An extract from this article can be found on page 217.

- **Telnet Feedback**: If you have problems while using telnet, you can select this option to write a message to the telnet Feedback department. A dialog appears, containing the names of available Internet Services. In this dialog, select the Outbound Telnet option. (You would select the Inbound Telnet option to report problems you have when connecting to CompuServe through your Internet site.)

  After a few seconds, the dialog shown in Figure 8.2 appears. After you have entered your name and the message, press the Send Message button.

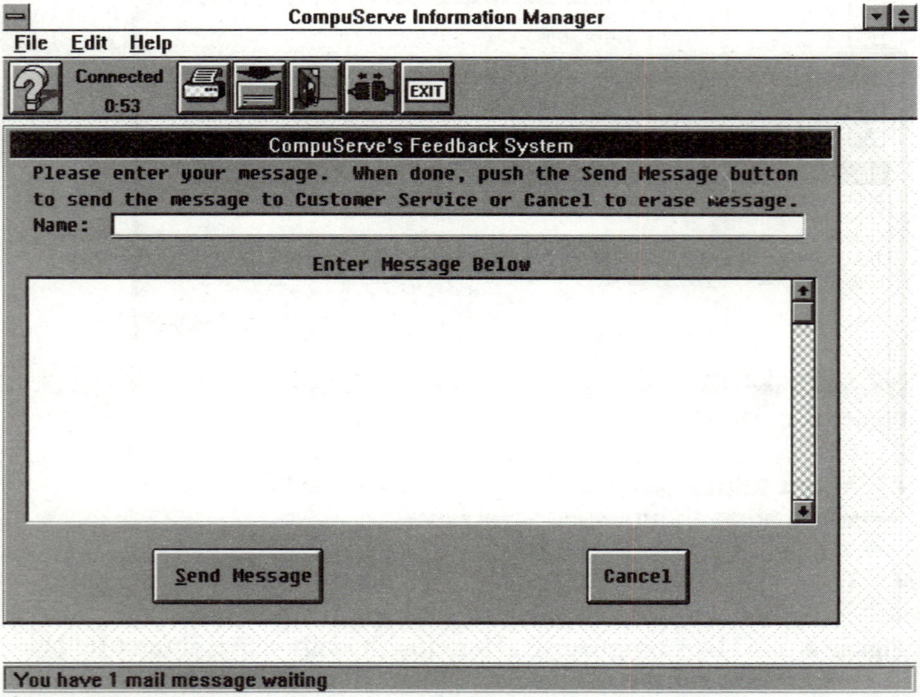

Figure 8.2 Use this window to send a message to the Telnet Feedback department at CompuServe

- **Access Telnet**: Select this option to enter the telnet area.

Using telnet

Important: To use telnet from CompuServe, you need terminal software that supports VT100 emulation. This emulation is built into WinCIM 1.4 and will be activated automatically.

After you have selected the List of Sites option on the CompuServe Telnet Access menu, WinCIM will display a list of available servers servers (see Figure 8.3 for an example).

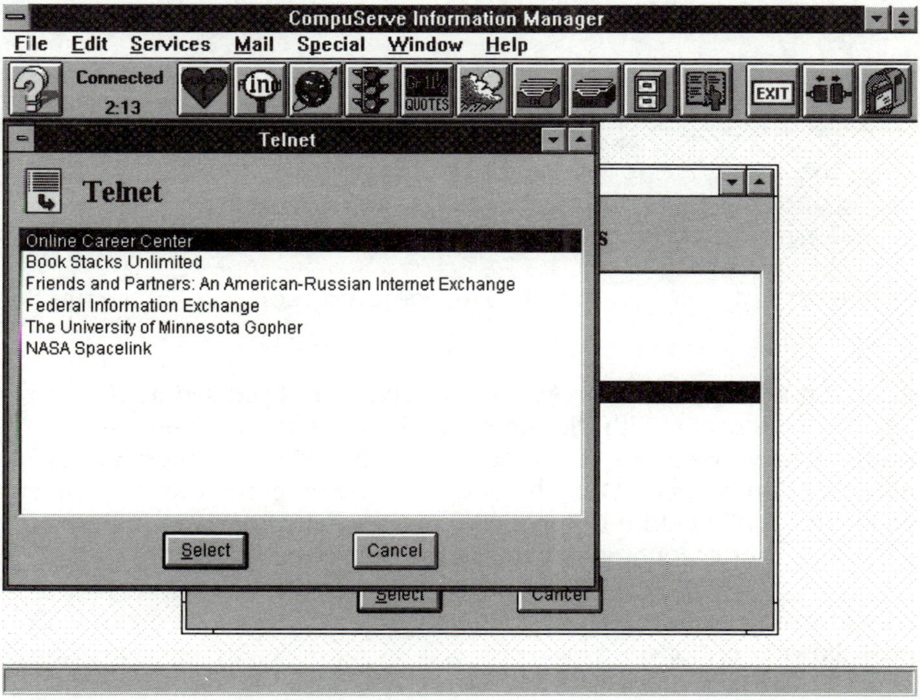

Figure 8.3 A selection of telnet sites recommended by CompuServe

Accessing a listed telnet server

To access one of the listed telnet servers, enter the corresponding number and press the Enter key. You will see another menu, with the following options:

- **Description**: Select this option to learn more about the server you have selected, before actually accessing it.

- **Logging on**: This option tells you more about login procedures for the server you have selected. Some servers allow you to use your name, whereas others want you to use the word **guest**.

- **Returning to CompuServe**: Select this option to learn more about how to return to CompuServe, once you are accessing the server. In all cases, you can press Ctrl-] (keep the Ctrl-key pressed down while you hit the] key) to return to CompuServe.

- **Access Site**: When you are ready to access the site, select this option. CompuServe will inform you that you're about to enter the Net:

```
You are about to establish a connection to
an Internet host.
The performance, reliability, availability and
content of Internet hosts is beyond
CompuServe's control.

Hit return to establish connection to Internet
host.
```

After you have selected the Access Site option and pressed the Return key, the connection with the server will be established. Follow the prompts on your screen; if you have any difficulties, just press Ctrl-] to return to CompuServe. Don't hang up by switching off your modem; it will take a while before CompuServe notices that you're not online anymore. Your account will therefore be billed needlessly.

Should you need to press Ctrl-], CompuServe will display a menu with the following options:

1 **Quit --- the current connection**

2 **Status --- display connection status**

Select option 1 to cancel the connection to the server. But remember: you are still connected to CompuServe. To disconnect from CompuServe, either press the Disconnect button on the Ribbon or select the Disconnect option on the File menu.

Accessing an unlisted telnet server

Most of the telnet servers available can be accessed from CompuServe, provided you know the server's exact Internet address. When the menu of telnet sites is displayed (in Terminal Emulation mode), type `telnet`, followed by a space and the name of the Internet server. For example,

```
telnet cix.compulink.co.uk
```

Whether or not you are actually granted access to the server depends on the server. If you don't have a user name and password, you could try using **guest** at the login: prompt.

Capturing data

In Chapter 7, you learned that you can use CompuServe FTP to download files from a large number of Internet sites. But when you use telnet, you can use WinCIM's File Capture option to store all retrieved information in a file on your hard disk. After you have disconnected, you can review or edit the file, using either Windows Notepad or your favourite word processor package.

To activate File Capture, either select the Record in File option on the Special menu or double-click on the label marked **Off**, next to the File Capture text on the Terminal Emulation window's status bar. WinCIM will ask you for the name of the file in which the retrieved information should be stored.

To switch File Capture off, repeat this procedure.

Frequently Asked Questions about telnet

- **What type of software is recommended for using the CompuServe telnet service?**
  Telnet sites generally expect that you will be running terminal emulation software that can emulate a VT100 terminal. While VT100 will be supported in WinCIM 1.4, WinCIM 1.3 or below may not meet your needs. MacCIM 2.4.1 (and earlier versions) supports

a subset of VT100 capabilities but it is not fully VT100 compliant. Version 3.0 will have full VT100 support. Other terminal emulators that have been used successfully with the CompuServe telnet gateway include Windows Terminal, Procomm, and Dynacomm.

- **How do I ensure that WinCIM 1.4 is in VT100 terminal emulation mode?**
  When using WinCIM 1.4 to access the telnet service, you will automatically be placed in full VT100 terminal emulation mode. You may notice that your screen changes color as VT100 is turned on. Upon exiting the telnet application, your default terminal emulation settings will be restored.

- **What do I do if I do not know the User ID and password to enter a site?**
  Many telnet sites allow people who do not have an account on their computer to login as a guest. Just type `guest` at the User ID prompt. In most circumstances you do not have to enter a password if you are a guest. Occasionally, this password is case sensitive. Also, make sure you read the descriptive text issued when logging on to a telnet site. Often, this text indicates the User ID and password to be used by visitors. Keep in mind that not all telnet sites allow guest access. You may come across some sites for which a legitimate User ID and password are required for access.

- **What type of performance can I expect when I connect to a telnet site?**
  Performance at telnet sites is subject not only to usage from the Internet, but also to local demand for resources. If many people access a site at the same time, performance can and will deteriorate quickly. Be prepared to wait for the remote site to respond to your requests if you are using it during periods of peak demand.

- **How do I disconnect from a site?**
  Typically, a telnet site will provide menu prompts and instructions on how to 'quit' or 'exit' the site. Once you leave a telnet site, you will be returned to CompuServe.

  If you have difficulty exiting the site, press the control key plus the "]" key to return to CompuServe.

- **What are the advantages of using the CompuServe telnet interface?**
  CompuServe presents a controlled view of the Internet. Access is gained through a menu system that provides information about a

site, as well as seamless menu-driven access to a site. In addition, members have the abilitiy to telnet to any site of their choice, even if it is not listed on the menu.

- **How do I telnet to a site not on the menu?**
  CompuServe members may telnet to any site they desire (even if it isn't on the menu) by entering the following at the ! prompt when viewing the menu of sites:

  ```
  telnet sitename
  ```

  In this example, sitename is the fully qualified domain name. For example, to telnet to CompuServe, you would enter:

  ```
  telnet compuserve.com
  ```

  Note: We do not recommend doing this since you are already logged into CompuServe!

- **How can I suggest a site to be included on the telnet sites menu?**
  If there is a site you think should be added to the menu, just issue your request via Telnet Feedback.

- **How is access to the telnet service priced?**
  Access to the telnet service is priced the same way as forums, at extended service rates.

Useful files

If you need more information about telnet, or if you are looking for interesting servers to access, GO INETFORUM to access the Internet New Users Forum. A sample of the files available in the forum libraries follows.

- *[70610,3354] Lib:11*
  ERIC.TXT/Text Bytes: 4367

  Title : ERIC database Internet sites
  Keywords: ERIC EDUCATION INTERNET TELNET

  Information about publicly available Internet sites for accessing ERIC databases via telnet. ERIC maintains information on a variety of educational topics. ERIC Clearing houses are sponsored by the US Department of Education.

- *[73177,3346] Lib: 8*
  EZOO30.EXE/Bin Bytes: 134462

  Title : Electronic Zoo - Version 3.0
  Keywords: ANIMAL COMPUTER RESOURCES INTERNET BBS

  The Electronic Zoo is a list of animal-related computer resources on the Internet and beyond, including mailing lists, telnet and FTP sites, Gophers, WWW, online services and BBSs. Current as of 5/94. Uploaded by the author.

- *[76703,407] Lib:11*
  MINUTE.TXT/Text Bytes: 716

  Title : Minuteman Library Network (Suburban Boston)
  Keywords: MINUTEMAN LIBRARY BOSTON MASSACHUSETTS

  Minuteman Library Network now online
  The Minuteman Library Network is a consortium of about 25 public and college libraries in Boston's western suburbs.

  They recently installed an Internet connection, which means you can now search the catalogs of member libraries via telnet. The address is mln.lib.ma.us and the log-in name is library.

Connecting to CompuServe through telnet

If you have access to the Internet through another access provider (your office, for instance), you can connect to CompuServe without the need to dial an access number. Starting with version 1.4, WinCIM offers complete support for inbound telnet. After you have connected to CompuServe, you will be able to read your mail, visit forums, download files etc. In short, all options are available to you, regardless of whether you use telnet or a regular dial-up node. There is only one condition: you need to have a SLIP or PPP account. Proceed as follows:

1 Start WinCIM. Select the Session Settings option on the Special menu. Next, press the New button to start a new session. You could call this one *Telnet*, so that you can identify it easily.

2 Check that the following fields contain the correct values:
- **Connector**: Winsock
- **Baud Rate**: 14400
- **Network**: CompuServe
- **Dial Type**: Direct

3 Press the LAN button. This will cause the Winsock Settings dialog to appear. In the Host Name field, enter `compuserve.com`. Leave the Host IP Address field empty and ignore the value in the Connect Timeout field.

4 Press the OK button to close the Winsock Settings Dialog. Press it again to close the Setup Session Settings dialog. You are now ready to establish a Winsock connection. You may leave the WinCIM application open, so that you don't have to start it later on.

5 Be sure that you are connected to the Internet (either with SLIP or PPP).

6 In the WinCIM application, select the Get Mail option on the Mail menu. Using TCP/IP, WinCIM will now connect to CompuServe. You will hardly notice the difference between this and the 'normal way' of dialing up to a CompuServe Network node!

7 When you've finished, disconnect like you normally do. If necessary, give the appropriate socket command to end your Internet connection.

Chapter 9

HTML: the language of the Web

- Features of HTML documents
- Ways to publish your HTML documents
- Software that you need to make HTML documents
- More about HTML elements
- A demonstration document
- The next step

CompuServe Internet Services

Although many people think (and say) otherwise, developing your own World Wide Web pages isn't difficult. Using a special **markup language** called **HTML** (the abbreviation for **HyperText Markup Language**), you create **source code** by adding a series of codes to new or existing documents. After you have inserted the source code, any HTML browser can display your HTML document.

Features of HTML documents

The nice thing about HTML is that you can make your documents as simple or complex as you wish. The following list shows some of the features that you can use to make your documents interesting, nice to look at and attractive to a large audience:

- **Headings** in different sizes, to indicate separate sections of the document.
- **Font attributes** to draw attention to a particular word, sentence or paragraph.
- **Lists** (numbered or bulleted) to summarize information.
- **Links** to other places in your document, to other documents that you have prepared, or to other documents on the World Wide Web. Creating a link involves nothing more than inserting one or two codes in your document.
- **Graphics** that the browser will display automatically. Inserting a graphic in your document is easy: you simply insert a code that contains the filename of the graphic.

Ways to publish your HTML documents

So what do you do with your HTML documents after you have created them? There are several options available to you for publishing your material.

- Place them on your hard disk and use them locally, without even connecting to the Internet. For instance, I have a local copy of my own home page on my hard disk, which contains a number of links to interesting sites on the World Wide Web.

- Place them on a diskette and distribute them. Anyone who has a World Wide Web browser can view those documents directly from the diskette! This is a nice and affordable way to publish material in a standard format.

- Upload them to a CompuServe forum. As with publishing material by diskette, this is an easy way to make your newsletters, e-zines etc. available to many people. Use a compression tool (like PKZIP, that can be found on a number of CompuServe forums) to combine all documents, graphics, sound clips etc. in one file that can be downloaded by anyone who wants it.

- And finally: publish them on the World Wide Web! Although this is the most logical option, it's the last one in this summary. The reason is that CompuServe doesn't offer World Wide Web publishing facilities for its members. But there is good news, too: more and more companies rent storage space to anyone who wants to have his or her documents available on the World Wide Web. In most cases, a few hundred kilobytes will be more than enough to publish interesting documents. Once you have hired disk space with a specific server, you can use FTP to place your files in your own directory on that server.

Software that you need to make HTML documents

If you have used CompuServe's Dial PPP feature, you already have all the software that you need to build HTML documents. This gives you:

- An editor. If you plan to use international characters, you might be better off using an ANSI editor like Windows Notepad. However, ASCII editors such as EDIT.COM (the DOS program) can be used too. And naturally you can use your favorite word processor software also, provided it can save documents in ANSI or ASCII format.

- A World Wide Web browser. After you have written and edited your HTML document, you will need a World Wide Web browser (such as Netscape or SPRY Mosaic) to view it. The browser software will interpret the **source code** (the document with HTML elements that you prepared) and show the results on your screen. Compilation is not required; unlike normal programming languages, documents that are written in HTML don't need to be compiled before they can be displayed by a browser. The browser interprets the source code and translates the HTML elements into viewable headings, images, links, and so on.

Although these two pieces of software are enough to get you started, you might want to take a look at the large collection of **HTML editors** currently available. These editors make inserting HTML codes easy and straightforward, and often contain help information about specific codes. The best place to look for HTML editors is the Internet Publishing Forum (`GO INETPUB`).

More about HTML elements

There are two types of HTML elements: **container elements** and **single elements**. Elements are indicated by **tags**: codes that are often placed between angle brackets (< and >). The text between the angle brackets is case independent; you can therefore use upper case, lower case or a combination of both.

Upper or lower case?
To make it easy to spot elements in a document, some HTML writers type them in upper case. However, some HTML utility programs use lower case. Feel free to develop the style that you are most comfortable with, even if that means that you use both upper and lower case.

Container elements

Container elements come in pairs: a **start tag** (like <H1>) and an **end tag** (like </H1>). As you can see, end tags are preceded by a slash (/). Anything between the pair of tags will be affected by them. For example, you would use the tags <B> and </B> to have the enclosed text displayed in a bold font. In some cases, additional **attributes** are used to provide more information about the way an element should behave.

Redundant end tags

In cases where it's clear that the end tag is not necessary, it can be omitted. You'll see some examples of this on the following pages.

Single elements

There are two types of single elements: **single tags** and **entities**, sometimes called **special character codes**.

Single tags

Single tags can be used to include images. An example:

```
<IMG SRC="test.gif">.
```

When displaying the document, the browser will use the *SRC* attribute to look for a file called *test.gif*. When the *test.gif* file is found, the browser will show its contents on the screen.

Entities or special character codes

Entities can be used to include special characters in your documents (like < and >, for instance). They begin with an **and sign** (&) and end with a semicolon.

Yes, they're case dependent

Note that, unlike tag names, some entities are case dependent. For instance, the entity to include an ö is `ö`, whereas the entity for Ö is `Ö`.

A few examples of frequently used entities are listed below:

Entity	**Character**
`<`	< (less than)
`>`	> (greater than)
`&`	& (and sign)
`"`	" (double quote)
`è`	è (e with a grave accent)
`é`	é (e with an acute accent)
`ë`	ë (e with an umlaut)

Other accent characters
In this list, *grave*, *acute* and *uml* are used to indicate letters with a grave accent, acute accent and umlaut, respectively. You can use this method to add accents to other vowels also. For instance, specify `Ü` to get an upper case Ü.

ANSI and accented characters
If you use Windows, and therefore the ANSI character set, you can simply type the accented characters, without having to worry about entities. Since HTML uses the ISO 8859 character set, which is identical to the ANSI set used by Windows, all accented characters will automatically show up correctly.

A demonstration document

Attention, Macintosh users
Although we'll refer to Windows applications in this chapter, you can also try these examples on your Macintosh, provided you have a World Wide Web browser and an editor.

In this section we'll use a simple document to demonstrate the most important features of HTML: paragraphs, headings, lists and graphics. We'll discuss the real power of HTML, **hyperlinks**, a little bit later.

Use your favorite editor to type in the following text:

```
<TITLE>Our first HTML document</TITLE>
<H1>Our first HTML document</H1>
Welcome to our first WWW page!
<P>
This demonstration document contains some important
HTML codes, used on almost every World Wide Web page:
<UL>
<LI>Lines
<LI>Headings (two of them, actually)
<LI>Lists (like the one you are reading right now)
<LI>Graphics
</UL>
<H2>Lines: one code does it all!</H2>
This document contains a line:
<HR>
```

```
Also, we have included a graphic: <IMG
SRC="klikhere.gif">
```

Save this text under the filename *demo01.htm.* You might want to save it into a temporary directory, for instance *\demo.htm.*

After you have saved the file, start SPRY Mosaic and click on the Open button, or select the Open Local File option on the File menu. Select the file and press the OK button. A few seconds later, your screen should look like the one in Figure 9.1. The chances are that an error message is displayed, indicating that a certain file couldn't be retrieved: ignore that error message for now.

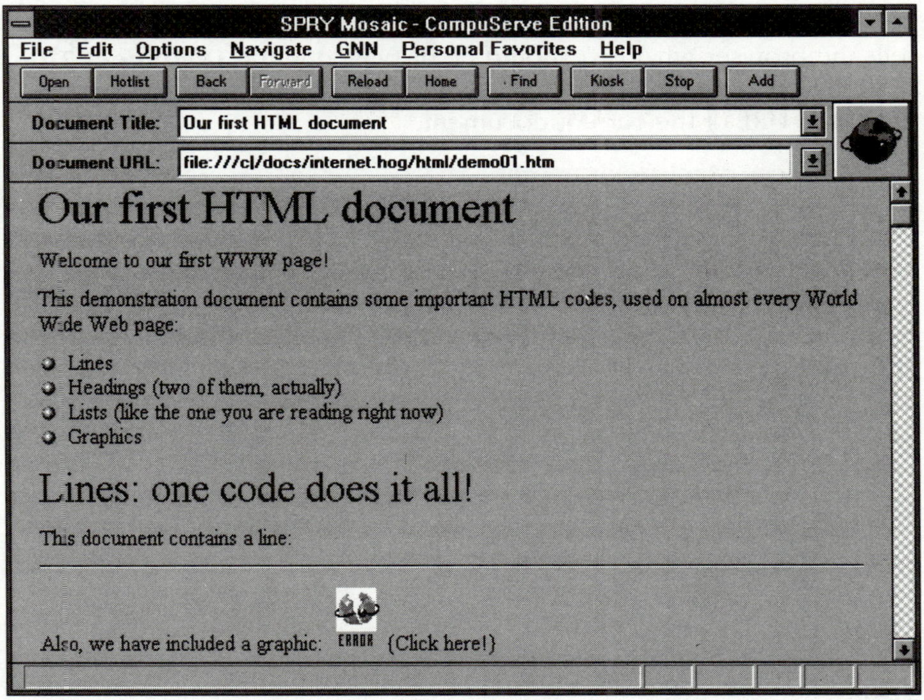

Figure 9.1 The contents of the *demo01.htm* document, as displayed by SPRY Mosaic

If your screen looks different, go back to your editor (don't close the SPRY Mosaic application) and check your document. Save the file again, switch to SPRY Mosaic and press the Reload button to view the revised edition of your document.

The HTML elements in our demonstration document

You probably notice that all HTML elements have been translated into their corresponding screen elements. The following sections discuss the elements that we have used in the demonstration document, in the order in which they appear. Also, a number of examples are included to demonstrate the elements in more detail.

Remember that most elements are **containers** and come in pairs: the end code is indicated by a leading slash (/).

<TITLE>

The <TITLE> container should appear at the top of the document. It tells the browser what text should be displayed in the **Document Title** field. If you omit the <TITLE> container, the Document Title field will show the URL of the current document.

<H1>

This is one of the six **heading tags** available. The digit after the H character indicates the **heading level**. If you want to see how the headings look on your screen, type in the following example, or look at Figure 9.2.

```
<TITLE>Heading demo</TITLE>
<H1>This is heading 1</H1>
<H2>This is heading 2</H2>
<H3>This is heading 3</H3>
<H4>This is heading 4</H4>
<H5>This is heading 5</H5>
<H6>This is heading 6</H6>
```

<P>

This is a very important element. Since normal carriage returns are interpreted as spaces, you need the <P> element to start a new paragraph. Your browser will insert a blank line and print the text following the <P> on the line thereafter. The following document demonstrates this:

```
<TITLE>Paragraph demo</TITLE>
This is the first paragraph of our document.
This text is still part of the first paragraph, even
```

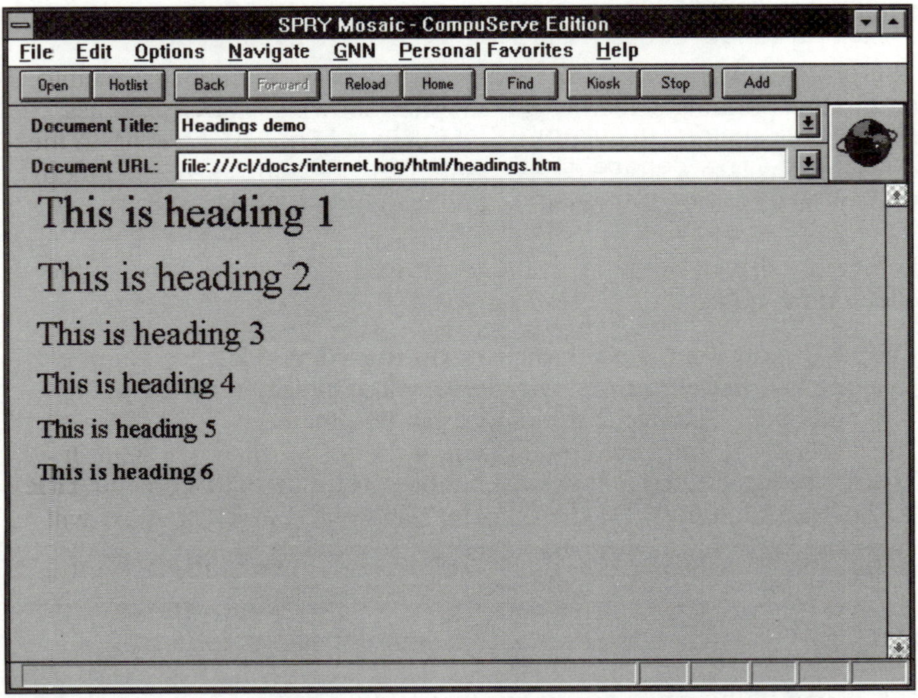

Figure 9.2 The six headings that you can use in an HTML document

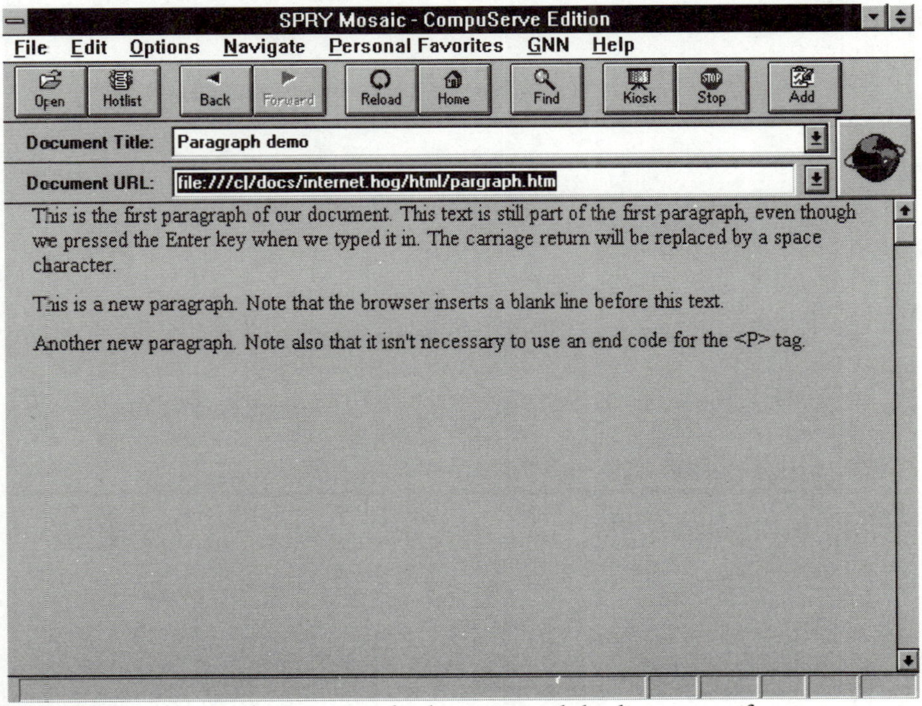

Figure 9.3 Paragraphs, paragraph elements and the browser software

```
though we pressed the Enter key when we typed it in.
The carriage return will be replaced by a space
character.
<P>
This is a new paragraph. Note that the browser inserts
a blank line before this text.
<P>Another new paragraph. Note also that it isn't
necessary to use an end code for the &lt;P&gt; tag.
```

<UL> and <LI>

The <UL> container is used to create an **unordered list**, containing one or more **list elements**. List elements are indicated by the <LI> tag. The end code </LI> for that element can be omitted.

The following example shows the simplest form that a list can have:

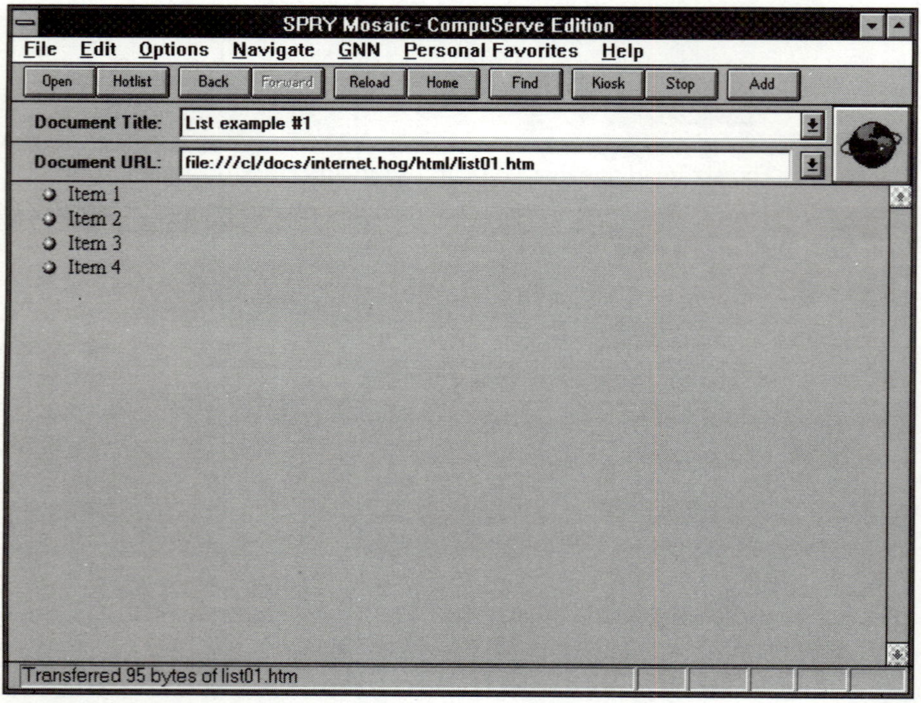

Figure 9.4 A simple unordered list

```
<TITLE>List example #1</TITLE>
<UL>
<LI>Item 1
<LI>Item 2
<LI>Item 3
<LI>Item 4
</UL>
```

List items can be as long as you wish. You can even include <P> elements to start indented paragraphs. The following example shows this:

```
<TITLE>List example #2</TITLE>
<UL>
<LI>Item 1
<LI>Item 2
    <P>
    This text "belongs" to Item 2. It is a new
    paragraph, but it is indented, just like Item 2.
    Note the blank line!
```

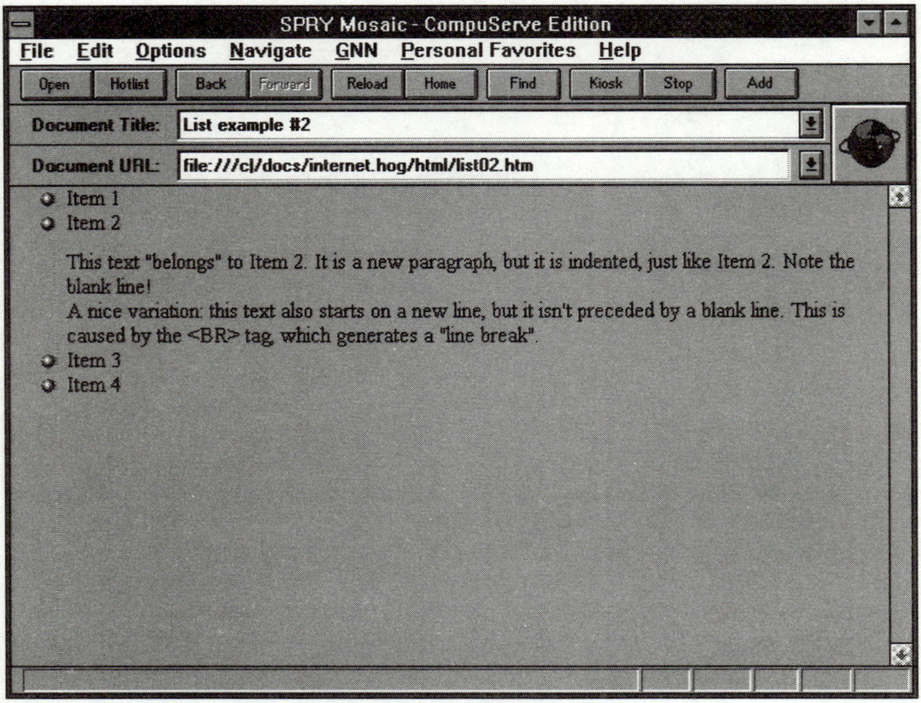

Figure 9.5 Using paragraphs and line breaks in lists.

```
    <BR>
    A nice variation: this text also starts on a new
    line, but it isn't preceded by a blank line.
    This is caused by the &lt;BR&gt; tag,
    which generates a "line break".
<LI>Item 3
<LI>Item 4
</UL>
```

This example also introduces the **line break** element: <BR>. The text following this element will be placed on a new line. However, it won't be preceded by a blank line.

Indent your source code
Note that since double spaces are ignored by browsers, indented lines in the source code don't have any effect on the way the document will be displayed. You can therefore indent lines to make your source code easier to read.

The following example demonstrates an interesting possibility: you can **nest** one or more lists. Note that each list has its own pair of <UL> and </UL> elements.

```
<TITLE>List example #3</TITLE>
<UL>
<LI>Item 1
<LI>Item 2
<LI>Item 3
    <UL>
    <LI>Item a
    <LI>Item b
         <UL>
         <LI>Item I
         <LI>Item II
         <LI>Item III
         </UL>
    <LI>Item c
    <LI>Item d
    </UL>
<LI>Item 4
</UL>
```

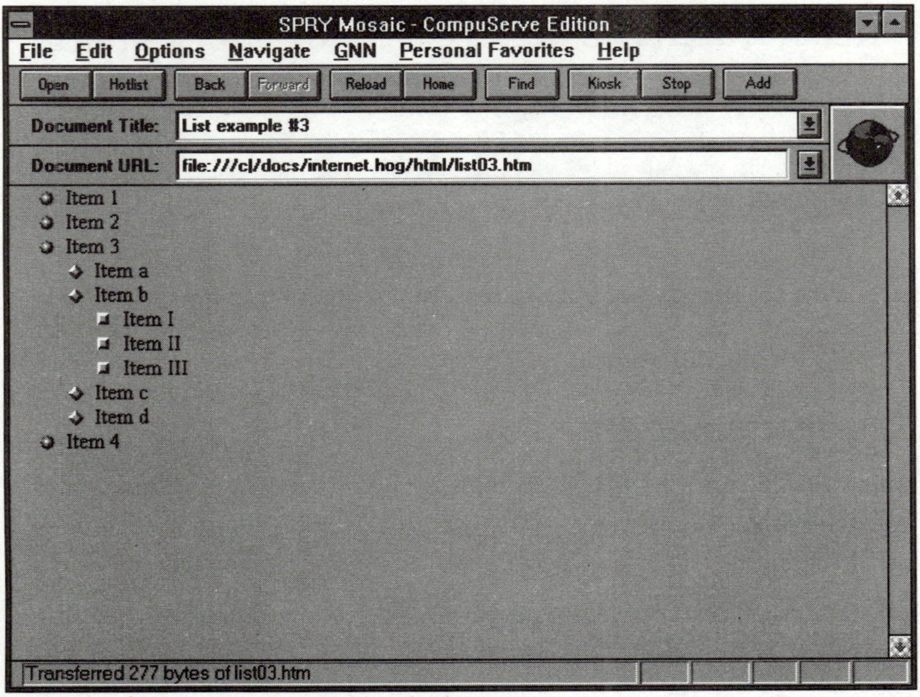

Figure 9.6 Nested lists, three levels deep

Until now, we have used only unordered lists. However, there are a few more list categories:

- **Ordered lists (<OL>)**: these are identical to unordered lists, except for the fact that the bullets are replaced by numbers.

- **Definition lists (<DL>)**: these lists are often used for glossaries, definitions of terms, and so on.

- **Menu lists (<MENU>)**: 'one-liners', often used to display menus with hyperlinks to other World Wide Web documents. Typically, items in menu lists shouldn't be longer than one line.

- **Directory lists (<DIR>)**: used to display short entries, like filenames or document names.

The following example shows a document with ordered lists, definition lists and menu lists.

```
<TITLE>List example #4</TITLE>
<H6>Ordered list:</H6>
```

```
<OL>
  <LI>Item a
  <LI>Item b
  <LI>Item c
</OL>

<H6>Definition list:</H6>
<DL>
  <DT>HTML
  <DD>HyperText Markup Language
  <DT>URL
  <DD>Uniform Resource Locator
  <DT>WWW
  <DD>World Wide Web
</DL>

<H6>Menu list:</H6>
<MENU>
  <LI>Item 1
  <LI>Item 2
  <LI>Item 3
</MENU>
```

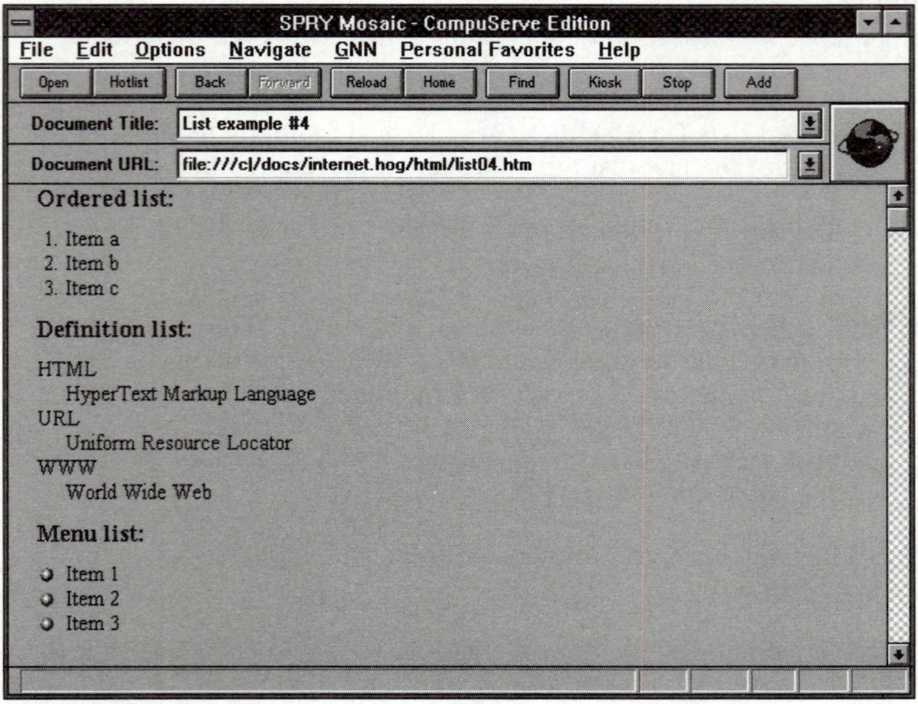

Figure 9.7 Various lists

<H2>

By now, this element should be familiar to you: it indicates a **level 2 heading**.

<HR>

This element inserts a **horizontal ruler** in your document: a horizontal line. Used sparingly, lines can make your documents more attractive and easier to read.

Displaying graphics

Our demonstration document shown on page 228 contains one more element that we haven't discussed in detail yet. Also, Figure 9.1 on page 229 shows that something is wrong: a graphic with the text *error* is displayed. And when you opened the document, your browser probably generated a 'Can't open file' error message, too.

The reason is that in our demonstration document, we have included a **link** to a graphic. The following element contains this link:

```
<IMG SRC="klikhere.gif">
```

The element is pretty straightforward: it tells the browser to display an image. It contains an **attribute**, **SRC**, that instructs the browser to use the source *klikhere.gif*, a GIF file. Since no such file exists the browser shows an alternative graphic, indicating that an error occurred.

Graphic file formats and the World Wide Web

Although **file viewers** can be configured to display virtually any type of file, most browsers provide built-in support to display files in GIF or JPG format. It is, therefore a good idea to convert your graphic images to one of those formats. The main differences between GIF and JPG are listed below.

- **GIF** is a **lossless** compression format: when you convert a graphic file into GIF format, no information will be discarded. The downside is that GIF files can be fairly large, depending on the resolution and the number of colors used. Also, the format of GIF files doesn't allow for more than 256 colors.

- **JPG**JPG is a **lossy** compression format: although the file size can be reduced significantly, some of the image information will be lost, which can result in images with a lower quality. However, JPG files allow for more than 16 million colors.

It's up to you to decide which format you want to use. Some HTML documents offer both formats; a small JPG file that gives you a good idea what the image is all about, and a larger GIF file that can be downloaded if you really like the image.

If you're a Windows user, you'll probably want to convert BMP files (the default graphic file format used in Windows) to either GIF or JPG. Since Windows doesn't provide built-in support for this, you'll have to use a conversion utility. One of the best utilities on the market is **Paintshop Pro**, a very popular shareware program. It can be downloaded from a number of CompuServe Forums: `GO PCFF` to access the PC File Finder and use the keyword *paintshop*.

Using Paintbrush I have created a button, like the ones you see in regular Windows applications. The actual Paintbrush image, *klikhere.bmp* is shown in Figure 9.8.

Figure 9.8 We'll include this button graphic in our demonstration document

Using Paintshop Pro, I have converted this button into a GIF file, called *klikhere.gif*. Assuming you have done the same or have a similar image that you can use, perform the following steps:

1 Copy the *klikhere.gif* file to the directory where the demonstration document, *demo01.htm*, resides.

2 Switch to your browser and re-open the *demo01.htm* document.

If all went well, your browser should now display the demonstration document with the button in place, as shown in Figure 9.9.

Adding support for non-graphical browsers
As a World Wide Web publisher, it is your responsibility to see to it that users of non-graphical browsers can enjoy your documents as well. Therefore, you might want to add some text to your document that will be shown on screens that can't display graphics. The <IMG> element provides an attribute to do this: **ALT**. Expand the

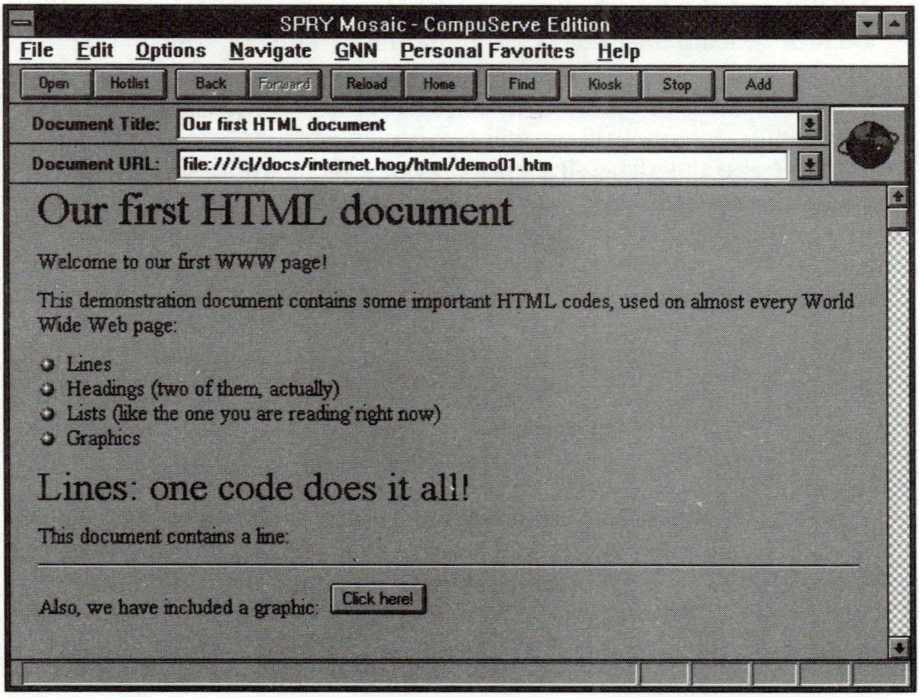

Figure 9.9 We've included a graphical image in our World Wide Web document

<IMG> element to include the following text:

```
<IMG SRC="klikhere.gif" ALT="Click here!">.
```

Although the button in our document displays the text 'Click here!', nothing happens when we click on it. The reason is that we haven't added any **hyperlink** functionality to the button yet. It's time to introduce the **anchor tag**: <A>.

Adding a hyperlink

A complete hyperlink consists of two so-called **anchors**:

- The **starting point**: the place where you click to reach the destination. Starting points can be text (often underlined and displayed in a unique color) as well as images. When the mouse pointer is located on a starting point, its shape changes into a hand with a pointing finger. On your own pages, you will want to include at least one, but possibly more of these anchors.

- The **destination**: the information (either in the same document or in another document) that will be displayed when someone clicks on the hyperlink. The simplest form of a destination anchor is a filename or a URL.

Inserting the starting point anchor

First, we'll include a starting point anchor in our demonstration document. Replace the last line of the document (the one with the <IMG> element) with the following:

```
Also, we have included a graphic: <A
HREF="nextpage.htm"><IMG SRC="klikhere.gif"></A>
```

To get a better look at what we're doing you could also format this line as follows (remember that carriage returns and double spaces are ignored by the browser software):

```
Also, we have included a graphic:
 <A HREF="nextpage.htm">
   <IMG SRC="klikhere.gif">
 </A>
```

You see that the <IMG> element is now embedded in the <A> container. The <A> container contains one element: **HREF**. This element is the **HyperText Reference** to our destination. The part that is embedded between <A> and </A> (the button image, in this case) will become the actual hyperlink.

Save this document as *demo02.htm*. The complete source code for our demonstration document now looks as follows:

```
<TITLE>Our first HTML document</TITLE>
<H1>Our first HTML document</H1>
Welcome to our first WWW page!
<P>
This demonstration document contains some important HTML
codes, used on almost every World Wide Web page:
<UL>
<LI>Lines
<LI>Headings (two of them, actually)
<LI>Lists (like the one you are reading right now)
```

```
<LI>Graphics
</UL>
<H2>Lines: one code does it all!</H2>
This document contains a line:
<HR>
Also, we have included a graphic:
<A HREF="nextpage.htm">
  <IMG SRC="klikhere.gif">
</A>
```

Now open the *demo02.htm* document in your World Wide Web browser. The result can be seen in Figure 9.10. The 'Click here!' button has a border, indicating that it is a hyperlink. You can easily verify this; when you place the mouse pointer on the button, it changes into a hand with a pointing finger. Also, the status bar shows the destination: the *nextpage.htm* file.

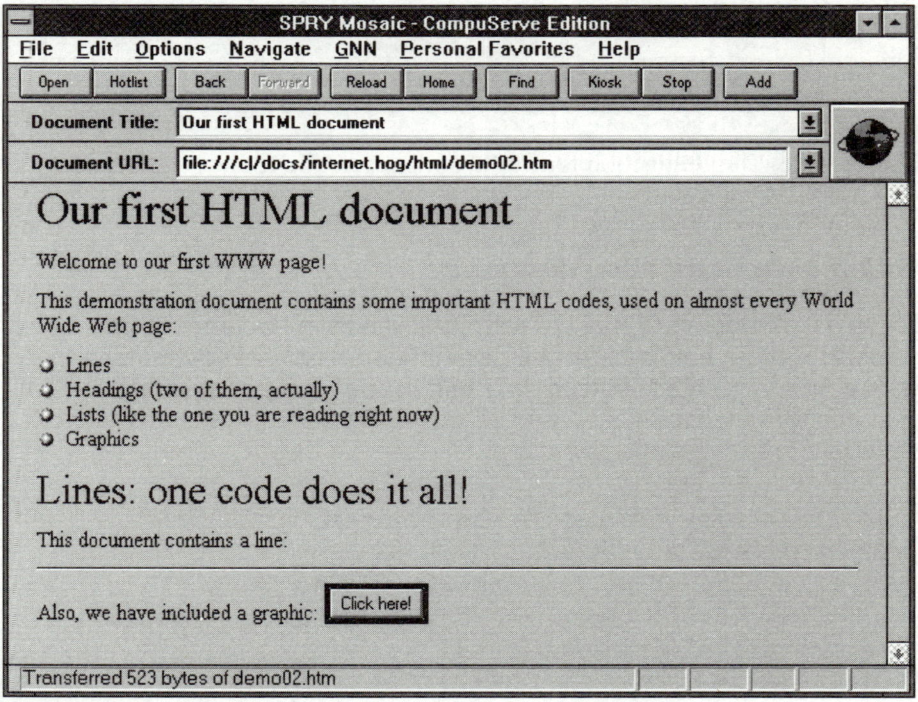

Figure 9.10 Our document now contains a hyperlink, which points to another file.

When you press the button, your browser will try to locate the destination file. Figure 9.11 shows the results: since the file doesn't exist yet, the browser software generates an error message.

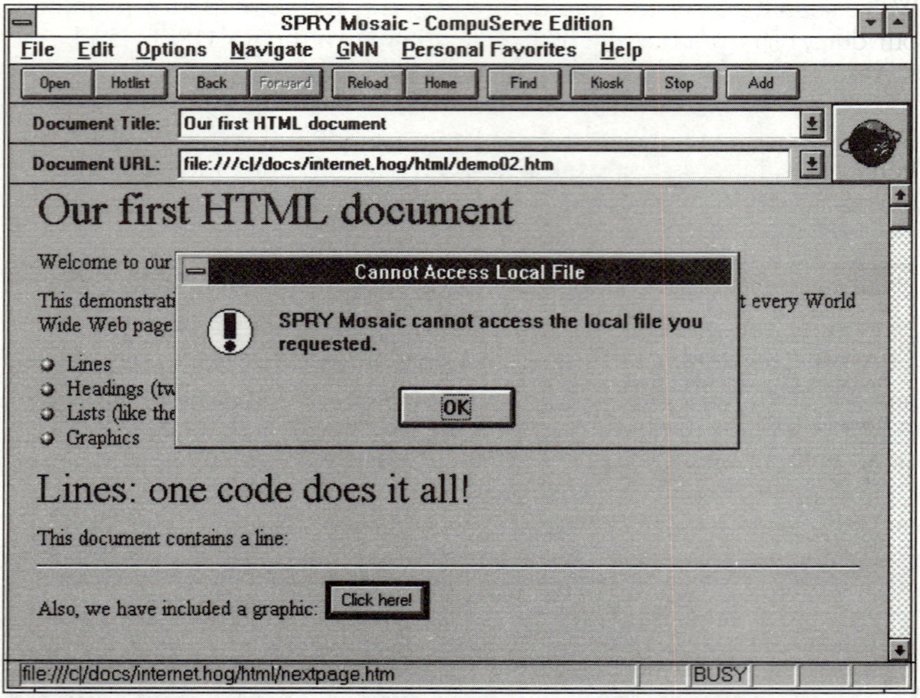

Figure 9.11 The destination for our hyperlink can't be found – it doesn't exist yet!

Creating the destination document

For this example, we'll make a simple destination document that contains a hyperlink back to the original demonstration document. In your editor, type the following text and save it as *nextpage.htm.*

```
<TITLE>Another demonstration document</TITLE>
<H1>You've made it!</H1>
You have arrived at the destination document. Click <A
HREF="demo02.htm">here</A> to return to the original
demonstration document.
```

The <A> container element deserves a closer look:

```
<A HREF="demo02.htm">here</A>
```

We've seen the *href* attribute before; it points to the revised version of our demonstration document. The text between the <A HREF> and </A> codes, *here*, will become the hyperlink.

Now go back to your World Wide Web browser and press the 'Click here!' button. If all went well, your screen should now look like the one in Figure 9.12.

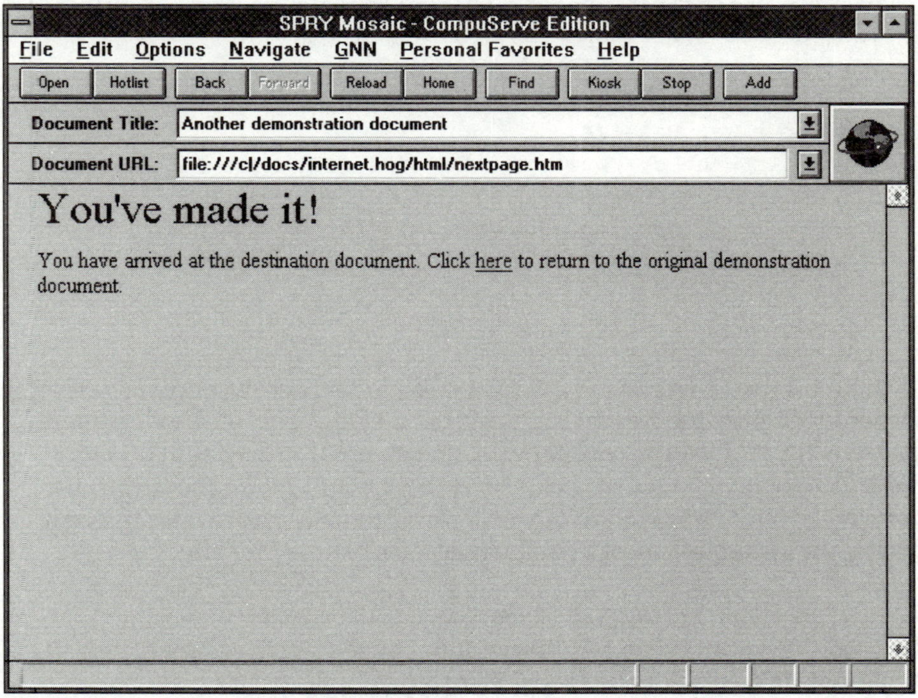

Figure 9.12 The magic of hyperlinks: we've reached our second document.

Now click on the *here* hyperlink; you should return to the original document.

Creating hyperlinks to real Web documents

Now that you know how to create a hyperlink to a local file, you're only a small step away from creating your own home page, filled with links to your favorite documents on the World Wide Web. Instead of filenames, simply specify the URLs of those documents and off you go!

The following HTML document, which you can save as *demo03.htm*, contains hyperlinks to three World Wide Web documents: the CompuServe Web Page, the SPRY Home Page and the home page of Thomson Publishing, were you can find the ***WebExtra*** for this book.

```
<TITLE>My first links to the outside world</TITLE>
<H1>Let's go outside!</H1>
This demonstration document contains links
to three interesting places on the World Wide Web. Simply
click on the hyperlinks to visit those places!
<UL>
<LI><A HREF="http://www.compuserve.com">The official
CompuServe Web Page</A>
<LI><A HREF="http://www.spry.com">The SPRY Home Page</A>
<LI>The home page of
<A HREF="http://www.thomson.com/intlitcp.html">International
Thomson Computer Press</A>, publisher of the book that has
taught me HTML.
</UL>
```

When you load this file in your World Wide Web browser, your screen should look like the one in Figure 9.13. To view one of the documents for which you have provided links, simply press its hyperlink. If you use CompuServe NetLauncher, you don't have to be connected to the Internet; your browser software will automatically launch the Internet Dialer and establish the PPP connection for you.

Hyperlinking to the max: image maps

If you have spent some time on the Web, it is likely that you have been surprised by **clickable maps**: graphical images that are 'roadsigns' to several places on the World Wide Web. A good example of such a roadsign can be found on CompuServe's own WWW home page (*http://www.compuserve.com*, see Figure 9.14). When you place the mouse pointer on the image, it changes into a hand with a pointing finger, as usual. However, several parts of the image all point to different places. This is achieved by the use of so-called **image maps**. In this final part of our 'demonstration section', we'll give you an idea of what image maps are all about.

Image maps: a Web-only feature

Unfortunately, it is not possible to test image maps locally. You'll need to put your World Wide Web documents on a server to use

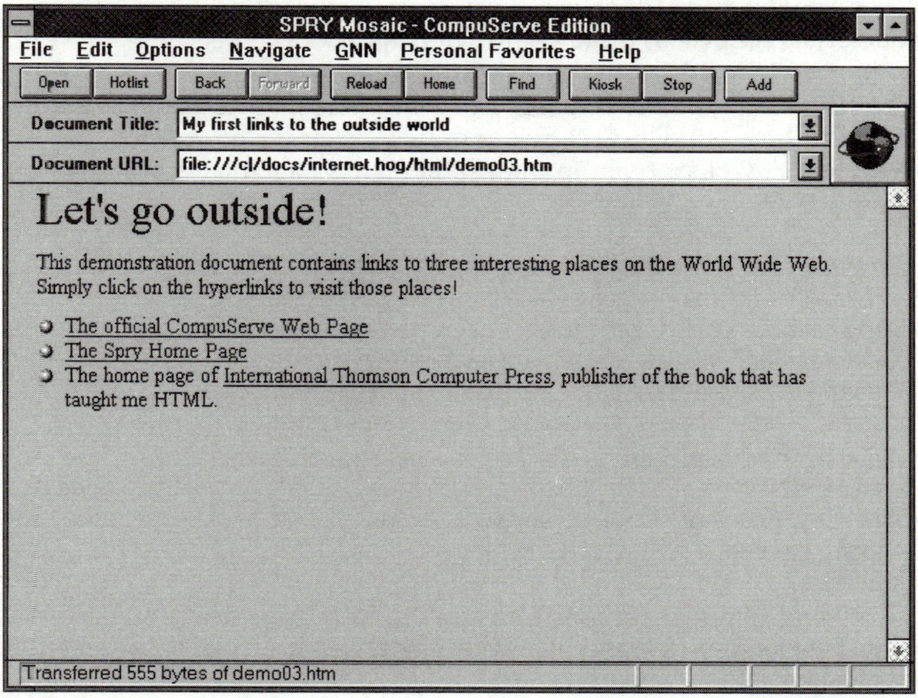

Figure 9.13 Hyperlinking to the World Wide Web isn't difficult, as this screen proves

Figure 9.14 An example of an image map, which can be found on CompuServe's Home Page on the World Wide Web

them. Therefore, the information in this section may not apply to you. If you don't have space on a server to publish your own World Wide Web documents, you might want to skip this section.

Basically, an image map is a normal image that is linked to a **map file**, a text file that contains pixel coordinate (*row, column*) information (hence the term 'map'). By dividing the image into several regions and specifying the coordinates of those regions in the map file, you can have the different parts of the map point to a number of hyperlinks. When someone places the mouse pointer in a certain region of the image and clicks on the mouse button, the correct destination for that region will be looked up in the image map file.

The following example contains a real clickable map: a GIF image that contains three buttons. Feel free to draw a better image yourself, or download my piece of art from the ***WebExtra*** page that is available for this book.

```
<TITLE>Clickable maps made easy</TITLE>
<H1>Let's click!</H1>
This demonstration document uses an <B>image map</B>, to
provide you with a real button bar. Simply click on the
appropriate button for the document that you want to view.
<P>
<A HREF="btnbar.map"><IMG SRC="btnbar.gif" ></A>
<P>
If your browser doesn't support graphics, click <A
HREF="textonly.htm">here</A>.
```

Save the example as *demo04.htm* and load it in your World Wide Web browser. Figure 9.15 shows the results. We have two new elements in this source code:

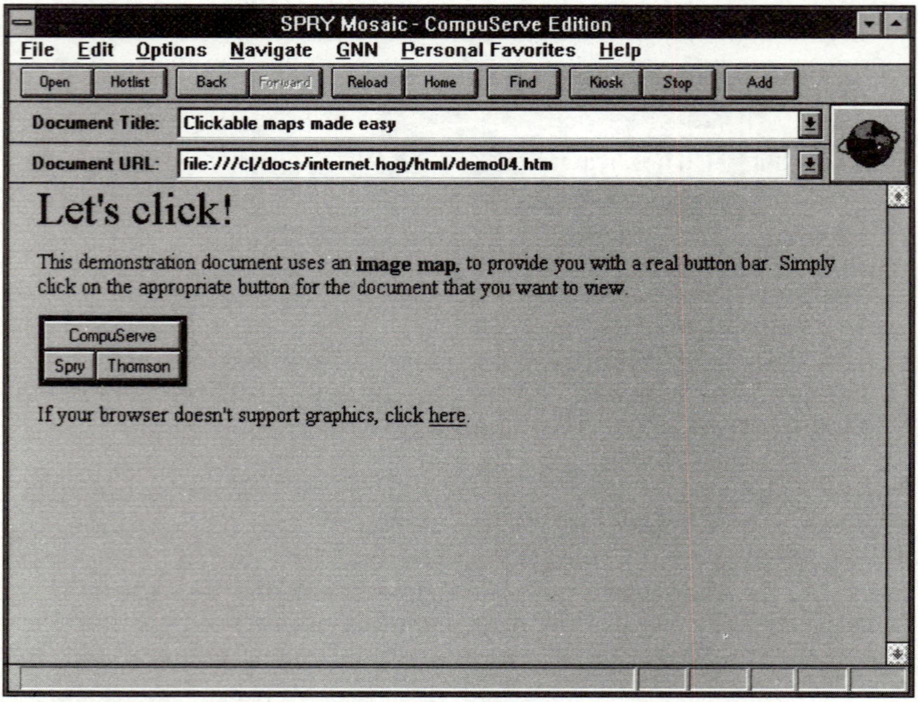

Figure 9.15 Incorporating a clickable map in our document

- **href="btnbar.map"**: instead of pointing to a destination, the hyperlink now points to a file called *btnbar.map*. This text file, which we will create in a few moments, should contain coordinate information as well as the hyperlinks that correspond to those coordinates.

- **ISMAP**: this attribute tells the browser software that the image is a clickable map. If this attribute is omitted, the complete *btnbar.gif* image would be nothing else than a hyperlink to the file *btnbar.map*. Therefore, clicking on it would merely display the contents of the *btnbar.map* file...

Consider text browsers, too!
People who don't use graphical browsers can't use image maps. Therefore, be sure to include a line like the last one in this example in your documents (the hyperlink could point to an alternative, text-only document), or provide text links as well.

Creating the map file

We're not done yet: we still have to create a file that contains the actual hyperlinks. There are three ways to retrieve the necessary coordinates:

- If your painting software can display the pixel coordinates, use that option to find out the top left and bottom right coordinates of each region.

- Use a software application that can create image maps for you. An excellent tool for Windows users is *mapedit*, written by Thomas Boutell. This program can be downloaded from *ftp://sunsite.unc.edu/pub/packages/infosystems/WWW/tools/mapedit/mapedit.zip*.

- Use your browser software! Simply place the mouse pointer somewhere on the graphic and look at the status bar for the actual coordinates. Easy, isn't it?

Regardless of the method you use, the coordinates for the button bar in this example are as follows. All coordinates are in (*row,column*) format, where (0,0) is the upper leftmost side of the bitmap.

- **CompuServe**: (0,0) (97,21)

- **SPRY**: (0,22) (36,40)

- **Thomson**: (39,23) (97,40)

Using this information we can now create our map file.

There are two standards that pertain to image maps: **NCSA** and **CERN**. Contact the system administrator of your server for information about the image map standard that you should use.

If your server uses the CERN program to interpret image maps, save the following text as *btnbar.map*:

```
rectangle (0,0)    (97,21)      http://www.compuserve.com
rectangle (0,22)   (36,40)      http://www.spry.com
rectangle (39,23) (97,40)       http://www.thomson.com
```

If your server uses the NCSA program, save the following text as *btnbar.map*:

```
rect http://www.compuserve.com  (0,0)     (97,21)
rect http://www.spry.com        (0,22)    (36,40)
rect http://www.thomson.com     (39,23)   (97,40)
```

You can now use FTP to upload these files (*demo04.htm*, *btnbar.gif* and *btnbar.map*) to your server.

Specifying other shapes

Besides rectangles, you can also define circles and even polygons (triangles, hexagrams etc.) as hyperlinks.

- **Circles**: To define a circle in a CERN image map, you specify the coordinates of the circle's center point as well as its radius, like this:

  ```
  circle (120,10) 20  http://www.compuserve.com
  ```

  In a NSCA image map, you specify two coordinates: that of the center point and one coordinate on the circle itself, like this:

  ```
  circle http://www.compuserve.com (120,10)
  (140,10)
  ```

- **Polygons**: To define a polygon, specify the coordinates of each adjacent corner, like this (for CERN image maps):

```
polygon (10,60) (50,20) (90,60)
http://www.compuserve.com
```

Or like this (for NSCA image maps):

```
poly http://www.compuserve.com (10,60) (50,20)
(90,60)
```

The next step

In the previous sections, we deliberately left out some of the important theoretical aspects of HTML. Although it is not really necessary to know about these aspects in order to make your own World Wide Web documents, they might help you to better understand why HTML documents behave the way they do, should you encounter any problems. They'll also help you to write consistent, well-structured documents in HTML.

If you want to do serious HTML programming, you should consult the Internet Publishing Forum (`GO INETPUB`) for more information. Also, be sure to take a look at this book's ***WebExtra*** on the World Wide Web for more information.

Index

Notes

Notes

Notes

Notes

Notes

Notes

Notes

Notes